▶ Skill Applications

**Decoding C
Student Book**

Siegfried Engelmann • Linda Meyer • Gary Johnson • Linda Carnine

**SRA
McGraw-Hill**

Columbus, Ohio

A Division of The McGraw·Hill Companies

Table of Contents

Photo Credits Cover Photo: KS Studios

SRA/McGraw-Hill

A Division of The **McGraw-Hill** *Companies*

Imprint 2002
Copyright © 1999 by SRA/McGraw-Hill.

Send all inquiries to:
SRA/McGraw-Hill
8787 Orion Place
Columbus, OH 43240-4027

Printed in the United States of America.

ISBN 0-02-674793-6

13 14 15 16 VHJ 05 04

1

count
counter
counting
counted

2

ai

A	B
sailed	bailing
painting	remain
pail	sailor
strain	nails
chain	wait

3

ou

A	B
out	shout
account	slouch
pounded	bound
grouch	sour
snout	

4

A	B	C
ir	Bert	turn
ur	clerk	jerked
er	Shirley	third
	buster	dirty
	thirst	shirt
	first	surf

5

1. stout
2. churn
3. perch
4. ail

6

felt laughed left sticking boats
woman anchor dollars didn't
don't without sooner catching
dragged thinking tired

Bert Meets Shirley

7

Bert had a job in a sailing shop. He was a clerk and he didn't like his job.[1] Every day without fail, he went to the shop and waited for people to buy things. Then people came to the shop. They picked up paint and nails and containers for bailing. But every day Bert said to himself, "I'm tired of this job."

Then one day a big sailor came into the sail shop. This sailor was a woman who spoke loudly. "Hello, buster," she said to Bert. "My name is Shirley. I am the best sailor you will ever see. * And I need a long anchor chain."[2]

"Do you have to shout?" Bert asked.

"Shout?" she shouted. "Don't be such a grouch." She pounded the table. "Get that chain. The sooner I sail, the sooner I will catch perch."[3]

"The chain is upstairs," Bert said. "Wait here and I will get it for you."

"No," Shirley shouted. "You don't look very stout. I'll go with you and carry the chain down."

So Shirley and Bert went upstairs. She grabbed the chain and gave it a jerk. Then she turned to Bert and said, "How much for this anchor chain?"

"Ten * dollars," Bert said.

Shirley said, "That sounds fair. I'll take that chain on account."[4]

"You haven't opened an account here," Bert said. "How can you take it on account?"

The sailor said, "I'll take it on account of I don't have any cash." She laughed and laughed. Then she turned with a jerk. "That's a joke," she said. "You'll get paid without fail. Don't stand there with that sour look."

Shirley dragged the chain down the stairs. When she was at the bottom of the stairs, she said, "You're out of shape. Get out of this sail shop. Go fish * for perch."

"I can't do that," Bert said. "I must remain here and do my job."

"Don't you thirst for the sound of the surf?[5] Don't you want to see the waves churn around your feet? Didn't you ever get out under the clouds and the birds?"

"Oh, yes," Bert said. "But—"

"Don't but me," she said. "Get rid of your slouch and fish for perch. It will fix what ails you."[6]

Bert found himself thinking of the birds and the waves. Then he said, "When can we go?"

"Now," she said. She pounded the counter. Then she slapped Bert * on the back. "Pick up the anchor chain and follow me."

When Bert tried to lift the chain, he said to himself, "This is a strain. I don't know if I will be much of a sailor."[7]

1 ai

A	B
main	faint
container	waist
bailing	afraid

2

A	B	C
ir	dirty	stir
er	turning	another
ur	perched	churn
	stern	further
		surf

3 ou

A	B
sound	around
pounding	shouted

4
1. sound
2. hull
3. stern
4. flounder
5. faint

5
wouldn't you'll you've should cannot
didn't don't that's can't tried tied
begin hear toward mast anchor
those these stitching side dragged
asked asks grapes could slapped
yourself sure bobbing grabbed
below knee deck hull

On the Open Sea

6

Bert had left the sail shop to go fishing for perch with Shirley. They went to the dock. Bert counted six sound boats at the dock.₁ The third boat didn't look sound. It needed paint. Nails were sticking out of the side of the boat. The deck was dirty. "This is my house," Shirley said loudly. "I can't wait to get it under sail."

"This boat is a turkey," Bert said.₂

Shirley said, "Be fair, Bert. This is a swell home."

Bert dragged the chain on board. "Some boat," he said.

"It's time to sail," Shirley said. "Run up the * main sail."

"Where is the main sail?" Bert asked.

Shirley slapped a big mast. "Here it is," she said.

"I can't run up that thing," Bert said. "I can't even climb up that thing."

"You don't run yourself up that mast," Shirley said. "You run the sail up that mast. I'll show you how."₃

So she did. And then, as Bert stood there, not sure what he was doing or why he was doing it, the boat began to turn and go out to sea.

Soon the boat was in the open sea, bobbing up and down in the surf. * Bert began to feel sick. But Shirley was singing. She was perched in a chair under the main sail.₄ And the boat churned a path in the surf. At last Shirley shouted, "Bert, grab a container, go below, and start bailing. Our hold must be filled with water."

Bert went below. The water was up to his waist.₅ He felt faint as the boat pounded this way and that way. He bailed and bailed and bailed. At last the water was only knee-deep. Then Bert went back to the deck.₆

"What ails you?" Shirley shouted. "You look like you * just ate sour grapes."

"I'm sick," Bert said.

"Take a turn around the deck," Shirley said. "The sea air will take care of what ails you."

Bert went to the stern of the boat. Just then the boat began to flounder as a big wave slapped the side of the hull. Bert fell into the water.₇ He came up just in time to see another big wave churn toward him. Before he could shout, the wave hit him like a train of water. He came up and tried to shout, but he had water in his mouth. "Blurp," he said. * The old boat and Shirley were farther away.

"Help," he yelled, but his shout was faint over the sound of the pounding sea.₈ Suddenly Bert was very afraid. But just then he heard somebody say, "Hello."

1 ai

A	B
afraid	brain
faith	pained
strained	faint

2

A	B	C
er	mermaid	swirled
ur	surfer	surfboard
ir	stirred	thirsty
		clerk

3 ou

A	B
out	sounds
surrounds	shouted
around	without

4
1. flounder
2. flail
3. fret
4. snout
5. swirl

5

won't don't didn't wasn't staring
weren't wouldn't starting swim
swam middle paddled yourself worry
shark anybody rather floating talking
submarine attack while hungry brushed

The Merman

6

Bert was flailing in the surf, but he was failing to get close to the old boat.₁ Then suddenly somebody said, "Hello."

Bert turned around and saw a head bobbing in the water. "You must be a mermaid," Bert said.₂

"Don't be a jerk," the head said. "Do I look like a maid?"

"No, no," Bert said. "You look like a man. So you must be a merman."₃

"Don't be a jerk," the head said again. "I am a surfer. I took the wrong turn and here I am, out in the middle of the sea."₄

The surfer paddled over * to Bert. Bert said, "I am afraid we won't be able to get back to the beach."

"Don't get yourself stirred up," the surfer said. "Things will take a turn for the better if you just keep the faith."

"How do you do that?" Bert asked just as a big wave swirled over his head.

"Grab hold of my surfboard and play it cool. Don't strain your brain. Somebody will come by if you just wait."₅

"How long will we have to wait?" Bert said as he reached for the surfboard.

"Don't be a pain, man," the surfer said. "Don't * worry about how long it will be. Don't start thinking about how we are shark bait sitting out here. Don't think about how thirsty you are. Think of how much fun this is. Like what would you be doing if you weren't out here?"₆

"I would be working as a clerk in a sail shop," Bert said.

"See what I mean?" the surfer said. "Anybody would rather be out here floating around like a flounder."

Bert said, "I don't know about that. I think I would rather—" Bert stopped talking. He was staring at a fin that was cutting a * path in the water. Bert said, "Isn't that a shark fin?"₇

"That's not a submarine," the surfer said. "Look at how that shark can swim. Wouldn't it be neat to swim that well?"

"But—but—won't that shark attack us?" Bert said.

"I'll tell you in a while," the surfer said. "But don't fret about it. If that shark is hungry, we will be its supper."

"But I don't want to be a shark's supper," Bert moaned.

"Well," the surfer said, "if you don't dig it here, why don't you just take the next bus home?"₈

Just then the shark * swam under the surfboard. The shark's snout brushed against Bert's foot. "I think I'm going to faint," Bert said.

"That's cool," the surfer said. "You'll feel better after a little nap."₉

Bert felt sick. He wished he were back in the sail shop.

1 ar

A	B
hard	tardy
start	park
armor	sparkler

2

explained countless faint clerk hours
wailed ground painful pouting aid
surround serve bounding surfer snail
perched complain around flounder

3

1. perch
2. wail
3. survive
4. strain

4

slipped climbed bucket strain
anchor tripped grubbed yawned
simply hanging hunger away
mount spotted craft ahoy

Back on Board

5

Bert was sick. He was hanging onto a surfboard in the middle of the sea. A shark was swimming around and around the surfboard. The surfer didn't seem to mind, but Bert felt faint.₁

He asked the surfer, "How many hours can we survive out here?"

The surfer said, "If that shark gets a hunger pain, you won't have to worry about surviving."₂

Bert asked, "What if I make loud sounds. Will it go away then?"

"Sharks dig loud things," the surfer said. "If you do that, sharks will surround us."₃

At that moment Bert spotted a sailboat bounding over * the surf.

"Look, look," Bert shouted. "A craft has come to our aid."₄

The surfer didn't look up. He simply yawned. "Oh, well," he said, "looks as if our fun is over."

Bert didn't feel that he was having fun. He looked at the sailboat, and he could see somebody perched on the main mast. It was Shirley.₅

"Ahoy," she wailed. "I see a pair of sick fish on a surfboard."

The boat seemed to move like a snail, but soon it was next to the surfboard. Bert left the surfboard and floundered over to the boat. Then he climbed * up over the rail. ₆

"Oh, that was painful," he said. "We were out there with sharks and we didn't—"

"Shut up and stop wailing," Shirley said. "Grab a pail and start bailing."₇

The surfer didn't complain. He slipped his surfboard over the rail and climbed up. Then he said, "When do we eat?"

Shirley said, "After you work. Grab a bucket and start bailing."

"Wait," the surfer said. "Let me explain. I don't work. I surf and I eat, but I don't work."₈

Shirley said, "And I don't serve eats to them that don't work."

"I dig," the surfer said. * "I don't feel much hunger, so I'll just sit in a deck chair and take a nap." And that's just what he did.

Bert bailed and bailed. Then he bounded up to the deck and said, "This life at sea is too much strain. Take me back to the sail shop."

"We came out here to fish," Shirley said. "And that's what we're going to do. Drop the anchor chain and get ready to count the flounder."₉

"I like the ground under my feet," Bert said. "It's plain that I'm no sailor. Take me back."

"Stop your pouting," Shirley said.₁₀* "There are countless fish out there just waiting for a fish line."

Bert wailed, "I can't stand the smell of fish. I can't stand the sound of the surf. Take me back to my job as a clerk."

The boat bobbed over the waves. Shirley handed Bert a long fishing pole. She slapped Bert on the back. "You'll come around," she said, "after you feel the joy of fishing."₁₁

1

ar

A	B
hardly	marks
jarred	started
tarnish	parts

2

surrounded spurted hounding sounded
first ground thirst mailed
another mouth jerked tiller around
wailed sputtered ouch survive

3

1. serious
2. termites
3. suddenly
4. tiller

4

line slump sawdust crack tossed
dropping rolled pulled tugged
splash fooling handle swam swing
splat races you've hasn't we're
haven't weren't I'll shouldn't didn't
I've wouldn't doesn't
couldn't don't I'm you'll

Thousands of Flounder

Shirley tossed a pail of little fish over the side of the boat. "This bait will get them," she said. Soon big fish surrounded the sailboat.₁

Shirley dropped her line into the sea. She jerked up and pulled a big flounder over the rail. She dropped the fish on the surfer. The surfer rolled over and said to the fish, "I was here first, fish."₂

Shirley pulled another fish from the sea and then another. Then she shouted, "Come on, Bert, you grouch, it's time to fish."

Bert dropped his line into the sea. He felt a tug. He jerked * up the fishing pole. But Bert didn't pull a flounder from the sea. The flounder pulled him into the sea. Splash. "Cut it out," Shirley yelled. "This is no time to fool around."

Water spurted from Bert's mouth. "I'm not fooling," he sputtered.₃ "That fish is too big to handle."

Bert swam back to the rail of the boat. He tossed his pole over the rail. The surfer grabbed it and said, "Is this work or fun?"

Shirley said, "This is more fun than playing in the rain."₄

"Then I'll do it," the surfer said. He jerked up on the * pole and pulled a stout flounder from the sea. The flounder swung around and hit Bert just as Bert was trying to climb over the rail. Splat. Bert fell on a fish that was on the deck.₅ He slid across the deck on that fish and went sailing over the other side of the boat. Splash.

"Cut it out," Shirley said sternly. "This is no time to play around."

Again water spurted from Bert's mouth. "I'm not playing," he said.

"I'm playing," the surfer said. "This is about as much fun as surfing."

The surfer and Shirley ate flounder that * night. Bert didn't eat. He sat near the main mast and talked to himself.

He was still talking to himself the next morning when Shirley shouted, "Now it's time to go back to port."₆

Shirley grabbed the tiller and turned it to one side, but the boat didn't turn. The tiller broke in her hand. Then she yelled, "Men, we've got termites on this ship. They ground the tiller into sawdust. I don't know how long it will take them to eat the rest of this fine ship."₇

"Oh, not that," Bert wailed. "I'm a clerk. Why didn't I just * stay and be a clerk? Why did I—"₈

"It's full sail," Shirley said. "We must reach port before the termites have ground this boat into bits."

"This is the life," the surfer said. "I dig races and I dig termites."

Bert got up to see what the termites did to the tiller. As he walked near the rail, he felt the deck begin to crack under his feet. Slump. A hole formed in the deck, and Bert fell into the hole filled with a thousand flounder.₉

"Stop clowning around," Shirley said. "This is serious."

"But," Bert hollered as he floundered * around with the flounders, "the termites really know how to eat wood."

"I just hope they don't eat the main mast," Shirley said.₁₀

1   ar

A	B
far	sharpen
aren't	sharpened
charming	starting
carpenter	

2   hour   sailor   chair   south
third   pouting   tiller   grounded
exclaimed   clerked   around

3   1. collapse
2. craft

4   shouldn't   hadn't   wasn't   suddenly
hasn't   you've   clattering   isn't   weren't
what's   couldn't   that's   into   onto
unto   tottered   serious   really   pointed
shore   rented   clowning   toward   passed
eaten   crafted   chewing   skidded
landed   filler   front   board   casting
place   raced   grabbed

A Race With Termites

It was a race between the termites and the sailboat. The termites had eaten the tiller and now they were working on the deck. Shirley was saying, "Let out more sail."

Bert was saying, "Why did I ever leave the sail shop?"[1]

And the surfer was saying, "This is really fun. I dig it."

Hour after hour dragged by. Then suddenly, the rail on the left side of the boat fell down.

"Look at those termites eat wood," the surfer said.

"Oh, no," Bert said.

"Let out more sail," Shirley said.

An hour later more rail fell down. Bert was * sitting in a deck chair talking to himself. "We're not going to make it," he was saying. Suddenly his chair collapsed, and Bert was sitting on the deck.[2]

"Stop clowning around," Shirley shouted.

Another hour passed. During that hour the rest of the rail around the boat collapsed. Shirley said, "Men, I think we're too far south to make it back to the dock. We're going to have to turn toward shore before water starts to spout through the bottom of this boat."[3]

The surfer said, "Why don't you go to my dock? It's over there." He pointed toward the * shore.

"Do you rent a dock there?" Shirley asked.

"No," the surfer said. "I own that part of the beach. My uncle left it to me. But I can't stand it because the surf is poor."

"Stop talking and start turning," Bert said. "I want to feel dry ground under my feet."[4]

So the boat turned toward the shore. Just then the top third of the mast tottered and fell over. The surfer said, "Those termites are something."

The boat came closer and closer to the shore, and the boat got lower and lower in the water. "I think we * spouted a leak in the hull," Shirley said.[5]

"I'll nail some boards over the hole," Bert said. He grabbed a hammer and some boards. He went down the stairs and flailed around in the water and the flounder. But when he tried to use the hammer, the handle broke. The termites had eaten holes in it. Bert was about ready to start pulling out his hair.

"We're going to make it," Shirley shouted from the deck. "I'll just run this craft aground next to the dock."[6]

The old boat was spouting new leaks. It was sinking lower and lower into * the water. Bert was chewing his fingernails. He ran up the stairs. And just when he got to the deck, the boat made a loud sound as it came aground next to the dock. The boat stopped so suddenly that Bert skidded on the deck and went sailing over the front of the boat. He landed nose first on the beach. His mouth was filled with sand. "We made it," he yelled.[7]

"Stop clowning around," Shirley said. "Bert, you just don't seem to know when things are serious."

1

ship
sheep
sharp
shark
shake

2

ge

A	B
strange	charge
gem	change
dodge	manage
gent	

3

lousy exclaimed started flounder
stairs fisher sharks sounding
parking around spark repair turned

4

1. business
2. surfer
3. respond
4. waist
5. skid

5

broken enough skidded responded
wouldn't didn't doesn't shouldn't
don't couldn't business picked
holding fishing pulled share poster
loan along across away replied
right following people period

What Will Bert Do?

6

Bert was on the beach yelling, "We made it." The boat was grounded next to the dock.₁ The surfer picked up his surfboard, turned to Shirley, and said, "That trip was a real treat." Just then the front of his surfboard collapsed and fell to the deck. He was left holding a third of his surfboard. "Hey," he said. "That's not fair. How can I go surfing with a broken board?"

Shirley slapped him on the back. "You're born to fish," she shouted. "Stick with me and we'll go after the big flounders."₂

Bert got up and spit sand from * his mouth. Then he yelled, "I'm not going with you. I'm going back to the sail shop. I'm a clerk, not a sailor."

Shirley said, "How can you go back to that place after you've had the sound of surf in your ears?"

"I dig," the surfer said.

"No, no," Bert yelled. "I like to feel the ground under my feet. I'm sick of the surf and I can't stand boats with termites."₃

The surfer tossed his broken surfboard on the beach. Then he grabbed a fishing pole and made a long cast along the beach.₄ In an instant he * pulled out a big fish. "This fishing is a lot of fun," he said. He swung the fish onto the deck. Then he cast again. He jerked up on the pole and pulled out another fish.

Shirley grabbed the fish and looked at it. "That's a shad," she exclaimed. "Are there always shad around here?"

"Yep," the surfer said as he made another cast. "This water is lousy with shad."

Bert said, "This water is lousy—period. I never want to see any more water. I'm going back to the sail shop."₅

Shirley said to the surfer, "How much of * this beach is yours?"

The surfer said, "About a third of a kilometer up the beach and about a third of a kilometer down the beach."₆

"Wow," Shirley exclaimed.

By now Bert was walking across the beach, away from the boat. "I'm leaving," he said.

"Stop pouting," Shirley said. "First you're clowning around when things are serious, and now you're pouting when things are beautiful."₇

"What's beautiful?" Bert shouted.

"Well come on back here and I'll tell you," Shirley responded. "I've got a plan that will make everybody happy. It will make you happy; it will make the surfer happy; * and it will make old Shirley happy."

Bert stopped and looked back at the boat. He was thinking.₈

1 ge

A	B
charge	range
stranger	large
barge	manager
gem	lodge

2 ce

A	B
force	price
cent	center
face	spice
cell	space
place	

3

farmer turning painted third

jar charge plaster aren't

lousy first hailed tarp

4

1. convert

2. purchase

3. probably

4. reply

5

behind ducked alive station chief

posters either business our shuffling

burp money replied game

booming rubbed hardly fire fired

your neither skidded

6 A Business on the Beach

Shirley told the others that she had a plan. Bert was standing on the beach shuffling his feet. The surfer was casting his line into the water. Shirley was waiting for Bert to make up his mind about leaving.[1]

Finally Bert shuffled over to Shirley. "Let's hear your plan," he said.

"Here it is," Shirley replied. "The surfer owns this beach. I own this boat. And you, Bert, are a clerk."

"Right," Bert said.

"Cool," the surfer said as he reeled in another shad.

Shirley said, "And this beach is lousy with fish. So what if we opened a business * right here on the beach? We could fix up the old boat and convert it into a sail shop. Bert, you could work in the sail shop. We could charge people to fish here. I could be in charge of the fishing. And we would pay the surfer for using his beach."[2]

"Cool," the surfer said. "I really dig money."

Bert rubbed his chin. "You may have something there," he said slowly. "We could sell sails and bait and anchors and all the other things you would buy in a sail shop."

"Right," Shirley said. "People would get a charge * out of coming to our shop. It would be a real boat right here in the water."[3]

The surfer said, "And I could take the money you give me and buy a new surfboard. And I could fish for free."

"Right," Shirley said. "And I could fish too and sell some fish."

Everybody began talking at the same time. They talked and talked.

On the following morning they began to work. They repaired the old boat. It wasn't in any kind of shape to go back to sea, but it was good enough for resting in water that was waist- * deep.

Bert got a loan from the bank and purchased goods for the sail shop.[4] Then he made posters. He plastered the posters all around. Some said, "Seashore Sail Shop— Marine supplies, diving equipment, fishing goods." Other posters said, "Fish at Seashore Sail Beach. Pay for the fish you catch. No fish, no pay."[5]

That's how the business got started. Hardly a month had gone by before the business was booming. And it's going strong today. Bert and Shirley are pretty rich. You can see them down at Seashore Sail Beach almost any time. But if you go down there, * you probably won't see the surfer. You'll probably find him up the beach about six kilometers, where the waves are good. He comes back to Seashore Sail Beach now and then, either to fish or to pick up his share of the money the business makes.[6]

So Shirley was right. The business had made everybody happy.

1 ce

A	B
place	piece
danced	cents
force	slice
rice	fence

2

Kurt jar strange faint general
counter surge plunger sound
thirst dodge experts
exclaimed announced departed

3

1. several
2. inspect
3. exclaim
4. future
5. unusual

4

I've we're wasn't those what chief
station these touched engines gong
causing arrived examined stunned
different major show glowing
mustard squint suddenly disappear
done picture minutes planet instead
gone toward slowly fighters appeared

The Mustard Jar

5

This is an unusual story in several ways. It is a story that takes place in the future, and it is a story about a mustard jar.[1]

The mustard jar looked a lot like any other mustard jar. It was made of glass, and it had a plunger on the top.[2] When you pressed the plunger, yellow mustard squirted out. This mustard jar was on the counter of a snack bar. Every day things were the same for the mustard jar. Every morning Kurt, the man who owned the snack bar, filled the mustard jar. People then came into the * snack bar. Some would order a hamburger. They would grab the mustard jar, press the plunger, and squirt mustard onto their hamburgers. Day after day, things didn't change.[3]

But one day was quite unusual. It started out like any other day, with Kurt filling the mustard jar. As usual, people came into the snack bar and squirted mustard on their hamburgers. In the late afternoon the people left the snack bar and Kurt began to clean up. Everything was quiet until suddenly there was a loud sound followed by a strange green light. The snack bar was filled with this * green light. Kurt ducked behind the counter and exclaimed, "Oh, no. They've found me."[4]

Suddenly a strange-looking woman appeared in the middle of the green light. In a husky voice she said, "You must come back to the planet Surge with me."[5]

"No, no," Kurt yelled. "I am happy here. I won't go back to that place."

"Then I will have to use force," the strange woman said calmly. A strange-looking gun formed in her hand. She pointed it at Kurt and—bong—a path of light danced from the gun into the snack bar as the room * rang with a wild sound. Kurt had ducked behind the counter and the dancing light had not hit him.

Instead, it hit the counter, and the counter began to burn.[6]

"You cannot hide," the woman with the gun announced. Again she fired at Kurt, who was dodging this way and that way behind the counter. Bong. The path of light hit the wall behind the counter and made a circle of flame on the wall. Bong. The path hit a picture on the wall, causing the picture to burn. Bong. The path hit the mustard jar, but the mustard jar didn't burn. It began to glow. *[7] Bong. The path of light hit Kurt and stunned him. "Aaaahh," he yelled and fell to the floor.

The strange-looking woman jumped over the counter, grabbed Kurt, and picked him up. Then, as she carried Kurt, she seemed to disappear in a bright circle of green light. They were gone and the snack bar was again empty.[8]

Within three minutes after the strange woman and Kurt had departed, fire engines arrived at the snack bar. Somebody had seen smoke coming from the shop. Within two minutes after the fire fighters arrived, they had put out the fires. * "We're all done here," the chief said. "Take the truck back to the station. I'll stay here and see if I can find out how these little fires got started."[9]

The other fire fighters left, and the chief began to inspect the place. She examined the walls and the windows. She examined the floor.[10] As she was inspecting the floor, she glanced to one side and saw the mustard jar. She stopped. "What is this?" she asked herself. "That jar is glowing." Very slowly she moved her hand toward the jar. Then she touched it softly. "It's not hot," she said. * "But I think I can feel it moving. It almost seems to be alive."[11]

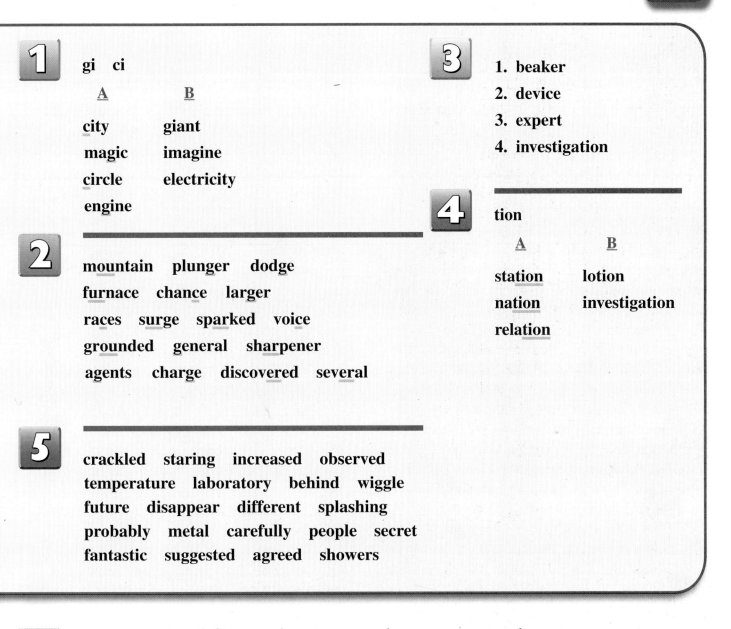

1 gi ci

A	B
city	giant
magic	imagine
circle	electricity
engine	

2

mountain plunger dodge

furnace chance larger

races surge sparked voice

grounded general sharpener

agents charge discovered several

3

1. beaker
2. device
3. expert
4. investigation

4 tion

A	B
station	lotion
nation	investigation
relation	

5

crackled staring increased observed

temperature laboratory behind wiggle

future disappear different splashing

probably metal carefully people secret

fantastic suggested agreed showers

6

Nothing Changes the Mustard Jar

The fire chief had discovered the glowing mustard jar in the snack bar.₁ She held it carefully by the plunger and took it to her car. When she got to the fire station, she called the police chief and told the chief about the mustard jar. The police chief called a major in the army. The major called a general, who called somebody in Washington.₂ While all this calling was going on, the mustard jar was in a glass case in the fire station. All the fire fighters looked at it and shook their heads. "It's almost alive," several of * them observed. ₃

Two days after the jar had been discovered in the snack bar, several people from Washington entered the fire station. They were experts on different types of matter. Each looked at the mustard jar, and each observed, "I've never seen anything like this before."

After all the experts had inspected the jar, the one in charge of the experts said, "We don't know anything about this jar.₄ We have never seen matter in this form. We must find out what makes it work." The experts returned the mustard jar to the glass case. Then they placed the glass * case in a metal box, which they took to a place high in the mountains. A large fence circled this place, and there were many signs on the fence. Each sign said, "Top Secret. Don't talk about your work."₅

The experts went inside to a laboratory, where they removed the mustard jar from the glass case in the metal box. Then they began their investigation. First, they put the mustard jar in a beaker of water. Nothing changed. The jar kept on glowing. Next, the experts put the jar in a freezer. Nothing changed. At last, they put the jar * in a furnace, which heated the jar far above the boiling temperature of water. Nothing changed. Still the experts increased the heat to a temperature that would melt glass. Finally, they turned up the heat as high as it would go. The mustard jar glowed just as it had glowed before. The glass didn't melt.₆

"This is fantastic," one of the experts exclaimed. "That jar should have melted."

"I have an idea," another expert suggested. "Let's try electricity."

"Yes," a third expert agreed, "electricity might work."

So the experts put the mustard jar in a giant device. Then they turned * on the electricity.

At first, they sent a charge of five thousand volts through the mustard jar. Nothing changed. They increased the charge again and again. "Let's give it all the electricity we can," an expert suggested. "This is our last chance." So the experts sent a charge of three million volts through that jar. Showers of sparks filled the room. The sound of electricity crackled and sparked. First, the jar appeared to wiggle and shake, then to smoke.₇

"Shut it off," one of the experts yelled. "It's burning up."

Suddenly the room became dark. The experts crowded around the * smoking jar. Everybody just stood there, staring at the jar and not speaking. Then one expert yelled, "Am I seeing things, or is that jar getting larger?"

"You're right," another expert agreed as she looked closer. "Look at it grow."₈

"And I'm alive," a voice said.

The experts looked at each other. "Who said that?" one woman asked. They looked back at the jar, which was now as big as a pop bottle.

The mustard jar said, "I said that. I am alive."₉

"I'm getting out of this place," one of the experts said. "I don't believe in talking mustard * jars." With fast steps he ran from the room. However, the other experts didn't move. They just stood there with their mouths open, staring at the huge mustard jar.

1 gi ci

A	B
giant	engines
changing	forcing
cinch	dodging
racing	cities
	excite

2 tion

A	B
relation	vacation
solution	imagination
invention	investigation

3
1. laboratory
2. crease
3. observe
4. sprout

4
piece sprouted experts change
darn chance voice spout spaces
huge nerve giant agents
force plunger announced

5
flatter quite adventure exactly
something fatter quiet future
actually squirt instead squirm touch
rough wiggled glowing enough replied
moved skidded flowed minutes stubby
tickled second cautioned

6

Glops of Mustard

Nobody knows exactly how long the experts stood with their mouths open looking at the talking mustard jar. But at last one of them worked up the nerve to talk to the jar. (If you don't think it takes nerve to talk to a mustard jar, try it.) The expert said, "How do you—I mean why are you—I mean what do you—?"₁

The mustard jar said, "I don't know. I just know that I am alive and I can talk."

"Can you move?" one expert asked.

"I will try." The mustard jar seemed to shake and wiggle. Then * it fell over. It shook some more and stood up. "I can move a little bit," the jar said.

"Maybe you can move more if you keep trying," one woman said.

So the jar tried and tried. After trying for a few minutes, the jar said, "I think I can change shape if I really try hard. I will look at something. Then I will change so that I look like that thing."₂

The mustard jar looked at a wall. The experts observed little glass eyes just under the base of its plunger. As the jar looked at the wall, * the jar got flatter and flatter. The jar didn't look like a wall, however. It looked like a flat mustard jar. When the jar was quite flat, it fell over. One of the experts began to laugh. "That was funny," he said.₃

The jar's eyes darted at the expert. The jar then said, "I will make myself look just like you." As the jar stared at the expert, the jar began to change. It got bigger and bigger and bigger. Then little legs began to sprout from the bottom. And little arms sprouted from the sides of the jar. The * mustard jar didn't look like the expert, however. It looked like a huge mustard jar with little stubby legs and arms. All the experts began to laugh.₄

"Stop laughing," the jar announced, "or I'll let you have it." But the experts were so tickled that they couldn't stop laughing. Suddenly the plunger on top of the jar went down, and a giant squirt of yellow mustard flowed out of the spout.₅

"Take that," the jar said. The experts were covered with glops of mustard.

"My new shirt," one woman said. But as she was talking—squirt—a second shot of * yellow mustard hit her in the open mouth. "Ugh," she said. "I can't stand mus—" A third shot hit her in the mouth.

"I'm getting out of here," one expert said and he began to dash toward the door. When he was about halfway there, however, a huge squirt of mustard landed on the floor in front of him. When he hit the slippery goop, his left foot shot out from under him. His seat landed in the mustard, and he skidded all the way out the door. He left an ugly yellow path on the floor.₆

"Now stop laughing," * the mustard jar cautioned. "I look just the way you do."

"Yes, you do," one expert said as she wiped mustard from her face. She was lying, but she felt that she had enough mustard on her face to last her for some time.

Another expert said, "You look fine, just fine."

The mustard jar smiled. You could see a little crease form in the glass when it smiled. Then the jar said, "Now that I look just like a person, I want to do the things that people do."₇

1 tion imagination inspection invention

2
repair chance sparkler imagine
nerves couches germ hardly largest
plunger general surround fence
crouch remained covered device

3
1. unfortunate
2. waddle
3. hesitate

4
slid slide spit quick suspect winner
behave blanket actually unbelievable
unfortunate waddled squirted
laboratory neither limited elephant
supply crowded unlimited pretended
believe built head coughing shoulder
escape jarred before either agreed
insisted eyes yellow sniffing

5 # The Spy Won't Split If the Jar Won't Spit

When the mustard jar told the experts that it wanted to do the things that people do, the experts agreed. "Yes, that's a fine idea," they insisted. They didn't think the idea was very fine, but they didn't want to get squirted with mustard again.₁

So the mustard jar and the experts left the laboratory. The jar, which had made itself about two meters tall, waddled along on its short little legs. Some of the experts started to smile and giggle, but when the jar's eyes darted in their direction, they pretended that they were coughing.

When they were close * to the huge fence that circled the top secret laboratory, they saw two people running across the grass. One was yelling, "Stop that man. He is a spy."

The experts looked at each other. They didn't know how to cope with a spy.₂ They worked with different kinds of matter, not with fists and guns. But the mustard bottle didn't hesitate. With a quick little waddle the jar moved across the grass. It stopped in front of the spy. The mustard jar remained still for a moment. Then the plunger shot down with unbelievable speed and out came a huge * gob of yellow mustard. The unfortunate spy didn't stand a chance when the mustard hit him. It covered him <u>from</u> head to toe like a yellow blanket and gooped up the grass surrounding him. First his left leg went flying. Then his seat hit the grass, and he slid right past the mustard jar, leaving an ugly yellow streak in the grass.₃

"The jar stopped that spy," one of the experts yelled.

Another expert asked, "What chance did he have in the face of the mustard jar?"

The experts ran to the spy. One of them said to the spy, * "If you don't behave yourself, I'll tell the jar and it will splat you good."

The spy said, "I won't split if that jar won't splat me with that stuff."₄

Another expert said, "That's a joke—the spy won't split if the jar won't spit."

The woman who had been chasing the spy ran up to the mustard jar and said, "I don't know what kind of clever device this is, but I'm grateful. What imagination—making a disguise as clever as a mustard bottle. Who would suspect a mustard bottle?"₅

The woman patted the mustard jar on the shoulder * (the part where the bottle gets wide).

Then she patted the mustard bottle on the other shoulder. "Yes," she said, "we are all grateful."

The mustard jar said, "Everybody loves me so much, it makes me sad." Then just below the mustard jar's eyes, a tear began to form. Of course it was mustard. The tear ran down the mustard jar's cheek. Then the mustard jar wiped the tear away with its stubby little hand.₆

One expert said, "There's just one thing that bothers me. If you keep blasting people with mustard, won't you run out of mustard pretty soon?"*

"Oh, no," the mustard jar said, wiping another mustard tear from its eye and sniffing through its little nose. "I have an unlimited supply of mustard. Watch this."

The mustard jar squirted out a pile of mustard that was bigger than a cow and almost as big as an elephant. One expert said, "I think I'm going to be sick."

Another expert said, "That's terrible. I've never seen such an unbelievable sight in my life."

The mustard jar said, "Isn't that wonderful? I'm still full of mustard."₇

1

changes   chances   reflection   pardon

grounds   starving   hailed   lousy

investigations   gentle   department

operated   naturally   directed   scarf

protection   apartment   device

2

1. flinch
2. unbelievable
3. innocent

3

bloop   label   flowing   flinched   grown

wag   squirted   cafeteria   built   sloshed

angrily   sorry   waddle   hesitate

business   suspect   demanded   either

stroked   covered   proof   gallons

wasting   bullets   laughing   breath

shower   neither   believe   poked

unusual   barely   suggested   peering

mound   lying   certainly   knees

4

The Mustard Jar Becomes a Spy

The mustard jar and the experts were staring at the huge pile of mustard the jar had just squirted onto the ground. The spy chaser said, "Say, I believe I can use this mustard jar on one of my investigations."

The mustard jar said, "Oh, wow, maybe I'll be a spy."[1]

The spy chaser stroked her chin with one hand and poked at the jar with the other. This device is a little strange, she observed to herself, but it seems well built.

The jar said, "And I can hide very well. Watch this. I'll make myself look like a * dog." The mustard jar got down on its stubby little knees. Then it grew a tail, which began to wag. The spy chaser began to laugh. "What in green hills and valleys is that?" she asked. She was laughing so hard that she almost fell down. "A mustard jar with a tail—I can't believe it." She grabbed her belly and bent over in a big hee-haw laugh. When she stood up to take a breath, she must have seen something very unusual. Imagine looking up in time to see a wall of yellow mustard flying at you so * fast that you barely have time to hold your breath and close your eyes. Then that wall of goop hits you— bloop.2

The spy chaser was on her back. She wasn't laughing any more. Her eyes peered out of the pile of yellow mustard. "What kind of device is this?" she demanded.

"Don't get too loud," one of the experts suggested. "There is a lot more mustard where that came from."

"All right," the spy chaser said angrily. She stood up and sloshed over to the mustard jar. "All right, I'll use you. But we'll have no more of this * mustard wasting. Remember there are people in parts of the world who would give a lot for the mustard that you waste. Save that mustard for the—" There was a loud bloop and once more the spy chaser was flat on her back with her eyes peering from a mound of mustard.3

About an hour later, the mustard jar and the spy chaser were in the spy chaser's apartment. The spy chaser had taken a shower and was now putting on clean clothes. "Here's the plan," she announced. "I want you to stand in the window of a department store * a few blocks from here. That store is operated by spies. We plan to raid the store soon, but we need an insider and you're it." The spy chaser looked at the mustard jar. "Well, maybe you're not a real person, but you look a lot like one." Naturally she was lying.4

The mustard jar said, "You certainly won't be sorry. I can do a lot of things that the usual spy can't do." The mustard jar pounded itself on the chest. "Bullets can't hurt me. Go ahead. Get your gun and take a shot at me."

"Not here in * the apartment," the spy chaser said, tying her scarf.

"Oh, go ahead," the mustard jar said. "You have to make sure that I'm bulletproof, don't you? It's for your protection. Go ahead. Shoot me."

"No, I really—" the spy chaser looked at her clean white shirt and she remembered how it felt to get hit with a huge mound of yellow mustard. She said, "Well, all right," because she didn't want that to happen again.5

She got her gun. She aimed it at the mustard jar. "Where do you want me to hit you?" she asked.

The mustard jar exclaimed, * "It doesn't matter. Just shoot me anywhere."

The spy chaser aimed right at the fattest part of the mustard jar's fat body. Then she squeezed the trigger. Boom . . . bloop.

The spy chaser was covered with mustard again. The mustard jar said, "I'm sorry. I didn't mean to squirt you that time. When the bullet hit me, I flinched and I must have pulled in my plunger." Then the mustard jar added, "But at least you know I'm bulletproof."6

"I'm really glad I found out," the spy chaser said. She didn't look too happy standing up to her knees in mustard. *

1

my
sly
sty
style
styling
spying
spies

2

ea

A	B
streak	clean
mean	real
hear	screamed
	clear

3

serve   center   swirl   turned
protection   aimed   enlarge   office
giant   charged   startled   strange
innocent   racing   gentle

4

1. helicopter
2. label
3. tremendous

5

pardon   ceiling   celebrate   strain   direction
can't   directly   couldn't   standing
throughout   observe   law   raw   move
climbing   dangling   member   pressure
secret   listened   earth   department
entirely   window   liter   briefcase   swooped
cafeteria   front   strolled   happening
angrily   spies   world   eight

Ugly Yellow Goop

6

The next day found the mustard jar standing in a window in a department store with a new label on its front. The label said, "Cafeteria—second floor." The mustard jar didn't like the label very much, but the jar was glad to be a member of the Secret Agents. The jar said to itself, "I'll bet I'm the only mustard jar in the entire world who chases spies."[1]

Throughout the day people walked past the mustard jar, but not one of them seemed to be a spy. The jar looked and listened, but it didn't observe anything that seemed * strange. Once it saw a man start to whisper something to another man, and the jar listened very carefully. But all the first man said was, "Pardon me. Do you know where the men's department is?"

Late that day a woman strolled by with her son. He was about seven years old. When he spotted the mustard jar, he said, "Mother, please buy me that jar."

"No," his mother said, "that jar is much too big for our house."[2]

"I want it," the boy said. "I want that mustard jar."

"Now stop talking so loudly," his mother said. "You must * behave yourself."

The boy began to cry. "I want a big mustard jar," he screamed, running from his mother. He ran up to the mustard jar. "I want it," the boy yelled. "Let me have it. Let me have it."

So the mustard jar let him have it with about a liter and a half of mustard that was aimed directly at the center of the boy's mouth. The boy must have been startled indeed, because he stopped crying and stared at the mustard jar. Then he ran back to his mother, who yelled, "How on earth did you get * covered with that ugly, yellow goop?"[3]

The mustard jar stood very still, posing as an innocent giant mustard bottle and trying not to smile. But just then there was a huge crash and part of the roof caved in. People screamed and began to run from the store. The mustard jar could see a helicopter through the hole in the roof. At that moment three people ran from an office on the first floor of the department store. A rope dropped from the helicopter, and the three people began climbing the rope. One of them had a briefcase.

Before the * mustard jar knew what was happening, eight Secret Agents ran into the department store and charged toward the people who were dangling from the rope. "Stop in the name of the law," they yelled.[4]

But suddenly, the helicopter swooped up in the sky, taking the three spies with it.

"They're gone now," one of the Secret Agents said angrily.

"Yes," another agent said. "We had better call for a plane to follow them."

"I will follow them," the mustard jar said, running toward the Secret Agents. "If I shoot out mustard fast enough, I move in the other direction. I * fly. Here I go."[5]

With a tremendous blast of mustard, the mustard jar went flying through the department store. It hit one wall and then another. It hit the floor three times and the ceiling once. Then it sailed through the hole in the roof. The entire department store was a sea of mustard by now. A Secret Agent who had mustard all over her said, "There have to be better ways of catching spies than this."[6]

1 ea

A	B
hear	screaming
disappear	meanwhile
squeal	beam
piecemeal	clean
	steal

2

circle   sponge   office   blurt
century   imagination   ground
straight   sharper   city   disturb   darted
celebration   generate   location

3

1. situation
2. stunt
3. continue
4. outfit

4

stained   direction   swirling   startled
protection   squirted   huge   tremendous
exclaimed   starting   trouble   through
helicopter   stunt   throw   couple
business   another   before   skidding
replied   landing   proof   below   glops
dive   breath   observed   unbelievably

The Chase

5

A great chase was taking place over the city as the mustard jar chased a helicopter. It was a very messy chase. The mustard jar had to squirt mustard out very fast in one direction to make itself move in the other direction. The mustard jar had trouble going in a straight line. So it zigged and zagged, and spun around like a pinwheel on the Fourth of July. Sometimes it would dive down, almost to the ground. But then it would turn around, squirt mustard at the ground, and shoot back up in the air.₁

The helicopter that was * carrying a pilot and three spies zigged and zagged to keep away from the mustard jar. Below, people were standing on the street, watching the great chase across the sky. From time to time, glops of mustard would fall on them. It was a messy situation. One man who got hit on the head with a large glop of yellow mustard said, "What kind of a stunt is this?"

Another man exclaimed, "It looks like mustard."

A woman observed, "It smells like mustard."

A little girl put some of the yellow stuff on her hot dog and said, "It *is* * mustard."

Then somebody yelled, "It is mustard gas. Run for your life. Mustard gas will kill you."

While people <u>were</u> running around or staring into the sky, the chase continued. The helicopter would dart in one direction as the mustard jar chased it. Then the helicopter would stop, and the mustard jar would go flying past it. When the mustard jar passed the helicopter, the helicopter would dart off in another direction.₂

As the chase continued, some of the streets below got pretty slippery. You have to remember that for the mustard jar to move, it had to shoot out * mustard very fast, and it had to keep on shooting out mustard. As all the mustard was landing on the city, cars were skidding around on the yellow streets. In one part of the city some boys and girls were sliding down a big mustard-covered hill. They sat in inner tubes and away they went. "This is great," they agreed. "This mustard is a lot better than snow."

A couple of blocks away workers were shoveling the mustard into trucks. These people worked for a mustard company. They were going to load up the mustard, take it to their * mustard plant, clean it, and sell it. These people weren't thinking too well. Mustard sales would be unbelievably poor in this city for a long time, because people would have enough mustard to last them for years.₃

Meanwhile the chase went on over the city. The helicopter stopped and the mustard jar darted by. The jar made a sharp turn. It was getting better at steering itself. The helicopter kept changing location. The helicopter darted to the left. The mustard jar darted to the left. Suddenly the helicopter stopped, but the mustard jar kept on coming. It was heading right * for the helicopter, and it was moving very, very fast.₄

1

ea

A	B
cleaning	scream
steal	meanwhile
hear	disappear

2

startled sprain outfit dangerous
device instruction enlarger beneath
remain imagine situation
information strain complaining
intersection burned range

3

1. collide
2. instant
3. holster
4. deceptive

4

celebration thousands giant enough
buildings behind spies proof chance
changes imagine tremendous shall
instant treasure waddling pressure

5

A Super Job

Over a thousand people were standing on the yellow streets below, watching as the mustard jar headed toward the helicopter. It seemed as if the mustard jar would collide with the helicopter. But at the last instant the helicopter dived down, and the jar did not collide with it. Instead, the jar went right over the top of the helicopter. When the jar passed over the helicopter, a great trail of mustard dropped onto the large blades of the helicopter. A helicopter cannot fly if its blades are covered with ice, so you can imagine what happened when they became * covered with nearly a ton of mustard. Sputter, sputter went the helicopter. And then down it went—zigging and zagging and turning around.₁

The helicopter landed in the middle of a street where some girls and boys were sliding on inner tubes. The helicopter, which had landed near the top of the hill, zipped down the hill. It slid further than any of the inner tubes had gone. It slid three blocks to an intersection where a police officer was trying to control traffic. The traffic was a mess because the cars were slipping and sliding around on the mustard. *2

The police officer had just allowed a long line of cars to creep through the intersection. He was ready to signal the cars going in the other direction when the helicopter came sliding down the street. The police officer got out of the way just in time. He took a big dive into the mustard and slid to the curb. Zip. The helicopter went through the intersection. Then—bang! It hit the back of a bread truck. The police officer got up and ran over to the helicopter. He pulled his yellow gun from his yellow holster and said to * the spies inside, "You're under arrest."3

One spy said to another spy, "I didn't know that the police dressed in yellow outfits."

The other spy said, "Oh, shut up."

When the spies were getting out of the helicopter, the mustard jar landed. By now a great crowd had gathered around the helicopter. The mustard jar waddled up to the police officer and said, "I am a member of the Secret Agents. I will take charge of these spies."4

The police officer looked at the mustard jar. He was going to say, "What is going on around here?" But he didn't. * Instead, he looked at the helicopter in the middle of a city street. He looked at streets and sidewalks and buildings covered with mustard. He looked at a talking mustard jar, as big as a person, waddling around on stubby little legs. When he saw all this, he said to himself, "This is so crazy, it can't really be happening."5

He slid his yellow gun into his yellow holster. He smiled at the mustard jar and he said, "I'm always glad to help the Secret Agents."

Later that day so many people called the Secret Agents that they burned out * the telephone lines. All these people were complaining. The chief of the Secret Agents called the spy chaser who had hired the mustard jar and complained to her. "That mustard device will cost us thousands and thousands of dollars," the chief said angrily. "Get rid of it. And don't hire any more devices like it."

That evening the spy chaser told the mustard jar, "Well, you did a fine job, but—" The spy chaser didn't want to make the mustard jar mad. "But—" the spy chaser said, "we want you to go undercover from now on. We're going to send * you to a quiet place far from this city. We want you to stay there until you hear from us."

The mustard jar smiled. "I did a super job, didn't I? I think I'll call myself Super Mustard."

The spy chaser smiled and said, "Yes, you did a super job. Now you must do this undercover work for us."

So the mustard jar went to the quiet place. And what happened there is another story.6

1

peaceful   celebration   intersection
sponge   rounded   dangerous   practiced

2

1. buoy
2. gear
3. occasional
4. gymnastics

3

Lopez   service   ceiling   deceptive
Florida   glided   Caribbean   unbelievably
Olympic   scuba   warn   taught   pressure
strain   Dubowski   accident   treasure
woman   classes   instructor   stripe
waddling   women   remembering
toward   coral   shadow

4

Jane and Doris

The water looked unbelievably blue to Jane. The sand beneath the water looked blue-white. From time to time a dark shadow of a fish glided over the sand. Everything looked very peaceful. The boat slowly bobbed and dipped over the waves. As Jane looked down to the bottom, she had to remind herself, "Don't be fooled. It is very deceptive down there."[1]

Jane Dubowski was a teacher. She taught gymnastics and swimming. At one time she had wanted to become an Olympic swimmer, but then she injured her leg in an auto accident.

She now has a brace on * her leg. She liked her teaching job, but for the past year she had been looking forward to her vacation. She wasn't sure when she first got the idea to dive for sunken treasure, and she wasn't sure when the idea became more than an idle dream. But sometime during the fall she had asked herself, "Why not? Why not go to the keys off the coast of Florida and dive for treasure?" The Florida Keys are little islands strung out from the tip of Florida into the Caribbean Sea.[2]

She had told a friend of hers, Doris Lopez, about * her idea. Doris, who was also a teacher, liked the idea. Doris and Jane studied maps that showed where people think ships carrying gold had sunk. One ship that had gone down off the Florida Keys was supposed to have carried over fifty million dollars worth of gold.₃

But Doris and Jane hadn't really thought that they would find the ship. They just thought that the diving would be fun. That winter they had taken scuba diving classes. They had saved their money, and when school was out, they bought airline tickets. They packed their scuba gear and flew to * Florida, where they rented a car and drove to one of the keys, named Key West.

When the women arrived at Key West, they rented a boat. It was an old boat, about seven meters long. It had an engine that sounded like a coffee grinder. The engine pushed the boat along at about four knots—not very fast. On their first two days the teachers took their boat out about two kilometers and made practice dives under the eye of an instructor. They set out buoys with diving flags. These flags are red with one white stripe cutting across * them, and they warn other boats that divers are in the water.₄

At first Jane and Doris went down only about ten meters. The pressure of the water hurt Jane's ears. After she had been underwater for twenty minutes, however, her ears stopped hurting. But her mask fogged up quite a bit and water kept leaking in around the edges of the mask. She wore a blue wet suit. Doris had a yellow wet suit. When Jane looked at Doris underwater, the suit looked yellow green, and shadows made by the waves drew little lines over Doris and over the * bottom.₅

"This is great," Jane said to herself. She followed a school of yellow fish along the bottom. She stopped and picked up a sponge from the bottom. She kept telling herself that she was having a good time, but she kept remembering all the things she had heard and read about diving near the reefs, which is where the treasure ships had gone down. She kept thinking about the next day when she would dive near the reefs. And she felt a little afraid. At the same time she kept thinking, "How blue this water is!"₆

1

northeast   information   giant

explained   dangerous   occupation

oxygen   ridge   peaceful

2

1. glimpse
2. pressure
3. prop
4. stranded

3

large   nervous   fences   patterns   sponge

muffled   slightly   swooning   sloshed

sandwich   adventure   coffee   creature

currents   coral   grinder   occasional

tomorrow   ocean   spare   great   worry

replied   loaded   fruit   shifted   front

compass   toward   shadows   beautiful

million   unlimited   escape   built

cafeteria   briefcase   couple

4

To the Coral Reef

Doris and Jane got up before six the next morning. Doris called the Coast Guard station to get weather information. The person told her that the day should be calm and that small craft should have no trouble. "But we expect a northeast wind to move in by tomorrow. If the air pressure drops today, it may come in sooner." A northeast wind was dangerous.

Doris asked, "How long will that wind blow?"

The person told her, "Maybe three or four days."

Doris hung up and shook her head. "We only have a week," she said. "And we may not * be able to go out after today for three or four days."[1]

"Nuts," Jane said. Jane walked to the window of their motel room and looked out. The sun was coming up over the ocean, and the ocean looked like a sheet of glass that was ruffled by an occasional wind. "Well, we'll worry about tomorrow later," she said. "Let's get going."

So Doris and Jane took their gear to the pier where their boat was docked. They filled the boat's main gas tank. Then they filled the spare tank. The woman who filled the tanks said, "Where are you * going today?"

Jane said, "Out to the coral reef."[2]

The woman whistled and shook her head. "That's dangerous," she said. Jane wished the woman hadn't said that. She knew that it was dangerous. She had read about the reef and about the water currents. She had read about how many people had been injured diving near that reef.

The woman explained, "Those currents are bad. They'll suck you down if you don't watch out."

Jane smiled and tried to act as if she wasn't bothered. "We'll be careful," she replied. Inside, she was saying to herself, "Maybe we shouldn't go." *[3]

Before seven o'clock the boat was loaded. Four air tanks were tied down in the front of the boat. Diving flags and markers were in the boat. On the middle seat was a large cooler filled with fruit, sandwiches, and soft drinks.

Jane started the coffee-grinder engine in the old boat. She shifted it into forward, and the boat began to move away from the dock. "Did you bring the suntan lotion?" Doris called from the front seat.

"Yes," Jane answered. "It's next to the cooler." But Jane wasn't thinking about suntan lotion. She was looking far out over * the ocean, trying to get a glimpse of the coral reef. She checked the compass and turned the boat slightly toward the south.[4]

Probably fifteen minutes passed before Jane yelled, "There it is." She pointed and Doris turned around. A large red buoy marked the reef. The reef stretched out for several kilometers, sticking out of the water in places, very white and very sharp.

Jane steered the boat to a place where the reef was just below the surface of the water. "Watch out," Doris said. "Don't let the prop hit that reef or we'll be stranded out here." *

Jane looked at the coral reef below. It was beautiful. It looked like a giant white ridge with a million patterns carved in it. It was a network of sharp knobs and knots and ridges and shadows. Jane could see little caves with fish swimming in and out of them. She said to herself, "It's hard to believe that anything so beautiful could be dangerous."[5]

1 ee

A	B
eel	screech
feel	steep
reef	peeling

2

charges   location   markers
surface   cautioned   sharpness
sponges   patterns   creature   mouthpiece

3

1. location
2. indicate
3. unsteady

4

attention   surge   breathing   burst
purchase   special   unsteady   nitrogen
current   grumbling   swayed   glimpse
watches   million   worth   die   razor
anchor   twenty   smiled   backward
bubbles   layer   sunken   sunlight
purchased   according   studied

5 Jane and Doris Take a Dive

According to a map that Doris and Jane had studied, a ship with more than fifty million dollars worth of gold had gone down at a location near the middle of the reef. That ship had gone down more than two hundred years ago, and nobody had ever found it. It was hard to say just where the ship went down because the reef changes shape from year to year. The reef is made up of millions of tiny creatures—some living and some dead. The coral shells of these little creatures can be sharp as razors.

"This looks like * a good location," Doris said as the boat moved between two lines of coral that stuck up above the water. Doris tossed the anchor over the side. Doris lowered the diving flags into the water. Then Jane slipped her arms into the loops on her air tanks.₁

"We'll stay down for one hour," Jane said. "Set your watch." Both Jane and Doris had large diving watches with special markers to indicate how long they had been underwater.

Doris cautioned, "Now don't get too adventurous. Stay on the east side of the reef. And don't go down more than twenty meters." *

Jane said, "Right. And don't get too close to the reef. That coral will cut like a razor."₂

Doris put her arm around Jane and patted her on the shoulder. "Good luck," she said. She smiled, but her eyes looked a little unsteady.

Jane sat on the side of the boat with her feet on the boat's floor. Then she fell backward into the water, holding her mask so that water wouldn't leak in. She looked around underwater and could see Doris in a cloud of bubbles. Jane waved. Doris waved. Then the women started to swim along the reef. * In some places large plants grew from the reef and swayed slowly in the current of the water, like grass bending in a wind. "Watch those plants," Jane said to herself. "They indicate how the current is flowing."₃

Suddenly Jane heard a funny grumbling sound. She looked around and saw that Doris was pointing to something. Jane swam over and looked. Three sponges were stuck to the reef about seven meters below Doris. Sponges are worth a lot of money. The sponges on the reef were probably worth two dollars each. Jane pointed down and then she swam down. She * pulled two of the sponges from the rock. Doris pulled off the other sponge. Then Jane and Doris returned to the surface. Jane's mask was fogged. She pushed it up and said, "Doris, we may get rich just finding sponges. Who needs a sunken ship?"₄

Doris smiled. Jane and Doris swam to the boat and tossed the sponges over the side. Jane explained, "I think I'll go back down there and see if I can find any more sponges."

Jane fixed her mouthpiece in her mouth, put her mask in place, and went underwater about ten meters. She passed through * a school of little silver fish that flashed in the sunlight. She peeked into the caves along the reef. She went down another five meters. She was looking very hard for sponges, but she was not paying attention to the plants and how they were waving in the current.₅

1 ee

<u>A</u>	<u>B</u>
eek	between
creek	succeed
screech	fifteen

2 breathing hurt pounding barge
started about creature grinder

3
1. surface
2. ledge
3. nitrogen

4
scream mound burst aloud squint
grumbling farther squirt drifting
tilted continued disk frightened
indicate tried meters current
moving surge suddenly oxygen
mouthpiece hidden heart nobody
hundred relax pressing razor bottle
bubbles sunken caught

5

Caught in the Current

Jane was about fifteen meters below the surface, swimming next to the reef and looking for sponges. Suddenly she felt something tug at her. It was the current. Her legs were pulled by the current that sped through a break in the reef. Jane could hear herself breathing very hard. She kicked and tried to swim up, but she could not move up. She was slowly drifting down. She kicked again and pulled with her arms as hard as she could, but now she was moving down even faster. She reached out and grabbed a ledge of coral. She felt * something cut through her rubber glove. She let go and slid down.₁

The current pulled Jane down about three meters. Then it began to move her east through the break in the reef. Jane wanted to scream for help, but she remained silent except for the bubbles that came from her mouth and the pounding of her heart. "I've got to get out of here," she said to herself.

"Relax," she told herself. "Don't panic. Don't panic." The current pulled her through the break in the reef. Then it started to pull her down again, but not as hard. Jane * tried to swim up again. She pulled with her arms. She kicked until her legs hurt, but it was no use.

"I'll have to go with the current," she decided. "I just hope that it lets me go pretty soon." The current continued to pull her down, deep into darker water.₂ Jane could not see the bottom below her. She could see only darkness. When she looked up, the sun didn't look like a white disk anymore. It looked yellow-green. "Relax," she reminded herself as she drifted with the current.

She looked down again. "I must be thirty meters * deep," she said to herself. "I must— what's that?" Jane looked down. The water was pressing Jane's mask against her face so hard that she had to squint to see the dark form that was on the bottom. Was it a mound of coral? Or was it too dark to be coral? What was that long thin line next to it? Jane was almost afraid to say it to herself, "It's a ship." But it was. The mast was next to the ship. The hull was tilted with part of it hidden under sand.

"It's a ship," Jane said to * herself. "I see a ship." She was all mixed-up. She was frightened. Her heart was beating like the coffee-grinder engine of their boat. She could feel goose bumps forming on her arms. "I am looking at a ship that nobody has seen in over two hundred years. Wow!" At the same time, part of Jane's mind was saying, "I just hope I live to tell somebody about it."₃

The current was pushing her past the ship, but now it seemed to be pushing her up. Again, Jane tried to swim up. This time she began to go up. * "Stop," she thought. "If you go up too fast, you'll get the bends."

When somebody gets the bends, bubbles form in the blood. When you open a soft drink bottle, bubbles form because the pressure on the liquid drops when you open the bottle. The same thing happens when divers come up to the surface too fast. As they come up, the pressure on the blood drops. If the pressure drops too fast, bubbles of nitrogen will form in the blood. These nitrogen bubbles can burst blood vessels and cause great pain.

Jane wanted to get to the surface so * that she could mark the spot where she saw the sunken ship. She was still drifting farther and farther from the ship. But she had to wait before going up to the surface. She waited and drifted.₄

1

ch sh wh

<u>A</u>   <u>B</u>

chin   whether

chip   which

ship   church

whip

2

surfacing succeed remained burnt

speech returned teachers

3

1. decide

2. gasp

3. sprawl

4. immediately

4

darkness thirty exclaimed pounding
shipper meant warm warn water glub
trembling wobbly intended gauge
might indicate drowned gasped speck
second closer pointed somewhere right
climbed scared caught grinder pressing
wrong trying realized however disk

5

Deep in Dark Water

Jane remained underwater for another five minutes before surfacing. During that time she tried not to drift too far from the sunken ship. But when she came up, she saw that she was far from the reef, which meant that she was far from the ship. Jane's boat looked as if it were a kilometer away. A yellow speck was in the boat. "That's Doris," Jane said aloud. Jane was glad to see Doris, even though Doris was far away. Jane waved and yelled, "Hello."[1]

A few seconds passed. Then Doris waved back. Jane put her mask down and started * to swim back to the boat. When she was about twenty meters from the boat, she yelled, "I saw a ship. I saw it."

Doris said, "What?"

Jane swam closer. Then she yelled, "I saw a sunken ship."

Doris dove into the water without her mask or air tanks. She swam over to Jane. Out of breath, Doris gasped, "Where is it?" Jane turned around and pointed to a spot on the east side of the reef. "It's right over there, somewhere."₂

"Show me," Doris said.

"Let me rest a minute," Jane said. "I got caught in the current and * it scared me to death."

Doris said, "Let's sit in the boat a minute, and you can catch your breath."

So the teachers swam back to the boat. They climbed in and Jane sprawled out in the bottom of the boat. The sun was a white disk directly overhead. It seemed to burn holes into Jane's eyes. Jane rolled over on her side. "I really saw it," she said. "It looked big and dark. I don't know why, but I got very scared when I saw it. I felt like I was seeing something that was trying to hide."

"Oh, * I can't wait," Doris exclaimed. "Let's go see it. Right now."

"OK," Jane said. She stood up in the boat. Her hands were trembling and her knees felt wobbly. She pointed to the east side of the reef. "It's over there, about fifty meters from the other side of the reef."₃

Jane decided they should swim to the other side of the reef and then dive down. Jane didn't want to let the currents take them past the ship. Before they went down, Jane said, "I think it's about forty meters deep or more, but don't go all the way * down. We don't have enough air.

Don't go below thirty meters."

Down they went through a cloud of bubbles. Down. The water was getting darker. Jane couldn't see the bottom, yet she knew that her eyes would get used to the dark in a minute or so. Down. She could hear her heart pounding, and she could feel the mask pressing against her face. The sound of the bubbles coming from her mouth was very loud—lub-u-glub-u-lub. Down. "Something is wrong," Jane said to herself. Then she realized that more than one thing was wrong. The water was too warm. * When she had passed over the ship before, the water was cold. And now there was no current. Were they in the wrong place?₄

Jane peered down. She couldn't see the bottom. She looked at the depth gauge on her wrist. "I've got to see the bottom," she thought. Down. Down. Jane kept looking and swimming. But she wasn't looking at her depth gauge or listening to the sound of her heart. She was now twenty-five meters down. Doris was above her, trying to signal her, but Jane was looking down and swimming slowly toward the bottom.₅

Suddenly Jane * stopped. She could see the bottom now. It was very far down. "This can't be the right place," she thought. "I had better go up." When she looked up, she realized that she had gone deeper than she had intended. The sun was green. Doris was a shadow above her. Jane looked at her watch and realized that she did not have enough air to stay underwater very long. If she returned to the surface immediately, however, she might get the bends.₆

1 th wh

A	B
then	swishing
when	bash
whistled	batch
chill	which
whether	switch

2 agreed   decided   hours
northeasters   breathe   smart

3
1. fierce
2. pleaded
3. advice
4. nervous

4
surround   turned   distance   seafood
mouthpiece   meant   business   weather
figure   wanted   valve   wasted   sprawl
signaled   above   worth   worry   enough
carrying   struck   warn   spare   bobbing
television   tried   spraying   morning
report   problem   goose   being   knot

5

A New Diving Plan

Jane had gone down too deep, and if she returned to the surface too fast, she might get the bends. But she didn't have enough air to go up slowly. She went up until she was above seven meters below the surface. She signaled to Doris, who was above her. Jane pointed to her tank and shook her head from side to side.

She said, "I'm running out of air," but underwater, what she said sounded like this, "Ibib-rur-n-obobub."[1]

Doris shook her head up and down and gave the OK signal with her right hand as if she understood. Then * Doris swam to the surface. Jane waited and waited. She began to get nervous. She had only about a minute's worth of air left. "Where is she?" Jane wondered. Then she saw Doris swimming toward her. Doris had gone back to the boat to get a spare air tank. She was carrying that tank and swimming toward Jane.

Jane took the tank, placed the mouthpiece in her mouth, turned on the air valve, and began to breathe air from the new tank. Jane gave the signal for "Thanks," and she meant it.₂

That evening Jane said, "We're not going at * this diving business in a very smart way. When we go back, we'll have to string some spare tanks at the end of the anchor line. When we need them, they'll be there, and we won't be in danger."₃

Doris agreed. The two women worked out their plan for the next day. They decided that they would go out unless the northeast wind was fierce. Doris said, "If we don't get out there tomorrow, we may never get another chance."

The next morning was gray and cold. The teachers went down to the dock. The boats were bobbing in the * waves. The woman at the dock said, "I won't rent a boat to you today. No way."

So the day was wasted. Jane and Doris walked along the beach. They drove to a seafood stand for lunch. They walked along the beach in the afternoon. Then they went back to their motel room and watched television. They didn't talk much.₄ Slowly night came and it was time for bed. But Jane didn't sleep well. The wind whistled through a crack under the door. In the distance waves were breaking on the beach, swishing and spraying.

The next morning was gray * and windy. Jane looked out the window and tried to go back to sleep. There would be no diving today. It would be another day of walking around, killing time, and waiting. "Let me see the sun,"

Jane pleaded. But there was no sun that day.

The next morning was gray, but the wind had stopped. "Get up," Jane yelled. "It's calm. We can go diving."

Jane wanted to get to the reef really fast. In the back of her mind she was afraid that the wind would start blowing again. The woman at the dock said, "I don't know. * The weather report says that there may be some more winds today."

"Come on," Doris said. "There's no problem. The water looks as smooth as glass, and tomorrow is our last day. We won't sink your boat."₅

"OK," the woman said, "but remember, I warned you. You never know about these northeasters. They can come up in the wink of an eye. My advice to you would be to forget it. Don't go out there, but if you want to go—"

Jane smiled at Doris. Jane felt goose bumps forming on her arms and neck. "This is it," she said. * "Today is the day we find that sunken ship."

"Yes," Doris replied. "Today is the day."

An hour later, the boat was near the coral reef again. Jane didn't have any trouble finding the place where she had anchored the boat before. Now all she had to do was figure out where that sunken ship was.

When Doris and Jane went over the side, a line of blue-gray clouds was far to the north. The clouds were moving toward the little boat and the two divers. Those clouds were being pushed by a wind of forty knots per hour. * ₆

1 igh

A	B
right	frightened
fright	fighting
brightness	sighted

2

latch which ouch fresh thrash
through while thought chance
navigation clearly charge motioned
carved investigation afraid
announced route nearest apart

3

1. announce
2. wispy
3. suspended
4. anchor
5. swayed

4

approached barnacles swirled glanced
surface buoys spotted hanging
panic sucking forehead quit
quiet directed slime peaking staring
caught yanked shadow
lying laying horizon

5

The Gray Ghost Ship

Jane and Doris set the diving flags in the water. They hung an air tank on the line leading to the anchor. "Now we should be able to stay down until we find that ship," Jane said when the last flag was in the water.

The plan was for the women to take the route that Jane had taken when she spotted the sunken ship. The women would anchor the boat in the same spot they had before. They would dive there, and let the current take them through the gap in the reef and past the ship. One of * them would then swim down to the ship while the other went to the anchor line. When the diver who went to the ship finished the investigation, the other diver would swim part way down with a fresh air tank and meet the other diver.₁

"Here we go," Jane announced. Both divers were in the water hanging onto the side of the boat. They didn't spot the line of blue-gray clouds to the north. Jane slid her mask over her face. Down she went. Doris was there next to her, moving through a mass of bubbles.

Down they went * through the warm water. Down. Then the pull of the current began sucking at their legs. "Don't panic," Jane said to herself. She turned to Doris and smiled, but Doris seemed to slip past her in the current. Down and to the east. Through the gap in the reef. Down, down. Cooler water now, and not as much downward pull.₂

Scan the bottom. Darkness and bubbles. "I wish the sun were out," Jane thought to herself. "It's so dark down here I can't see anything."

"What's that?" A dark line—dark black against the almost-black bottom. The mast. There * it is, Jane motioned, but Doris was looking the other way. Jane grabbed Doris's leg. "Look. Look," she exclaimed.

Jane pointed to herself and then pointed down. "I'm going down." And she did. Through the cooler water. Ouch. Her ears hurt and she felt a sharp pain in the middle of her forehead. The mask seemed to be pushing her face out of shape. Down.₃

Suddenly she could see the ship. It was covered with wispy plants that swayed and swirled in the current. The ship looked like a dark gray ghost. "Maybe I don't want to go down there," * Jane thought. She looked up. Doris was a dark figure suspended in the water far above her. "I've come this far," Jane thought, "so I won't quit now."₄

Down. Jane could now see parts of the ship clearly. There was a rail made of heavy carved timbers, covered with barnacles. There was part of a cabin with a door. The deck seemed to be covered with slime and long strings of seaweed. As Jane approached the door of the cabin, she reached into the pouch on her belt and pulled out an underwater flashlight. She turned it on and directed * the beam into the cabin. There were stairs covered with slime. There were some boxes and what looked like a broken chair. And there was a pile of—bones. Part of a skull was peeking through the slime. The eye sockets seemed to be staring at Jane.₅

She dropped the flashlight and swam. Her arms and legs went as fast as they could go. A string of seaweed caught on one of her arms. She yanked it off. She swam up and up and up. Then she looked back. Below her was the dark shadow of the ship with the * even darker mast lying next to it. She stopped and began to talk to herself. "Be calm. It was only a skull, only some bones." She began to swim fast again.

Doris met her about twenty meters from the surface. Doris gave her a fresh tank of air. Jane stayed there for five minutes. From time to time she glanced down at the ship below, but she could no longer see it because the sky was getting darker and darker.

When they reached the surface, Jane told Doris, "I'm not going back down there."₆

Doris pointed to the horizon and * said, "Jane, look." Jane looked at the sky.

1 al

A	B
alter	salty
falter	almond
calling	install

2

while whether weather thrash
slightly bright tightly wheeling
together faintly agreed faster
seemingly feast cloudy first gently
emerging placed salvage

3

1. protection
2. suggest
3. glance
4. breaker
5. venture

4

afternoon patterns flounder mound
huge hours inspection jerking worse
jagged ruffled horizon plumes wilder
towing aboard spare bluff kilometer
responded rolled forming continued
liters whistled designs during flight
impossible whipped evening venture
believe neither slime

5

Trapped in the Storm

There was a line of dark clouds to the north, and there was a line of whitecaps on the horizon under the clouds.

"We're in for it now," Doris exclaimed.

"What are we going to do?" Jane asked. "Those waves are going to hit us in a few minutes."

The women swam back to their boat, towing the spare air tank. They climbed aboard. Jane started the engine, and the boat began to move slowly along the reef. Jane explained, "I don't know where to go. We've got to find some protection from that storm, but I don't see any * protection."₁

"Let's keep moving along the reef," Doris suggested. "Maybe we can find a place where the reef is high enough to protect the boat."

Jane glanced back. The clouds were closer, and the whitecaps seemed to be bigger and wilder. The old scow continued to move slowly along the west side of the reef. Jane glanced back at the clouds again.

"Look," Doris said. Doris was pointing ahead. "There seems to be a coral bluff ahead."

Jane could see it. It looked like a gray-white mound emerging from the sea. The boat was about half a kilometer from the mound. *₂

"I wish this boat would move faster," Jane shouted. Before Doris could respond, however, a gust of cold wind swept past the boat, making ruffled patterns in the water. The boat turned slightly when the wind hit it.

"Here it comes," Doris shouted. Jane could hardly hear Doris's voice above the wind. Already whitecaps were forming on the other side of the reef. The wind was blowing the tops of the waves into a fine spray. Jane felt the side of her face getting wet. She licked her lips. They were salty.₃

The waves were now starting to roll over * the low places along the reef. As the waves rolled under the boat, the boat began to rock from side to side. The rocking, which was gentle at first, became more violent. From time to time one of the waves would splash against the side of the boat and send warm water streaming into the boat. Doris was bailing. The boat was only about a hundred meters from the coral bluff now; however, the boat was moving quite slowly as it climbed over the waves, rolling from side to side.₄

"If it gets any worse," Doris yelled, "we'll have to * turn the front of the boat so that it faces into the wind. We're going to flounder if we keep going in this direction."

But the boat continued along the coral and Doris continued to bail. Just before the boat was alongside the coral mound, a huge breaker hit the side of the boat and dumped about eighty liters of seawater into the boat. "Bail," Jane shouted as she began to splash water from the boat with her hands.

Now the boat was behind the mound. Huge breakers were smashing against the other side of the mound, sending plumes of * spray into the air. But the boat was in a protected place. Doris tied a rope around part of the mound. Then she and Jane sat in the front of the boat, close to the coral, as the surf pounded and the wind whistled through the designs in the coral.

The wind blew for more than two hours. During that time the women waited. From time to time they tried to talk, but it was almost impossible to hear what was said above the wind and the surf.₅

Then almost as suddenly as the storm had started, the wind died * down. Huge waves continued to roll over the reef for another hour, but the waves became smaller and calmer. They were no longer being whipped into jagged shapes by the wind.

At around five o'clock that evening, the waves were small enough for the women to venture back to the dock. Jane said, "I sure won't forget this day for a long, long time."₆

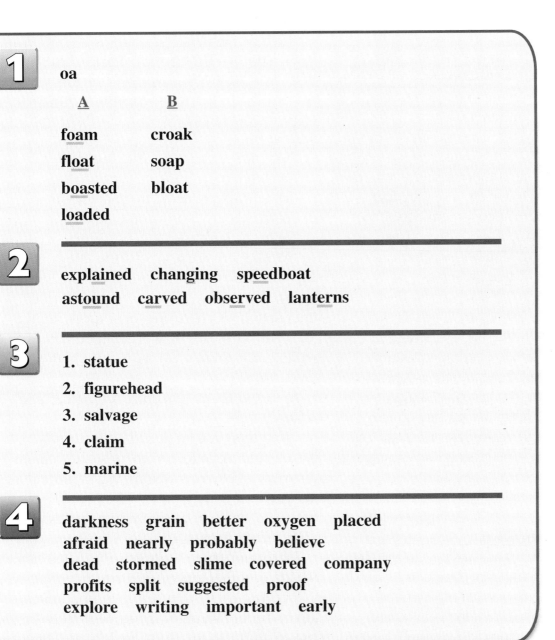

1

oa

A	B
foam	croak
float	soap
boasted	bloat
loaded	

2

explained   changing   speedboat
astound   carved   observed   lanterns

3

1. statue
2. figurehead
3. salvage
4. claim
5. marine

4

darkness grain better oxygen placed
afraid nearly probably believe
dead stormed slime covered company
profits split suggested proof
explore writing important early

5

Exploring the Ship

Jane and Doris made it home safely from the reef. When the women returned to their motel, Jane was very tired but still excited from her adventures. She and Doris had dinner at the motel restaurant. As they waited to be served, they began to talk. The more they talked, the faster and louder they talked. They made plans about going back to the sunken ship. About a hundred times Jane said, "There is no way I'm going back inside that ship. I just won't do it." She explained that the storm frightened her, but not nearly as much as * that ship had—down in the dark sea, covered with slime and filled with bones.₁

"OK," Doris said. "Let's go back early in the morning and put up a salvage-claim flag. Then we'll make a deal with some salvage company to go out there and explore the ship. We'll split the profits with them."

"Hey," Jane said. "That's a good idea. Let's do that."

And they did. The next morning they rented a speedboat—not that old scow that they had been using. The speedboat cost them fifty dollars, which was most of the money they had. The women * agreed that it was better to have a fast boat, even if that meant paying more money.₂

The ride out was a lot of fun. Doris drove the boat, and Jane sat in the back, feeling the spray made <u>by</u> the boat as it cut a path along the surface of the water. Jane watched the little waves zip by. Then the women placed a red salvage flag along with the diving flags over the spot where the sunken ship was resting.

Jane took a picture of Doris and the salvage flag. "That's just for proof," Jane said. "We have * just claimed a sunken treasure. I don't believe it."

"Me neither," Doris agreed.

By noon, the women had made arrangements with a man from a marine salvage outfit. His name was Mike. By two o'clock that afternoon, Mike, Doris, Jane, and two other men were anchored above the sunken ship. They were in a boat that looked like an old tugboat. Mike was in diving gear. He and one of the other men explained that they would go down and explore the ship.₃

By four that afternoon, the divers returned to the surface. Mike's mask bubbled up from the sea. * He pushed the mask back and smiled. "Well, you found a sunken ship, all right," he explained. "But I'm afraid there's no gold on this ship."

"Oh, no," Doris said. She turned to Jane and each woman shook her head.

"But," Mike added, "there are some things on board that are worth some money."

"What?" Jane asked.

"Well, there are a lot of little things. This ship was probably built around seventeen-eighty. It was probably carrying grain and other supplies. There are some bottles in the hold that are probably worth ten dollars each. I would guess there are * a hundred bottles down there."

Jane and Doris looked at each other and smiled.

"And there are some old navigation instruments. A couple of them seem to be in fair shape. They're probably worth more than one hundred dollars each." Mike listed other things—a statue, a carved figurehead, some writing instruments, some old lanterns.₄

Doris and Jane didn't get rich. Their trip to Florida cost them more than five hundred dollars. But each woman got eight hundred dollars for her share of the salvage from the sunken ship. On the flight back home, Jane felt pretty proud. "We may * not be rich," she observed, "but we did it. Instead of sitting and thinking about it, we did it. I think that's the most important part."₅

1 un

A	B
unreal	unable
unseen	unloaded
unbelievable	unfortunate
uncertain	

2

bright   easily   interesting   contained
distance   gigantic   although   falter
fifteenth   branches   approaches   flights
matches   bloating   frightened

3

1. tunnel
2. fluttered
3. snaked
4. drizzly
5. emerged

4

sequoia   canopy   foliage   building
swirled   darkness   drifted   develop
survive   through   swayed   Pacific
November   create   covered   arrangements
suggested   instruments   neither

The Redwood Tree

This is the story of a redwood tree that is living today in Northern California. That redwood, like many others, has had an interesting life.

Its life began with a seed contained in a cone. A redwood cone is about as big as a quarter. The cone starts to grow in early summer. By late summer it is full-sized and bright green with many seeds inside. The cone is not yet full grown, however. As fall approaches, the cone begins to change color, turning brown. Small flaps on all sides of the cone open, and as they do the * tiny seeds fall out. The seeds are so small that ten of them would easily fit on the end of your finger. If you wanted half a kilogram of these seeds, you would have to collect about 120 thousand of them.[1]

It seems strange that a seed so small can grow into the world's tallest tree, but it's true. Redwoods are the tallest trees, although a cousin of the redwood—the giant sequoia—has a thicker trunk than the redwood. Some giant sequoias have trunks so thick that people have constructed tunnels through them and these tunnels are so big * that cars can pass through them. The giant sequoia, however, does not grow as tall as the redwood. To get an idea of how tall the bigger redwoods are, imagine what it would be like to climb a flight of stairs as high as these redwoods. Imagine climbing five flights of stairs. Imagine how far down it is when you are five stories high. A big redwood is much taller than a five-story building, however. So imagine going up to the tenth floor, the fifteenth floor, the twentieth floor. From up here you can see a long distance, and * it's a long, long way down. However, if you were on the twentieth floor of a building, you would not be near the top of a big redwood. You would probably be tired from climbing twenty flights of stairs; however, to reach the top of a big redwood, you would have to climb another fifteen flights of stairs. That's right. A very tall redwood is about as tall as a thirty-five-story building. A person standing down at the base of the tree would look like an ant. The base of the redwood's trunk is so big that eight * people could stand next to each other and hide behind the trunk. And that gigantic tree develops from a seed smaller than a grain of wheat.[2]

It was on a sunny November day that the seed of the redwood tree in this story fluttered from the cone. The parent tree stood on the bank of a small creek that snaked among the giant redwoods. The weather had been cold, and a drizzly rain had been falling for days. During the rain, the flaps of the redwood cone swelled up and closed. But now the sun emerged, and a brisk wind * swirled through the tops of the redwoods, bending their tops to the south. As the top of the parent tree swayed in the cool wind, the cones began to dry out, and the flaps began to open. Below, the forest was deeply shaded by the foliage of the giant redwoods, which formed a canopy of green that extended as far as one could see. In the distance was the sound of the Pacific Ocean.

Late that afternoon, a sudden gust of wind pushed through the forest, bending branches of the redwoods. When that wind hit the parent tree, six of * the cone's forty seeds fluttered down and drifted down, down, into the dark forest below. One of those seeds would develop into a giant. The others would not survive.[3]

1

A	B
citing	exciting
act	exact
ample	example
tended	extended
plain	explain
posed	exposed
change	exchange

2

un

A	B
untold	unthinking
unbelievable	uneasy
unable	unfinished
unfortunate	unfaithful
unaware	

3

1. slime
2. litter
3. moles
4. severe

4

slightly boasted crunch installed
astounded alternate cloudy always
seeming inspection alter person
flight white hours exceptionally
produce survive branches coated

5

wrist severe midst obviously developed
neither fertile receive canopy
adventure continued occasionally lodged
quite quiet pinpoints remained
exposed feast contained strength event
tightly creating worse jagged ruffled

The First Winter

During a good seed year a large redwood will produce over six kilograms of seeds, which is nearly a million and a half seeds. And the year that our redwood seed fluttered from the cone was an exceptionally good year. The parent tree produced over eight kilograms of seeds that year, enough seed to start a forest that would be ten square kilometers in size. However, only a few redwood seeds survived. In fact, only three of the seeds from the parent tree survived their first year and only one lived beyond the first year.[1]

Obviously, our seed was lucky. * It was a fortunate seed because it was fertile. If a seed is not fertile, it cannot grow, and about nine of every ten redwood seeds are not fertile. Our seed was also fortunate because it landed in a place where it could survive. If it had fallen on a part of the forest floor covered with thick, heavy litter, it probably would not have grown. If it had fluttered to a spot that became too dry during the summer, it would have died during that first year.[2]

Our seed landed in a spot where moles had been digging. They * had made small piles of fresh brown dirt, and our seed landed on the edge of the dirt. Later that winter another fortunate event took place. The top seventeen meters of a nearby tree broke off during a severe <u>windstorm</u>. When the top, which weighed more than three elephants, crashed to the forest floor, it tore the branches from the trees that were in its path. The fallen top left a large hole in the green canopy that shaded the forest floor. This event was fortunate for our seed because it would receive sunlight. Some trees are capable of growing * only in bright sunlight, while other trees survive only in the shade. Redwoods are unusual trees because they can survive in either shade or sunlight; however, they don't grow well in deep shade.[3]

To give you an idea of how much faster redwoods grow in the sunlight, let's say that we planted two seeds, one in the deep shade, the other in the sunlight. When we look at the trees fifty years later, we observe that the tree exposed to the full sunlight is over thirty-five meters tall. The base of its trunk is almost one meter across. The * tree grown in the shade, however, is only about two meters tall, and its trunk is not as big around as your wrist.[4]

During the winter that our seed was resting on the mole diggings, the weather was cold and rainy. Most of the rain came in the form of a fine mist that would feel like tiny pinpoints of cold against your face. Occasionally, however, large drops of rain would rattle through the northern California forest, creating tiny streams on the forest floor. Our seed was much smaller than a drop of water, and it was pushed around by * the water quite a bit during the first part of the winter. At one time it seemed as if a heavy rain would wash it away from the mole diggings. However, it became lodged in a small crack between two mounds of dirt. And there it remained, ready to grow when days became warmer in the spring.[5]

1 un

A	B
unfaithful	uneven
unexpected	unfastened
unequal	unfailing
uneventful	unfinished

2 ly

A	B
occasionally	quietly
fortunately	unbelievably
obviously	slightly
exceptionally	easily

3
1. swell
2. torch
3. charred
4. smoldering

4
screech smallest cheap section watch
toasted brightened approached
straighten received crushed squirrel
wonder whisper seedling convert

5
visible connected height unfortunate
ignited exciting motionless thought
impossible celebration pancake strength
centimeter stretched changed bounding
flooding created sapling though
blazed developing emerged through

6 # Seedling to Sapling

In April something exciting happened on the floor of the redwood forest, just as it happened every year. Some of the redwood seeds began to develop into baby trees, which are called seedlings.₁

The forest floor was soaked by the winter rain, and the rain was still falling; however, the days were becoming warmer. In early April our seed began to change. At first it began to swell slightly as the inside of the seed changed. The hard inside of the seed changed into a white pulp that looks and feels something like pancake batter. Parts of this white blob * then began to become harder and take on a form. One end of the blob began to take on the shape of a tiny green plant. The other end became pointed and began to look like a tiny root. The root end pushed out through one end of the seed and began to worm its way down into the soft ground.₂ When the seedling was less than three centimeters long, it started to straighten up. The top of the seedling was still inside the seed, and the seed was in the soft mud. The only part of the seedling that * was visible above ground was the stem that connected the root to the seed. The seedling looked something like a person bending over in shallow water, with only the person's back above the water. The seedling looked like this:

As the seedling grew a longer root, it had enough strength to pull its top from the seed. The empty seed remained in the mud and the top slowly began to stand up. It was only about a centimeter tall, with two little leaves, stretched out to the side like two little green arms. A squirrel could have stepped on that * seedling and crushed it. But not far from that unbelievably small seedling was the parent tree, standing 130 meters tall.₃

During the seedling's first summer, it grew to a height of about six centimeters. On sunny days, the sun's rays came through the hole in the forest's canopy and flooded the ground around the seedling with sunlight. Trees, as you know, need sunlight to survive. They take the incoming sunlight and convert it into food. Without sunlight they starve because they can't manufacture food. Our seedling was fortunate because it received a fair amount of sunlight through the hole created * by the falling treetop.₄

Things went well for the seedling for six years. By the end of the sixth year our young redwood was no longer a seedling. It was now what is called a sapling—a young tree. And it was growing quite rapidly. You might think that redwoods are very slow-growing, but they actually grow faster than most trees. At the end of its sixth year, our redwood was nearly four meters tall and it was reaching straight up to the top of the forest, which was still a long, long way above the sapling. But the * sapling was now ready to grow nearly a meter a year.₅

That fall, however, something unfortunate happened. Late one evening lightning struck a nearby tree. A burning branch fell and ignited the litter on the forest floor. Soon a hot, orange fire blazed through the forest. That fire didn't reach even the bottom branches of the bigger trees, because those branches were more than thirty-five meters above the forest floor. However, the fire burned the smaller trees to the ground. It swept over our redwood sapling and within a few seconds, the sapling was a torch. Within a few * minutes, the sapling was a charred stick smoldering in the forest.₆

1 oi

A	B
oil	noise
point	pinpoint
voice	soil

2 ly

A	B
quickly	completely
certainly	uncertainly
occasionally	severely
frequently	gently
unbelievably	obviously

3
1. original
2. shading
3. toppled

4
suggestion   although   investigation
sprouts   furthermore   cloaked

5
burls smolder charred slime continued
smoldered creating once burnt
disease germs natural original
survived telephone knotty extended
seasons towering ago causes

6 # Toward the Towering Green Canopy

No fire fighters came to put out the fire in the redwood forest because that fire took place long ago. In fact, it took place more than two thousand years ago. At that time there were no houses or roads in the area now known as northern California. Nobody put out the fire. So the fire burned. After it flashed through the forest, the flames died away; however, parts of the bigger trees and large fallen branches continued to smolder for nearly a month. A fire smoldered at the base of the redwood's parent tree, creating a charred hole that * was big enough for a person to sit in. Many other large trees also had smoldering bases.

But when the heavy rains came in the late fall, the smoldering fires died out and the forest was once more calm with the sound of gentle rain falling on the charred forest floor.[1] The forest remained calm until the next spring when the trees again began to grow. Our redwood was among the first to start growing. Although it had been burned to the ground, it was not dead. Its roots were alive, and those roots sent up three shoots. These shoots * were quite thick and very fast-growing. By the middle of July, the tallest of the three was nearly two meters tall, growing right next to the charred trunk of the tree that had been burnt.

Fires often kill <u>young</u> trees, but fires don't often kill young redwoods because the redwoods simply send up new sprouts. Furthermore, there is no insect or disease that kills redwood saplings. While germs and different kinds of bugs kill other types of trees, no natural enemy kills the redwood.[2]

So our redwood continued to grow. Within three years, it was taller than it had * been before the fire. By now, one of the original sprouts had become the main trunk and it was growing quite rapidly, while the other sprouts were hardly growing at all. Six years after the fire, the two slow-growing sprouts were dead. Only the main sprout survived. Our sapling was now taller than the roof of a single-story building. Twenty-five years after the fire, our redwood was twenty meters tall, still growing at the rate of about one meter a year. Its trunk was now as big around as a telephone pole, and it had several large * burls on it. Redwood burls are knotty growths on the trunk and the branches. They look like big lumps. Smaller burls are as big as your fist. Larger ones may be a meter across and extend half a meter out from the tree. These burls are masses of buds. If you take part of a burl and place it in water, the buds will sprout, and a bunch of tiny redwood shoots will begin to grow from the burl.[3]

The largest burl on our redwood was right under one of the side branches. It was about as big as two * fists held together. By now, our redwood was starting to look like a forest tree. Young redwoods are shaped like Christmas trees. If they grow in a forest, however, the bottom branches don't receive any sun, because the higher branches of the tree block much of the sunlight. This causes the lower branches to die. As the tree continues to grow, the higher branches keep shading the lower branches, and the lower branches keep dying. Soon the trunk of the tree may be free of branches for some distance. When our redwood was twenty meters tall, only the top ten * meters of the trunk had living branches. The bottom ten meters of the trunk had either dead branches, or no branches.

The seasons followed each other—rain, warmth and sunlight, and more rain. By the time our redwood was eighty years old, it was over seventy meters tall—which is about as tall as a twenty-story building. The base of its trunk was two meters across. Its trunk was bare of branches for over thirty meters. And its top was near the green canopy created by the towering older trees.[4]

1 ure

A	**B**
treasure	pleasure
picture	nature
mature	assure
sure	pressure

2

noisy installed actually exceptionally
uncertainly severely occasionally
unexpectedly unbelievably foiled emerge
furthermore unfortunately boiling survive
approaching latches alternate crouched

3

1. mature
2. leveled
3. deafening

4

thorough through tough thought
though strewn sugar toppled
producing producer height reached
leveled frightening flared swirling
gigantic toothpicks including swayed
great burnt natural towering
continuing knotty change racing
parent unfailingly exchanged
joint particularly unfaithfully

Another Fire

5

When our redwood was eighty years old, it was producing seeds; however, less than one of every hundred seeds was fertile. Our redwood did not become a good seed producer until it was over two hundred years old. Then it continued to produce fertile seeds until its death.

After our redwood reached the height of seventy meters, it began to grow more and more slowly. It had become a mature tree. When it was two hundred years old, it was growing only a few centimeters a year, but it was already more than ninety meters tall. By the time it * was four hundred years old, it was growing at the rate of less than two centimeters a year.₁

It was during our redwood's 420th year that a terrible fire swept through the forest. This fire was not like the one that had leveled the small trees years before. This was a fire that rolled over the tops of the tallest trees in the forest, sending up flames more than 130 meters into a sky that was dark with smoke. The roar of the fire was deafening. Its speed was frightening. It began in a pile of dry litter near the * base of a young tree. The fire flared up in a few seconds. Within a minute it was climbing the smaller trees, then the larger ones. When it reached our redwood, the fire was a rolling, swirling mass that <u>was</u> hot enough to melt metal. With a rush it burned all the green needles from our redwood. It burned the branches and burned the trunk.₂

That fire smoldered for three months. A few trees toppled during the fire, particularly the very old ones. The parent of our redwood was one of those that toppled. The parent tree was more than * two thousand years old and had lived through five great fires. But most of the big trees remained standing. They looked like gigantic charred toothpicks sticking up from the black forest floor.

Not all of the trees in the forest were redwoods. Some were sugar pines, and there were a few oaks. The fire swept over all these trees. And when the following spring came, the older oaks were dead and the older sugar pines were dead. But the mature redwoods, including ours, were still alive.₃

The fire never reached the part of the tree trunk that was alive. The * living part of a tree trunk is a very thin layer just under the bark. The rest of a tree trunk or a branch is not alive. The wood inside is not alive. It is dead matter with a thin layer of living matter around it. The oaks in the forest were dead because their bark was about two centimeters thick. The fire burned through their bark and burned the layer of living matter just under the bark. The same thing happened to the sugar pines. But the mature redwoods have very thick bark. The bark on the trunk of * our redwood, for example, was about twenty centimeters thick.₄

1 un   ly

A	B
ridiculously	unfamiliar
particularly	uncertain
tightly	unnatural
actually	unexpectedly
exceptionally	

2 treasure exaggerate examine sure broil
occasionally probably stalled
situation voiced nature boasted
moist injure mature brighten insure

3
1. adapt
2. sprouts
3. canopy
4. strewn

4 through thought thorough though
tough colony colonies earth slaughter
Atlantic continent realize adopt
consider ordinary continued dense
century terrible surroundings loose
danger destroyed narrower
disturbed sugar endure

5

A Green Toothpick

*To realize how amazing the mature redwoods are, you have to remember that most other older trees become very fixed in their ways and would not adjust to the changes a fire would cause. Most young trees, whether they're redwoods or sugar pines, can adapt well to different situations. If you were to pile up dirt thirty centimeters deep around the base of a sugar pine sapling, the tree would adjust and keep on living. However, if you piled up dirt only ten centimeters deep around the base of a mature sugar pine, you would probably kill the tree.

Mature * trees often become so set in their ways that they die if the trees next to them are cut down. When these other trees are cut down, sunlight reaches the base of the mature tree, and the tree dies.₁ Now consider the mature redwood. Remember, our redwood was 420 years old when the fire burned every needle from it. You would think that a tree so old could not survive. But the redwood is no ordinary tree. And our redwood did survive.

The forest looked very strange the next spring. The charred trees that had looked like black toothpicks now * looked like green toothpicks. Little green sprouts shot out from the trunk of every mature redwood—from the ground to the top of every tree. Sprouts also shot out from what was left of the top branches. The trees <u>looked</u> very strange, almost as if somebody had painted the trunks and the remaining branches green.

The shoots grew very fast. By the end of the summer, some of them were almost three meters long. They continued growing rapidly during the next several years. The shoots near the bottom of the trees became shaded and died off. Those near the top * of the trees slowly took the shape of a cone. Within twenty years after the fire, the mature redwoods looked quite normal again, with long, bare trunks and green, full, cone-shaped tops.₂ Once more a canopy of green shaded the forest floor. The canopy was not as dense as it had been,

which meant that some of the younger trees that sprouted from the ground after the fire had a chance to grow more rapidly than young trees did before the great fire.

Century after century went by. When our tree was seventeen hundred years old, it lost its * top during a terrible windstorm. This happened the year before Columbus sailed across the Atlantic. The top thirteen meters of our redwood crashed to the forest floor, tearing branches from the surrounding trees and leaving a large hole in the canopy of green. That hole made it possible for some of the younger redwoods to grow. One seedling that sprouted the next year came from a seed of our redwood. That seedling was growing in the loose dirt dug up when the top of our redwood crashed to the forest floor. The seedling looked ridiculously small next to our huge * redwood.

Our redwood did not grow its top back quickly. Over two hundred years passed before the redwood was as tall as it had been before the windstorm. By now, British colonies were being settled on the other side of the continent.₃

Things remained peaceful in the redwood forest for the next three hundred years. Three smaller fires swept through the forest, and one left a large hole in the base of our redwood. Over the years a lot of animals used that hole, mostly squirrels and rabbits. It was big enough for three people to sit in, but it * didn't really harm the tree. The wood from redwoods doesn't rot even if it is exposed to the rain. Water will rot most other woods. Boards made from pine or fir must be treated if they are to be exposed to the weather. Not so with boards of redwood.₄

1

ly   un

A	B
suddenly	uneventful
severely	unstable
particularly	uncontrolled
rarely	unfortunately

2

exaggerate   unfailingly   assure   jointly   groans
exceptionally   unexplainable   creature
unfaithfully   hoist   lecture   surrounding
location   choicest   loaning   termites

3

1. polite
2. remarkable
3. outskirts
4. brittle

4

county   country   beautiful   shaped
contains   continues   becomes   forever
protected   gravel   narrower   edge
mature   destroy   contact   shallow
furniture   excellent   fault   dangerous
shrink   material   fences
building   square   bothered

The Redwoods Today

As you've seen, redwoods are remarkable. Fire can't destroy them. Even if young trees are cut down, they sprout up again. Redwoods are not bothered by termites or any insect that destroys other trees. The wood from redwoods is as remarkable as the trees. The wood will not rot if it comes in contact with wet earth. Even after the wood has been soaked for years, it won't rot. The wood is soft and easy to work with, so it makes good furniture and excellent siding for houses.₁

The redwood seems like a perfect tree, except for two faults. The * first fault is that the roots of redwoods are very shallow. They rarely go down more than ten feet. The roots fan out to the sides like great hooks or claws that hang on to the soil. When redwoods grow in forests, the roots of one tree lock under the roots of surrounding trees. When no trees surround the mature redwood, however, it becomes unstable. The first strong wind that hits the tree might blow it over.₂

Because redwoods have shallow roots, the trees are dangerous near cities. Let's say that a huge redwood—200 feet tall—is growing next * to some houses on the outskirts of town. And let's say that there are no surrounding trees. One night there is a great storm, and the redwood comes down.

The second problem is that the wood in older redwoods becomes brittle. It may split or crack. If that happens, parts of the tree may come down during a storm.₃

Because of these two problems, the redwood forests began to shrink up during the past 60 years. The great redwoods came down to make furniture, fences, and other building material. But even as early as 1921, the State of California began * giving money so that redwood parks could be formed. The old redwoods within these parks would be protected.

Our redwood does not live in one of these first parks. It lives near Arcata, California, in an area called Redwood Creek. And our redwood was lucky, because in 1968, the whole Redwood Creek area became part of a new park—Redwood National Park. The park contains 430 square kilometers of mature redwoods.₄

Our redwood is not the tallest tree along Redwood Creek. There is one that is more than 130 meters tall. But our redwood is one of the biggest trees. * It's not easy to find because there is no road that leads to it. To find it, you have to park your car on the gravel county road and walk along the edge of the creek, through the ferns and the soft litter on the forest floor. Look at the bigger trees and you'll see one with a base so big that you could hide three cars behind it. You'll see a cone-shaped hole near the bottom of the tree. And when you look up, the trunk seems to go up forever. But if you look closely, you'll see * a place near the top of the tree where the trunk suddenly becomes narrower, marking where the top had broken off long ago. And when you stand there in the silent forest looking at our redwood, you'll probably feel proud. You will be certain of one thing, however—you're looking at one beautiful tree.₅

1 conditioner Bruce office manage
furthermore grouchier occasionally
exceptionally simply curling
unbelievable pinched choice suburb

2
1. insurance
2. freeway
3. bothersome

3 sore phony polite insects world
vice president newspapers freeways
something usually timer everything
oven concrete simple neighbors
peaceful humming ocean groves
bananas coconuts jungle canopy
wearing pretend sour

Bruce the Grouch

Bruce Celt had a good job as vice president of an insurance company. Furthermore, he had a nice home. However, he was not happy. He didn't like to drive in his car on the freeways. He didn't like the food that he ate. He read the newspapers only occasionally because everything that happened in the world seemed bad.

Every day Bruce Celt went to work, and every day he worked hard. He worked through the lunch hour because he didn't like eating out. Sometimes he ate an apple or an orange.

After work he left the office, but he didn't * smile on his way out. He simply drove down the freeway. Honk, honk. Stop and go, and stop again. Honk. Every day it was the same.₁

Bruce lived alone. By the time he got home, his eyes were sore, and he had a pain in his head. Usually he parked his car in his garage and went into his house and sat. Occasionally he looked outside and watched what his neighbors were doing. But his neighbors didn't interest him. Sometimes he would sit outside in his yard, but the air was filled with smoke, and somebody was always trying to * talk to him. For example, one of his neighbors would say, "Hey, Bruce, have you seen my new car? It's nice. Come on over, and let's go for a spin in it." Bruce would try to be polite, but <u>he</u> couldn't help himself. He was a grouch.

After the sun went down, he would turn on the lights. But he didn't like lights because they seemed phony. They weren't sunlight. Usually he ate a frozen dinner. He took it from the freezer and popped it into the oven. When the timer on the oven went ding, he pulled out the * dinner and ate it.

After dinner Bruce would go for a walk. He would try to listen to the sounds of the birds and the insects. All he could hear, however, was the roar of cars on the freeway. Bruce usually walked for an hour. Then he would return to his home and go to bed.2

He was unhappy with his bed. It was too soft and too big. Furthermore, sleeping was not easy for Bruce. He would lie in bed and listen to the sound of the air conditioner. Occasionally he would hear the sound of the motor in * the freezer. And as he lay there, Bruce would find himself making the same wish night after night. "I wish I lived a life that was simple. With all my heart I wish that I could live with plants and animals, not with cars and concrete, not with television sets and freezers."3

But then something very strange happened. One night Bruce was sadder and grouchier than he had been for a long time. Things seemed very bad at the office. He couldn't stand another frozen dinner. His neighbors seemed exceptionally bothersome.

And that night he said to himself, "I'm going * to wish as hard as I can wish. I'm going to wish myself out of this place. I shouldn't have to spend the rest of my life being so unhappy. I'm going to wish harder than I've ever wished before."

So Bruce pressed his eyes shut as hard as he could and he wished. He made a picture of a place in his mind, and he wished for that place. It was a peaceful place—an island with trees and sand and warm ocean water. "Take me there," he wished. "Please, get me out of here."4

Bruce didn't remember falling * asleep that night. He only remembered wishing and wishing and wishing. When he woke up the next morning, however, he couldn't believe his eyes. He wasn't sleeping on his soft bed, and he wasn't in his bedroom listening to the humming of the air conditioner. In fact, he wasn't in his house; he was on a sandy beach. Not fifteen meters from where he sat was the ocean. Its gentle waves came curling along the beach. In back of him were groves of tall trees. He could see bananas and coconuts beneath the trees. He could hear the sound of * jungle birds in the canopy of green. This is unbelievable, Bruce said to himself. He pinched himself on the arm, but the trees, the sand, the ocean, and the exciting sounds did not go away. "I can't believe it," Bruce said to himself, and he stood up. He was wearing a pair of shorts and nothing more. There were no footprints in the sand.5

1 re

A	B
rebuild	require
regain	remember
reopen	reply
reappear	responsible
restate	remaining
	receiving

2 fertile particularly original especially
swirled slowly excited survive
future except thirsty moisture

3
1. deserve
2. breadfruit
3. bored

4 prove approval problems somersaults
earth parrots crickets fourth edge
bubbled fortunate restless wonder
worry tackle unfortunately coconuts
healthy realize although
handfuls smolder shoving among

A Dream Come True

Bruce walked slowly along the beach, stopping many times to look at the crabs and the seashells. He felt the warm morning breeze in his face. "I hope this is true," he thought. "I hope this is really true." Bruce wanted to jump up and down and yell, "Yippee." He wanted to turn somersaults in the sand. But in the back of his mind he kept thinking, "Maybe this isn't really happening. So don't get your hopes up."

Bruce stopped at the edge of the water and swirled his hand in it. Then he licked his fingers. Salty. The water * was salty, so the water was ocean water.₁

By the evening of his second day on the island, Bruce was getting used to the idea that he was not dreaming. By then he had walked all the way around the island and proved to himself that it was an island. He had eaten coconuts and bananas from the trees. He had also eaten breadfruit and berries. He had fallen asleep in the sun on the beach, and he had a sunburn to prove it. Later he had slept in the shade of a big coconut tree. He had watched parrots * and monkeys. He had breathed clean air and listened to the sounds of the waves, the crickets, and the bees. He had gone swimming in the ocean. Fortunately, he had found fresh water near the shore. It came from a refreshing spring. The water bubbled from the rocks and ran down the hill in a little stream. It was the best water Bruce had ever drunk.₂

After his third day on the island, Bruce felt less fortunate and a little more restless. He didn't enjoy watching the crabs on the beach as much as he had on the first two * days. The parrots in the trees didn't seem as exciting. While the sun seemed a little too hot, the shade seemed too dark.₃

And that evening when the sun was setting, he found himself saying, "I wonder what I'm going to do now?" He didn't want to go to sleep because he wasn't tired. However, there was no television to watch, no books to read, no lights to turn off.

The fourth day was even less exciting than the third. "I wished for this, so I guess I deserve it," he said to himself. "But there is nothing to do * here. If only there were some problems in this place. If only there were something to worry about. I wish there were other people on this island—even if I didn't like them."₄

No sooner had Bruce made the wish than he saw a group of women and men walking down the beach. "That's strange," Bruce thought. "I've looked over this island from one end to the other, and I haven't seen a single footprint, except the ones I've made. Where did these people come from?"

"Hello," Bruce called. He waved.

They waved back. Then one of them said in * a high voice, "Unk, unk."

Bruce walked over to the people. Bruce pointed to himself. "My name is Bruce," he said. "Bruce."

A tall woman wearing a long robe replied, "Unk," and pointed to her mouth.

"If you're thirsty," Bruce said, "let me give you some water. Follow me." He led the others to the spring in the grove of trees. But when he got to the spot where the water had been bubbling up from the rocks, there was no water. There was no stream.

"Unfortunately, there is no water," Bruce said. "However, we can always drink coconut milk." * He looked around for coconuts on the ground. He couldn't see any healthy ones. There had been hundreds of them, but now they all looked rotten.₅

1

un ly re

A	**B**
return	repeat
reply	remodel
require	report
remember	receive

2

**thirsty expecting situations glanced
survive silently except logical**

3

1. disturbed
2. provides
3. heave

4

strangely realized immediate solve
fighters although probably branches
unafraid insurance smoldering extended
collecting decided pry pried forehead
bored signs ankle among
scoop handfuls shoving tasted

5

More Problems to Tackle

One man pointed to his mouth and said, "Unk, unk."

Bruce said, "You're probably hungry. Well, we certainly should be able to find some breadfruit or bananas. Follow me." The others followed, but all the trees seemed to be bare. Bruce was becoming disturbed. Where had all the bananas and breadfruit gone? What had happened to the water? And what would happen if he didn't find water pretty soon?

Bruce knew that he would probably die within five days without water. He knew that he could go a long time without food. In fact, he had read about people who * had gone thirty days without food. However, people can't live very long without water.₁

Bruce turned to the other people, and suddenly he found himself talking to them. He was explaining the situation, even though he knew that they didn't understand what he was saying. "Let's look at our problem," Bruce said slowly. "We have no fresh water. It is impossible for us to drink water from the sea because the water is salty."

Bruce glanced at the strangers. They were standing silently, watching him. Strangely enough, Bruce was unafraid. In fact, he felt excited about solving a problem. For * an instant he remembered situations in which he had solved problems for his insurance company. For an instant Bruce realized how much he had missed those problems.

"We don't have to worry so much about food," Bruce said aloud, "because we can survive a long time without food. Our water problem is more immediate."₂ The strangers stared, and Bruce paced back and forth in front of them. "We can solve this problem if we're logical."

Bruce pointed to the sea. "We could boil seawater and collect the steam, which would turn into fresh water. Or we could dig for water. * In either case, we will need tools."

Bruce turned to the strangers. "What do you want to do?"

"Unk."₃

Bruce decided that it would probably be easier to dig for water than to boil seawater. He and the others walked to the place where the spring had been. Bruce found a rock with a sharp edge that he used to make a point on the end of a stout branch. Then he walked to the pile of rocks where the spring had been. He wedged the point of the stick between two rocks; then he pushed down on the stick * and pried a rock loose. Bruce picked up the rock

and tossed it aside. "See?" he said. "Use this to dig. Dig."₄

"Unk," one woman said. Soon everybody was working with long, stout branches. Some of the people pried up rocks, while others heaved them aside, making a hole where the stream had been. "If we dig deep enough, we should reach fresh water," Bruce explained as he wiped his hand across his forehead. The work was heavy, and the day seemed exceptionally hot, but Bruce was not bored. He was solving a problem and that was exciting.₅

The hole * became deeper and deeper. At first the bottom of the hole was dry. By the time the hole was waist-deep, the rocks were damp, and there were signs of moisture in the hole. When the hole was neck-deep and only two people could work in it at a time, there were more signs of water. The rocks that were being heaved from the hole now were soaking wet.₆

Finally, the two people working in the hole were standing ankle-deep in fresh water, and the hole was beginning to fill. Some of the other people didn't want to * wait for the water to reach the level of the ground. They jumped into the hole and began drinking the water, which was still muddy. Bruce was among them. He jumped into the hole and managed to bend over and scoop up handfuls of water. The hole was only a few meters across, but there were five people in it, shoving, pushing, and trying to drink. But the water tasted great to Bruce. He smiled, laughed, splashed water on the other people, and drank until his sides hurt. He felt unbelievably happy and refreshed.₇

1

re   ly   un

A	B
exceptionally	responsible
refreshed	uncertain
particularly	fortunately
unfortunate	repeated

2

moisture soaking easier wedged

sharp explained replied occasionally

expect painted thirsty

unbelievably stout injure

3

1. flexible

2. shortage

3. suitable

4. procedure

4

disappeared ordinary single surface

sharpened average constructed serious

waded waddled severe branches

solved choice provided furthermore

probably practice difficult fitted

instead feast stray

rapidly removed announced

5

Finding Food

That night, when the well was full of fresh water and the people were no longer thirsty, Bruce thought about the things that had happened. He tried to figure out how his life had changed when the things on the island had changed. Here's what he figured out: To live, you need some things. You need food and water. When the island had plenty of food and water, Bruce didn't have to do anything to stay alive. He didn't have to hunt for food, and he didn't have to hunt for water. But when the food and water disappeared from * the island, Bruce had to do something. He had to figure out a way to get water. He dug a well, but before he dug the well, he had to make tools. Bruce hadn't made tools during his first three days on the island because he hadn't needed them to stay alive.₁

Bruce and the others had solved the water problem. The next problem they faced was the lack of food.

"We can make tools for hunting the animals in the jungle," Bruce said, "or we can make nets for fishing in the sea." He looked at the jungle and * then at the sea. "I think we'll start with the tools for hunting birds and rabbits."

The tools were bows and arrows. Bruce made five bows from stout, flexible branches.₂ The bowstrings were vines tied to each end of the branches, and the arrows were long, straight sticks, sharpened on one end against a flat rock and fitted on the other end with parrot feathers.

Now it was time to practice shooting with the bows and arrows. After an hour's practice, some of the strangers were quite good. Bruce was probably about average at hitting a target made of grass. *₃ Things were far more difficult when they went hunting in the jungle, however. They searched for five hours, and in the end the hunters had killed only two rabbits and one bird.

Even before the hunt was over, Bruce said to himself, "I think that we should try to get food by fishing instead of by hunting." The hunters had spent most of their time trying to find the stray arrows that they had shot.

Although the hunters had started out with twenty-one arrows, they had only three left when the hunt was completed.₄

"This won't be a big * feast," Bruce announced, "but it will probably be a good one." To cook the dinner, Bruce made a fire. He made it in the way the Indians would build fires. He looped the bowstring around a stick and twirled the stick back and forth by moving the bow. One end of the stick was pressed against a rock. That end began to get hot as the stick turned rapidly. Small bits of wood placed on the rock next to the hot end of the stick began to smoke. Suddenly, the wood bits burst into flame. The strangers shouted "Unk, unk" * and smiled.

After dinner Bruce was still hungry. Something had to be done about the shortage of food. He said, "We'll probably have better luck fishing than hunting." And he was right. The group made nets from vines collected in the coconut grove. Four people waded into the ocean, tossed the net over a school of fish, pulled the net toward shore, and caught two fish. They repeated the procedure and caught three more fish.₅

That evening Bruce again thought of the events. "First we solved the water problem, which was the most serious problem," he said to himself. "Now * we have solved the food problem." As Bruce lay there near the fire with a long stalk of grass between his teeth, he thought, "I just wish that the other people could speak English. I'm tired of listening to 'Unk, unk.' "

At that moment, one woman walked over to Bruce and said, "That was a particularly good fish dinner."₆

returning   temperature   chattered

remarkable   judged   unusually

repeated   mature   severely   celebration

Centa   survival   extreme

1. tingly
2. site

breaking   delighted   strewn   shelter

group   younger   discovered   hollowing

serious   huddled   covering   shivering

already   remain   blazed   bear   suitable

probably   strangers   dancing   protect

jogged   feasting   located   replies   feathers

coals   learned   reporting   particularly

rethink   blowing   concluded   surroundings

Fighting the Cold

4

For some unknown reason all the strangers could speak English. Bruce was delighted. "This is remarkable. It calls for a celebration," he announced. There was a great celebration with racing, dancing, singing, telling stories, and a lot of feasting.

Bruce slept well that night. When he woke up in the morning, he was shivering.[1] It was snowing, and the air was unusually cold. Bruce judged the temperature to be below zero. The ocean was gray. The waves were breaking loudly, and the whitecaps were rolling far up the beach. The trees looked different because they had lost their leaves. Small * drifts of snow were starting to build up here and there.

"What's this?" Bruce said. Two people standing near him were shivering, too. One of them was a woman named Centa. Bruce had learned her name the day before.

Centa said, "If we can't find some way to stay warm, I'm afraid we will all die. Already some of us are getting sick."[2]

Bruce thought for a moment. His teeth chattered every time he tried to say something.

At last he said, "Let's build up the fire." The people gathered wood and threw it on the fire. The fire blazed * up in big, orange flames. Showers of sparks and smoke rose into the air.

"We need a shelter," Bruce said, standing close to the fire and rubbing his hands together. "We'll never survive this cold unless we build a shelter."

"What is shelter?" Centa asked.

Bruce explained, "A shelter is a place that is warm and dry. We could build a place that would protect us from the wind and cold. Maybe we could dig a cave in the side of a hill, or we could construct a shelter out of branches and vines and dry grass."₃

Bruce, Centa, and * the others jogged off to find a suitable site for the shelter. Centa found a steep hill that faced away from the sea.

"Bring the digging tools over here," Bruce said. "We'll hollow out this part of the hill. After we've made a little cave, we'll cover the front of it with some material that will break the wind."

Three people began hollowing out the side of the hill while Bruce and Centa started to make a covering for the front of the cave.₄ "Let's weave long branches together," Bruce suggested. "Then we can cover them with leaves and grass * and whatever else we can find."

One young woman kept the fire going. From time to time people working on the shelter would run over to the fire and warm up. Then they would return to their work. The group worked very fast. Before an hour had gone by, they had hollowed out the side of the

hill. By then Bruce and Centa had made a covering for the front of the cave.

Bruce and Centa fitted the "door" they had made over the front of the cave. Then Bruce used a tool to drag hot coals to the shelter. * "We don't want a big fire in our shelter," he told the others. "If the fire is too big, it will make a lot of smoke, and we'll have trouble breathing."₅

As everybody huddled together inside the cave, Bruce announced, "The next thing we have to do is make warm clothes. We can use the skins from the rabbits we hunt. Maybe we can also use feathers from the birds."

Unfortunately, the problem with rabbits and birds, as Bruce realized, is that they are small. To make a coat from the hides of rabbits, a person might need as many * as twenty or thirty rabbits. The hide of one large animal like a bear, however, would make two or three coats.₆

The next morning the wind was blowing particularly hard. As Bruce sat in the shelter waiting for the wind to die down, he began to rethink the things that were happening to him. He concluded, you need some things to stay alive. You need air, warmth, water, and food. Unless you have all of those things, you die. If you don't want to die, you've got to do something. You've got to build something or change your surroundings in * some way.₇ If you don't have enough warmth, you've got to do something so that you can stay warm. If you don't have enough water, you've got to do something that will give you enough water.

1

dis

A	B
dishonor	displease
disjoin	distract
displace	dislocate
distance

2

ch<u>oi</u>ce appr<u>oa</u>ched <u>ner</u>vously <u>dis</u>gusted

3

1. chores
2. comment
3. hoist
4. chimney

4

whispered sneak spotted squealing calm
hooves thread cloth yarn pounded
braced fan-shaped clothes obviously
remained fibers splitting reported
create howling hollowing pleasantly
notice tingly surprised
nervous collected narrow

5

Life Problems

Bruce looked outside. He could hear the wind howling. It made him shiver just listening to it. He remained in the shelter and began to think again. He thought, "Air, warmth, water, and food are survival problems. If you have more than one survival problem at the same time, the first problem you solve is the problem that would take your life first. If you have a water problem and a food problem, you solve the water problem first, because the water problem will take your life first. If you have a water problem and an air problem, you obviously * would solve the air problem first, because the air problem will take your life first."[1]

Centa went to the door of the shelter and looked outside. "I think the wind is dying down," she reported.

Bruce said, "Good. This is our chance to gather the material that we need to make warm clothes."

Bruce, Centa, and one of the men left the shelter. Bruce braced himself for the cold, and at first he was pleasantly surprised. The air didn't seem as cold as he had thought it would be. However, as he jogged along with the others toward a place * where dead vines lay in tangles on the ground, he began to notice the cold. His legs were becoming tingly. The tips of his ears and fingers began to hurt. "Let's keep moving," he said to the others. "It is very cold out here."₂

Bruce collected vines, while Centa picked up the skins of the rabbits they had eaten the day before. The other man peeled bark from some of the trees.

Then they returned to the shelter with their materials. Bruce looked over the materials, and he said, "We can pound the bark with rocks and make cloth out * of it." Bruce showed two others how to do it. As they pounded away on the bark, Bruce told another woman, "Pull the fibers from the vines. We can use those fibers as thread or yarn." So the woman began pulling the fibers from the vines.

Bruce said, "I'll use them as thread to lace the rabbit skins together, but first I'll need a needle."₃

Centa ran to the beach and found some fan-shaped shells. She took one of the shells and hit it gently with a rock, splitting it into long, narrow pieces that were pointed at one * end. "This will work as a needle," she said, handing one of the pieces to Bruce.

Bruce tied the vine fiber around the fat end of the needle and pushed the needle through one of the rabbit skins. As Bruce worked, Centa commented, "We'll need a lot more skins before we can make clothes from these skins. Let's make cloth clothes first; then we'll go hunting for some larger animals."

"Yes," Bruce said. "If we find larger animals, we can make clothes faster."₄

Early the next day, when the sky was growing light gray, Bruce and two other people went * hunting. On the far side of the island, a long distance from their shelter, they found tracks made in the snow by a large animal and examined them. Following the tracks, they soon came to a hill near the beach. A large wild pig and two baby pigs were standing there. "Don't kill the baby pigs," Bruce whispered as he and the other hunters began to sneak up the hill.₅ The large pig spotted them and began to run away. A woman shot an arrow, hitting the pig in the side. The pig turned around and began to squeal loudly. * Bruce shot an arrow that struck the pig in the chest, and the pig fell over.

Bruce felt sick as he walked over to the pig. It disgusted him to kill animals. He wouldn't have killed the pig if he'd had a choice, but what was he to do?

The little pigs ran nervously around the mother pig, squealing loudly. They did not run away when Bruce and the others approached.₆ One hunter picked up both of the baby pigs. He held one under each arm. As soon as he picked them up, they stopped squealing, and they seemed to * calm down.

Bruce and the others tied the large pig's front hooves together with a vine. They also tied the back hooves together. Then they slid a branch between the pig's legs. They hoisted the branch and carried the pig back to their shelter.₇

1 dis

A	B
dislike	dislocate
disjoin	distract
distrust	disbelief
	distaste

2

obviously   arrangement   chores
exception   unbelievable   piece   mounted
occasionally   nearly   attached
chowder   investigation   starting
particular   charred   relaxed   probably

3

1. examine
2. chowder
3. husks
4. verses
5. remodel

4

chimney   scraped   skinned   preparing
commented   bowl   plenty   tackled   tusks
started   giant   caught   busy   sang   chorus
comfortable   sense   vines   solved   unfortunately

Problems of Comfort

Bruce said, "We will try to keep the young pigs and raise them. But that means we will have to find food to feed them. And we must build a shelter for them."

For the rest of the day, the people took turns making a shelter for the pigs next to the shelter for the people. There was a pen in front of the pigs' shelter. The pigs could stay in their yard or go inside their shelter.

Bruce and Centa dug up some plants that had survived the snow. They threw the plants inside the pen. "These will give * the young pigs something to eat," Bruce commented.₁

Later that day Bruce and the others were huddled inside the shelter. The large pig was cooking over a small fire. It had been skinned. The skin had been scraped and was hanging on one wall of the shelter.

There was a lot to do—feed the pigs, hunt for food, get water and wood, make clothes, and make the shelter more comfortable. Work would be done faster if each person had a specific job.

Different people were given different jobs. One woman was given the job of preparing the pigskin by * pounding it with rocks until it was soft. One man did the chores around the shelter. Other people were given the job of fixing up the shelter. They were to make it bigger and to build a chimney so that the shelter would not be smoky. Bruce and Centa were to take care of the hunting and fishing. They would go out and find food for the others.₂

The day after the three pigs were found, Bruce and the others rigged up a way to catch fish without getting wet. They reworked their fishing net so that it looked like * a giant bowl that was attached to a long pole. Standing on the shore and holding the pole, Bruce and Centa could move the net along under the water. Fish swam into the open end of the net.

In one day Bruce and Centa caught thirty-six fish. The biggest was nearly a meter long.₃ They also made three crab traps. They dug deep holes on the beach, lined the walls of the holes with sticks, and waited. Bruce said, "When the tide comes in, these holes will be underwater. Then the tide will go out. Some crabs should fall * into the holes, and they won't be able to get out."

That evening the people had bowls of crab chowder. The bowls were made of coconut husks and the spoons they used were seashells. There were bits of seaweed and other plants in the crab chowder. After the chowder came fish, and after the fish everybody relaxed.

Bruce looked around at the shelter that the others had made larger. There was a chimney above the fire. The chimney was made of mud and of rocks tied together with vines.₄

As the people were sitting around, Bruce thought, "Obviously we solved * the problems of life first. Those were the problems of water, food, and warmth. After we solved these problems, we started to solve problems of comfort. We didn't have to raise pigs to stay alive; however, raising pigs is easier than hunting for them. We didn't have to make the new nets, but it is much more comfortable to catch fish from the shore with the new net. And we didn't have to remodel the shelter, but the chimney makes it more comfortable in the shelter."₅

Bruce looked at the pigskin mounted on the wall. Then he said to himself, * "We solved the life problems first. Then, after we solved the last life problem, we began to solve problems of comfort. That makes a lot of sense.₆ If we didn't solve all of the life problems first, we wouldn't have to worry about the problems of comfort. Unfortunately, we would be dead."

Just then one young woman said, "Let's sing songs." That sounded like a good idea, so everybody sang. One of the older men made up a song about the shelter. Everybody sang it.

"Oh, the shelter is warm,
the shelter is good.
We've got plenty of food
and * plenty of wood.
Our shelter is fine.
Our shelter is fine.
When we're in our shelter,
we have a very good time."

Different people made up verses. Then everybody repeated the chorus of the song.₇

Late that night Bruce woke up. He hadn't thought about this before, but he realized now that he didn't mind talking to people on the island. He didn't mind his job; in fact, he didn't think about his job much. There were things that had to be done, and Bruce was excited about doing them. There were problems to solve, and he tackled them. He * didn't have time to think about whether he was happy or sad. He was too busy to be a grouch.₈

1

A	B	C
un	distinct	disappeared
ly	discovery	displeased
re	disbelief	discomfort
dis		disagreement

2

1. extension
2. argument
3. deadlocked
4. hammock

3

achieved figure remodeling completed

loose combination referred original

rattle consisted thoughtfully

procedures particularly warmer

charge collected obviously switched

continued connecting entire leaned

specific occurred examine announced

arrangement prepared exceptional

unbelievable agreement individual

caution comfortable unfortunate

usually decision involved

4

The Trees Are Dead

The days were cold for about two months. The weather then became obviously warmer. Spring was coming and by now the shelter had been remodeled three times.

The first remodeling occurred about three weeks after the weather had turned cold. This remodeling was achieved by digging another hole next to the original one and then joining the two holes, forming a shelter that was about twice the size of the original one. The second remodeling began almost as soon as the first had been completed. It consisted of a large extension with a flat roof and a large fireplace. The * people referred to this area as the porch. It became the workroom. Animal skins and tools hung on the grass-and-wood walls. The last remodeling consisted of a second story, which was dug out of part of the hill above the original cave and connected with it by a roof and a ladder.₁ The second story became the sleeping area, and the entire downstairs became a combination workroom, kitchen, and dining area.

Everyone had specific jobs, but some people had switched jobs with other people. It turned out that one older man was very good at making clothes, so * he switched jobs with the man who had been making them. Also, the procedures for taking care of the animals had changed. By now there were four young pigs, two wild dogs, over thirty monkeys, and ten rabbits in a large, open pen. The monkeys were not doing well. They couldn't seem to stand the cold weather. The woman in charge of the animals collected plants and seeds for them to eat, made sure that they had plenty of water, and cleaned the animals' shelter.₂

One day, when the weather was particularly warm, Centa and Bruce were out checking their * traps. Bruce pointed to the trees. "Unfortunately, I think these trees are dead," he said. He took his ax and chopped through the bark of the tree. He looked at the layer that was just beneath the bark. "See," he said. "If this tree were alive, it would have a bright green layer beneath the bark. The layer on this tree is gray, which means that the tree is dead."₃

Bruce and Centa checked the other trees. All were dead. Finally Bruce said, "We probably won't have coconut, banana, or breadfruit trees this summer. Furthermore, all of the animals that * live off the trees will have no food, so they will either die or leave the island."

Centa said, "What are we going to do if we don't have food this summer?"

Bruce said, "We may be able to live off the sea animals. But we will have trouble keeping the land animals if we can't find plants for them." Bruce leaned against a dead tree and continued thoughtfully. "Maybe we should think about building a boat and leaving the island."₄

That evening Bruce sat on his hammock in the shelter and thought, "When people move from place to place, * they do so because they figure that the new place will be better than the old place. The old place probably doesn't give them enough comfort. Things are too hard in the old place. They don't know what things will be like in the new place, but they figure that there is a place where things are better. So they go out to find that place. If the old place gives them the comfort they want, there is no reason for them to move. If the old place doesn't give them the comfort they want, they may think about moving * to another place. If the old place has a life problem, they must move from the old place, because if they don't, they will die."₅

The days were getting warm now. Some grass was beginning to grow, so the group decided to turn the animals loose and let them hunt for their own food. Each animal had a rattle around its neck that was made from little bones and coconut shells. You could hear the animals even if you could not see them. However, most of the animals stayed near the shelter.₆

1
agree
agreed
agreement
argue
argument
argued

2
dis ly re un

A	B
displeased	dissatisfied
replied	exceptionally
exactly	disagreement

3
whether cheered unbelievable scratched
unusually cautioned announced original
survived choice maintain future exactly

4
1. decision   2. solution   3. enforce

5
involved deadlocked possible almost
decided property obviously excited
occasionally meant particularly
protected risk exceptionally decisions
individuals agreements unfortunately

6

Their First Real Argument

*The people had their first real argument that spring. The group disagreed about whether they should remain on the island or move. To move, the group would have to build a boat and sail across the sea. Obviously, there was some risk involved in moving. The question was whether there wasn't as much risk in remaining on the island.

Centa didn't want to move. She spoke for the others who agreed with her. She said, "There is some grass on the island, which means that there will be some food for the animals. We will probably discover that we can * survive here."

Bruce was in favor of building a boat. He spoke for those who agreed with him. He said, "Even if we don't use the boat, we should be ready to move if we have to. I think we should build the boat and then see what happens."₁

"No," Centa argued. "Building a boat will take a lot of time. We should use that time for planting seeds and growing crops."

Bruce said, "I don't agree with you. It is possible that most seeds won't grow after the cold winter. Furthermore, some seeds need years and years to grow * into plants that will have fruit."

The argument continued for days. At last Centa said, "We've got to figure out some way to settle this argument. Since there is an even number of us, we are deadlocked. Half want to build a boat; half don't. If there were one more person, we could never be deadlocked."₂

Then everybody began to argue about how to settle the disagreement. Some people said that Bruce should have two votes. Centa and the people on her side said that Centa should have two votes. But the people on Bruce's side said, "No way."

On * the third day of the argument, Bruce stated, "We should figure out a fair way to settle this argument." Everybody agreed, and here's their solution. They found a flat stone and on one side of it scratched an X. They placed the stone inside a coconut shell. Then they shook the shell and turned it over. They had agreed that they would build the boat if the stone landed so that the X was showing. If the other side was showing, they would not build the boat.₃

The side without the X showed. Everybody on Centa's side was excited and * cheered.

One woman on Bruce's side of the argument was displeased. She said, "I don't care what the stone says. I'm going to build a boat. The rest of you can do anything you want."

Bruce said, "No. We agreed that we would all do whatever the stone said. That means we're all going to do it."₄

Bruce was thinking there were many laws in the city where he had lived—traffic laws, laws about how to do business, laws that protect people and their property. On the island there were no laws at first. Bruce and the others had * just made one—a law about how the group makes decisions. This law told every person that, even though each person has some rights, the group has rights, too. Individuals can not do what they want if it hurts the group.

"I changed my mind," the woman said.

"No," Bruce said. "If we live together, you can't change your mind about some things. What if you decided to kill all of the animals? That would hurt the rest of us, so we couldn't let you do that. What if you decided to take somebody's clothes? That wouldn't be fair to * that person. So we can't let you make that choice."

"Who's going to stop me?" the woman asked.

"We will," Bruce said. "The rest of us must enforce the rules."₅

"That's not fair to me," the woman replied.

Bruce said, "Well, it's not fair to us if you break your agreements."

The woman walked away and acted angry for many days. She did her job, but she was pretty dissatisfied and grouchy about it.

1

un re dis

A	B
removed	unbelievably
uncertain	discovered
responded	replied

2

excellent surface thorns
pressure enforce peacefully
shapely solution decision advice

3

1. prevented
2. barge
3. minnows
4. evaporate
5. remarked

4

patches paddles smoldering exceptionally
hundred tiller occasionally narrow
quite cove quiet prevented quit
signaled caught argued piece
obviously stretch attached constructing

5

Visitors

As the days got hotter, Bruce and the others planted seeds. First they had to make new tools for plowing up the land. Then they planted the seeds they had found during the winter. After the seeds had been planted, the people waited. Some plants came up, but unfortunately they had bitter stems and bitter roots. Everybody agreed that there would not be a good food crop. The grass on the island grew in little patches; however, these patches were far apart. Between them was bare ground. There were a few bitter plants growing among the dead trees, but there * weren't many of them. There were some other plants that grew exceptionally slowly.[1]

Then one day one man came running to the shelter. He yelled, "A boat! There's a boat coming to the island!" Bruce and the others ran down to the beach. The boat was over ten meters long and very narrow. The people on the island jumped into the water and swam out to meet the boat. The people in the boat were smiling and waving their paddles.

When the boat was on the beach and everybody had greeted the people in the boat, a woman from the * boat said, "We have come to look for fish—we have no fish near our island."₂

"We have lots of fish," Centa said.

The woman said, "We will give you gold for your fish."

Bruce said, "We don't have any need for gold. Do you have anything that we need?"

"All we have with us is a boat full of bananas. That is the only thing that grows on our island."

Bruce and the others smiled. "Bananas?" Bruce asked. "We will trade for bananas. We will give you one fish for every five bananas."₃

"That is fair," the woman said * as she started to count out five hundred bananas. Bruce counted out one hundred fish, and the trade was made.

When the visitors left the island, they said that they would come back within two weeks with at least two thousand bananas. After the boat had left, Centa said, "We must start catching fish. We will need four hundred fish for the trade."

"We will need a place to keep those fish alive," Bruce remarked. "If we kill them, they will all be rotten by the time two weeks have passed." That made sense to the others.

Centa said, "I * discovered a narrow cove on the north end of the island that will make an excellent sea cage."₄

The little cove was shaped like the letter U. "This cove is perfect," Bruce said. "If we stretch a net across the mouth of the cove, the fish will be prevented from swimming away."

After fixing the sea cage, the people began constructing more nets. They made nets for catching small fish that would be used as bait for large fish. The people made fishhooks from the thorns that they removed from dead bushes. They attached minnows to the thorns, and they * attached the thorns to a line. A piece of wood attached to the line worked like a bobber; when it went underwater, it signaled that a fish had been hooked.₅

The people continued to fish night and day; however, after one week had passed, the group had caught only sixty-five fish. Bruce announced, "We've got to figure out how to catch fish at a faster rate. And I think I have an idea. The fish are not near the shore; therefore, they must be out in deep water. We've obviously got to go out and get them."

"How are * we going to do that?" one woman asked.

"We'll build a little fishing barge," Bruce replied. "We'll make the barge big enough for two people who will go out and catch fish. They'll store the fish on the barge and return when the barge is loaded with fish."₆

Two people began to argue. One woman thought that it was a good idea to build a barge. But one man said, "There are more of us than there are of them. When those people come with the bananas, we'll take what we want."

Centa responded, "The people won't want to trade * with us after we do that."

Bruce said, "Let's take a vote. And let's give Centa two votes so that we don't have a deadlock."₇

Everybody agreed, and they voted. There were more votes for building the barge. That afternoon they chopped down trees, gathered vines, and tied the tree trunks together with the vines. They worked all night. Occasionally some people would rest for three hours while the other people worked. Then they would switch; those who had been resting would work while the others rested.

1

thought
through
tough
enough
ought
brought

2

steering   returning   tiller   regain
probably   displeased   unlikely   balanced

3

1. shad
2. bargain

4

floated   fortunately   restate   unfair
remarked   kilograms   evaporate
centimeters   smolder   finally   smiling
handfuls   spotted   cheat   branches
pointed   argument   weigh   weighs
weighed   weight   attractive

5

A Smart Trade

By noon the next day, they had completed the barge. It wasn't a very attractive barge, but it floated. The bottom of the barge was made up of seven logs tied together. Each log was about eight meters long. In the back of the barge was a tiller for steering. There was a small sail made of grass and vines and bark.

And in the middle of the barge was a large box. The box was about four meters long, two meters wide, and one meter high. It would hold many, many fish.[1]

Bruce and a man named Jonas went * out on the barge with nets and fishing lines. They planned to be gone for as long as a week, returning in time to trade for bananas.

Fortunately, the barge didn't have to go far before the men spotted schools of fish. Most of the fish were more than a meter long. Jonas threw handfuls of small minnows into the water. Just then Bruce had a fish on his line. It pulled so hard that it began to move the barge. "Drop your bait and help me with this fish," Bruce yelled. Jonas pulled in his line and grabbed onto * Bruce's line. Finally, the contest was over, and the men had a fish that was three meters long. It probably weighed more than one hundred kilograms.2 It was not a shad; it was a big, blue tuna fish.

That was the first tuna fish the men caught, but not the last one. Before the sun went down they had thirty shad and twelve tunas. Most of the tunas were two meters long; however, one was even larger than the first one they had caught.

Finally, the barge box was filled with tuna fish, but Jonas and Bruce did not have * hundreds and hundreds of fish. They had only forty-two fish.

Jonas remarked, "We made a deal with the woman to trade one fish for five bananas. But most of these fish must be worth one hundred bananas each. Some of them must be worth five hundred bananas."3

A week later the woman and her friends returned to the island. They came in three boats; each boat was loaded with bananas. When Bruce and Centa met them on the shore, Bruce was holding a pan full of minnows. Also in the pan was a fish that was about thirty centimeters * long. This was the size of fish the woman had traded for when she came to the island before.

After Bruce and Centa greeted the woman and the others, Bruce held up the fish that was thirty centimeters long.4 Bruce said, "Do you remember what we said we would trade for?"

"Yes," the woman said. "We said that we would give you five bananas for every fish."

"Good," Bruce said. "This fish is worth five bananas. Is that right?"

"Yes," the woman said. She was smiling.

Bruce held up one of the minnows. "And this fish is worth five bananas," * he said.

The woman stopped smiling. "Are you trying to cheat us?" she said. "That fish is not even a fish. I won't give you five bananas for that little thing."

"You are right," Bruce said. "We must be fair." Bruce walked over to a scale that he had made from two branches. The branches formed a T. Bruce placed the first fish on one end of the T. Then he placed a rock on the other end, and the scale balanced. Bruce picked up the rock and said, "Why don't we call the weight of this rock one fish?" * 5

"That is fair," the woman said. "So you would have to place many of those tiny fish on the scale to balance the weight of the rock."

"That is right," Bruce said. Then he signaled the others to bring out the largest of the fish from their sea cage. Bruce pointed to the big tuna. He said, "This fish weighs as much as seven hundred of these rocks. So we have to treat this fish as if it were seven hundred fish."

At first the woman looked displeased. Then she smiled and said, "That is fair, and that is a * lovely fish."

1

re un dis

A	B
unfortunately	unnoticed
regain	displeased
uneventful	uncertain
reflection	require

2

spoil shade amount occasionally
cleaning particularly probably several
certainly salted furthermore barges

3

1. demand   2. disapprove   3. encounter

4

shore excellent announced smolder
frowned trouble evaporating firewood
demand fresh stacked pieces bargain
shad price severe partly simple similar

5

Another Sharp Trade

Bruce and the woman decided to trade again. After the three boats left, Centa said, "We should go out for the tuna and shad again. The fish may move away from here, and we won't be able to trade for bananas."

Bruce agreed. Before two people could leave on the fishing trip, everybody helped build a shed for storing the dead fish. They called it the shad shed. One woman said, "We built the shad shed in the shade so that the tuna would not spoil."[1]

Jonas and another man went out in the barge for two days. When they * returned, they had fifty fish on the barge. Everybody spent most of the day cleaning the fish, removing bones and the insides, and feeding the insides to the pigs and wild dogs. The people stacked the fish in the shad shed and made a hot fire in the shed. When the fire was blazing hot, they threw wet grass on the fire so that the fire would smolder and produce a great amount of smoke. After smoking the fish for more than twenty-four hours, they rubbed salt all over the fish. They got the salt by evaporating seawater. They * smoked the fish again, this time for over a week. The smoke and the salt kept the bugs away from the fish.₂

Several days before the boats were to return to the island with bananas, some of the people complained. An old woman said, "We put a lot of work in on this batch of fish. We had to clean them and store them, then we had to salt them and smoke them so that they would keep. Yet we agreed to trade for the same price we traded for before. That's unfair to us."

Bruce replied, "That's an excellent * point. I have a plan, and for this plan we need small shore fish."₃

A week later Bruce and Jonas met the boats from the other island. Centa and the others were sitting in the shade near the shad shed eating smoked fish. Next to Bruce were the small shore fish, which were rotting and smelled particularly bad. They were covered with flies and other bugs.

After the boats were on the shore, Bruce announced, "We're ready to trade."

The woman looked at the fish next to Bruce and said, "Those fish are rotten. We certainly won't trade for them." *

Jonas said, "Well, the only other fish we have are smoked fish, and I don't think it would be fair to trade those at the fresh fish price."₄

The woman was displeased and frowned. Bruce called for Centa to bring over some pieces of smoked fish. Centa passed these pieces to the people who had come to trade. "This tastes unusually good," the woman said.

"Yes," Centa said. "And since they are smoked, you certainly don't have to worry about them rotting. They will keep."

The woman frowned again and said, "Yes, some of the fish in the last batch * began to rot before we could eat them. However, we wouldn't have that trouble with these fish."

Bruce said, "Do you think it would be fair to trade one smoked fish for nine bananas?"₅

"No, I disapprove," the woman said. "One fish for six bananas."

Centa laughed. "That's not fair," she said.

Centa, Bruce, and the woman bargained for a long time. At last they agreed that one fish for seven and a half bananas was a fair price.

Things were going particularly well on the island. Trading boats came to the island every month during the summer. By the * end of the summer there were plenty of bananas for the winter. Life was almost uneventful.₆

Centa, Bruce, and Jonas had caught enough fish to last for a long time. These fish were smoked and salted and hung in the shed. Furthermore, during the summer the women and men had found other animals. Now the people on the island had more than fifty animals. Also they had cut down many dead trees, and there was lots of firewood for the winter.

Occasionally, Bruce would think about what had happened. The people on his island could catch fish. There was a * demand for fish on the woman's island. The people on her island had lots of bananas. There was a demand for bananas on Bruce's island, so the people traded. The people on Bruce's island got bananas, and the people on the other island got fish. Bruce said to himself, "The price of things goes up when there is a demand for those things. If somebody needs fish, the price goes up. If they have plenty of fish, the price goes down."₇

1 un re ly dis

2 pre

A	B
pretest	prepare
preview	prevent
precaution	preserve
predetermine	

3 salted survival experienced
unusual certainly suddenly

4
1. exceptionally
2. circulation
3. incident
4. protest
5. carnivorous

5 particularly company encounter solve
griping hammock stared realize
started comfortably blankets warmth
glanced though trimming logical
operator emotional thought

A Changed Man

One evening Bruce was lying in his hammock thinking. After he had thought about the island and the things that happened, he began to think about his home in the city and his job. He thought, "People paid me to do my job because there was a demand for insurance. People wanted insurance. They paid for the insurance. But it takes a lot of money to run an insurance company. A lot of people must put in a lot of work to give people insurance. I helped people get insurance, so the people had to pay me for my work." *1

Bruce thought about his home and his car. He said, "Most of the problems I had to solve were not problems of survival. I had to solve problems of comfort. I had a car, but I didn't need a car to live. I had air conditioning and other things; however, I didn't need those things to live. I needed them to be more comfortable. But you don't think about comfort until your survival problems are solved. All of my problems of survival had been solved. I had enough to eat, I had a house that was warm when the weather * got cold, I had warm clothes, and I certainly had good water to drink."₂

As Bruce lay there in his hammock, he began to wish that he was back in his home. He said to himself, "If I were back there, I would look at things differently. I wouldn't be as grouchy; I would realize that my life was exceptionally easy. I didn't have to work fifteen hours a day. On the island I work fifteen hours a day, and I am happy. Maybe I would be happy in my old home if I worked more. Maybe I wouldn't try * as hard to live comfortably. Maybe I would spend more time doing things and less time thinking about how bad things are. I probably made things worse by griping about how bad they were."₃

The next morning he woke up and rolled over. He ran his hand across his pillow and threw back the blankets before he opened his eyes. Then he noticed the hum of the air conditioner.

He opened his eyes quickly and sat up. He was back in his home. It was quiet and clean. He sat there for a moment trying to figure out what had * happened. Then he ran to the telephone, dialed the operator, and asked her the date.

She told him, "August fourteenth."

"What year?" he asked.

She told him the year, and then Bruce knew that it was the same day that he had gone to the island. Perhaps the whole thing had been a strange dream. Bruce glanced out of the window. A neighbor woman was trimming her bushes. Bruce waved and smiled; she waved back.₄

"It was all a crazy dream," Bruce said to himself. "But I'm glad to be back."

He ran to his dresser and opened it. He * was thinking, "I'm going to get dressed and go outside. I'm going to talk to my neighbors and walk around." Suddenly he stopped and stared at something on the dresser. It was an ax made out of a tree branch and a sharp rock. He picked it up and looked at it. It had initials scratched on the handle—B. C.

"Bruce Celt," Bruce said to himself. "This is my ax. I made it on the island."

Bruce felt a little dizzy. Did it really happen, or was it a dream?₅

After a minute Bruce said, "I guess I'll never know * how it happened, but I'm glad it did happen. I found out a lot of things on that island. I found out a lot about people and why things are the way they are."

And from that day on, Bruce was a changed man. First of all, he didn't hate his job. He always worked to do a better job. And he was no longer a grouch. People who knew him said that he was a good friend. He saw a lot of things about his city that he didn't like. But he didn't gripe about them. Instead he did * things to make them better.₆ He followed this motto:

We all need each other to solve our problems of life and our problems of comfort.

Bruce knew that people must work together. He knew that everybody has a job and that all jobs are important. Some people bring you food and water, some bring you warmth, and others help you live more comfortably.

1 aw au

A	B
law	awful
haul	crawl
saw	draw
claw	fault

2 tri

triceratops

tricycle

triangle

3 re un pre dis

4 eastern armor prehistoric

snout Celsius carnivorous

emerged vegetable extended

5
1. grazing
2. reptiles
3. mammals
4. thrash
5. herd
6. predator

6 ornithomimid scene leopard occasional

rhinoceros territory dinosaur crocodiles

hippopotamus watermelon spine

adulthood shoulders glide buried

incredible fierce wiggled

7

A Prehistoric Plain

The white-hot sun beat down on the great plain. The plain was covered with grass and occasional trees, and you could see heat waves rising from the ground. The grazing animals, moving slowly across the plain, looked as if they were melting in the heat waves. The heat was almost unbearable, although the animals didn't seem to mind it. The temperature was more than forty-five degrees Celsius.[1]

A few of the animals were mammals, but most were reptiles. From time to time, some flying reptiles would glide over the grazing animals looking for a baby or a weak * animal they could attack. Everywhere there were insects, some as big as your fist.

If it weren't for the types of animals on the plain, the scene would look quite similar to one you might see in eastern Africa today. Thousands of animals were grazing in herds, each herd moving in its own territory at its own pace. And each herd was taking its turn at the water hole.

Also, like today, there were predators on the plain. The predators today are carnivorous mammals like lions and leopards. But back then the predators on the plain were reptiles, including gigantic * dinosaurs.2

One of the most incredible types of predators lived in a large swamp twenty kilometers north of the plain. These predators looked like the crocodiles you might see in Africa today. They were different in one respect, however. Though today's crocodiles are only three meters long, the ones that were in the swamp when our story took place were as long as fifteen meters. This means that they were longer than a line of five elephants. Their mouths were so big that a baby hippopotamus could probably fit inside.3

The ocean north of the great swamp also contained many * fierce animals. Some of them were sharks that looked just like sharks you would see today. Others looked like large dinosaurs with flippers instead of legs. Some of the fish you see today were in the ocean back then—the dogfish, the garfish.

Several eggs were buried in the sand near a high cliff at the edge of the plain. One of the eggs was ready to hatch. It didn't look much like a chicken's egg. It was much bigger than any egg you have ever seen. In fact, it was probably bigger than a watermelon, and its shell was * about a centimeter thick. Suddenly the egg wiggled and moved under the sand as the animal inside tried to get out. The animal's pushing made a crack in the shell, and as it pushed again, the crack became larger. The animal thrashed and kicked for over a minute before its head emerged from the shell. Its head looked like an armor shield, with three horns—one at the end of its snout and two larger horns on its brow, one above each eye. The armor plate of the skull was formed by thick bone, and the plate extended behind the * head, covering the upper part of the animal's spine.4

This animal was known as a triceratops. The *tri* in its name indicates that it had three horns. A triceratops was a dinosaur and one of the largest grazing animals on the plain. You could see many full-grown triceratops moving across the plain—they looked like tanks. Of the animals that are alive today, the one that looks most like a triceratops is the rhinoceros; however, a big rhinoceros would look like a midget next to a triceratops.5

The triceratops that emerged from the egg already weighed sixteen kilograms. If * none of the predators killed it before it reached adulthood, it would grow up to weigh eight metric tons—the weight of several elephants— and it would measure more than six meters high at the shoulders. As an adult, it would eat more than a ton of grass and other forms of vegetable matter each day. But growing up on the plain was not easy, and the chances of our triceratops reaching adulthood were pretty poor.6

1

tri
triangle
triceps
trimester

2

A	B	C
au	taught	crawl
aw	drawing	caution
	caught	sprawl

3

differently   attention   rhinoceros
frightened   extinct   instinctively
disturbance   overgrown   motionless

4

1. foul-tasting
2. programmed
3. roamed
4. keen
5. taut
6. extinct

5

tongue   brontosaurs   inhabited
ornithomimid   galloping   Tekla   vision
muscles   designed   straight   triceratops
elephant   hippopotamus   grazing   territory
blazing   shoulders   ostrich   lizard   scrambled
predator   successful   shallow   caught

6

Triceratops Meets Ornithomimid

There were twelve triceratops eggs buried in the sand near the cliff. The first to hatch was Tekla. She squirmed free of the egg, dug her way to the surface, and looked at her world for the first time. She felt warmth and hunger. Her mouth was filled with sand. She moved her tongue, trying to spit out the foul-tasting sand.

Tekla would never know her mother. She didn't have to learn how to walk. Unlike mammals, she was programmed to walk from the moment she was born. She was also programmed to search for food and to fight; * she would have no fear of most animals. Only faintly would she realize that she was a triceratops, and not one of the other animals that roamed the plain. She would know only that she felt more comfortable around other triceratops than she did around the other animals. Like most grazing animals, she had a keen sense of smell and sharp vision.₁

Still trying to remove the sand from her mouth, she rolled on the hot sand. It felt good on her back. She looked up at the sun, white and blazing. The sun felt good. Suddenly, however, Tekla sensed * danger. Instinctively she scrambled to her feet and faced into the wind. Danger, danger, something screamed inside her. Danger. She put her head down and stood motionless with her muscles taut and her heavy elephantlike feet planted firmly in the sand.₂

She seemed to be looking straight ahead, but grazing animals are designed differently from predators. Predators have eyes on the front of their heads so they can look straight ahead. They look straight ahead when they attack, and they must attack to survive. Grazing animals, however, have eyes that are on the sides of their heads. A grazing animal * like a cow or a horse may seem to be looking only straight ahead, but its right eye can see everything on its right side and its left eye can see everything on its left. The animal can even see its own back end.₃ The eyes are designed to protect the grazing animal from attack. It doesn't have to worry about looking straight ahead as much as it has to worry about predators attacking from behind.

Run, run, something screamed inside Tekla. Instinct was telling Tekla what to do. She had never seen an ornithomimid, the predator who loved to * eat dinosaur eggs. She had never smelled an ornithomimid, yet she knew instinctively what to do. She ran from the cliffs toward the other grazing animals on the plain. She could run quite fast, nearly as fast as a horse.₄ Tekla looked like a fat little rhinoceros, her stubby legs galloping through the heat waves toward the distant line of grazing animals. She was very frightened. Her heart was pounding, but her mind had one thought—escape.

And she did escape. Her brothers and sisters were not as lucky. The ornithomimid sniffed around in the sand. That sand was once * a beach, and the cliff had been on the edge of the beach. When the great brontosaurs lived on Earth, Tekla's plain was a large, shallow body of water, and it was inhabited by thousands of brontosaurs. By the time Tekla was born, the great brontosaurs had been extinct for more than sixty million years.₅ The water had dried up, and all that remained were the cliffs, the great sand beach, the bones of some brontosaurs buried deep under the sand, and the shells of sea animals that once inhabited the plain.

The ornithomimid looked something like an overgrown ostrich * with a long lizard tail and sharp teeth. It wasn't usually successful at finding eggs in the sand because they were often buried quite deep. But the disturbance that Tekla caused caught the attention of the ornithomimid. Quickly it ran over to the spot where the pieces of Tekla's shell remained on the sand. The ornithomimid sniffed the shell, and then began to dig in the sand.₆

1

A	B	C
aw	law	caution
au	because	draw
	crawl	fault

2

exposing thundered emerging feared
unlike absolutely crunching survived
screamed silenced several

3

1. leisurely
2. aroused
3. feasting
4. scavengers
5. ignore
6. slither

4

tyrannosaur heavy occasional building
predator frozen lizard finished instincts
distance constantly instinctively

5

Ornithomimid Meets Tyrannosaur

The ornithomimid dug in the sand, exposing three eggs. One of Tekla's brothers was emerging from his shell. Snap, went the jaws of the ornithomimid, and Tekla's brother never saw the sun or ate the rich grasses on the plain. The ornithomimid ate three eggs.

Suddenly, the ornithomimid stopped and stood up. It looked almost frozen as it sniffed the air. Then it began to run. It ran faster than a horse, but not fast enough.

Another animal thundered behind it—the most feared animal on the plain. It was a tyrannosaur. Like an ornithomimid, it stood on two heavy * legs with a long lizard tail behind it. Unlike an ornithomimid, a tyrannosaur was taller than a two-story building. A tyrannosaur was a predator able to kill nearly any other animal on the plain. It was fifteen meters from the tip of its nose to the end of its tail. Its head was very big. A tyrannosaur looked strange with its tiny front legs that were much smaller than its head.₁

Although the ornithomimid was swift, the tyrannosaur overtook it after the two animals had run less than twenty meters. The jaws of the tyrannosaur closed on the upper * back of the ornithomimid with a crunching sound that could be heard far across the plain. The ornithomimid thrashed and screamed for a moment, but another bite from the tyrannosaur's jaws silenced it.

The tyrannosaur leisurely picked at the dead ornithomimid as several of Tekla's sisters and brothers freed themselves from their eggs. None survived, however. The smell of blood and food had aroused many predators, some large and some small. Some would wait for the scraps left by the larger animals. Others were bigger and bolder. They were ready to steal the kill from other animals—but not from a * tyrannosaur.₂ By the next morning, little remained of Tekla's brothers and sisters except a few pieces of egg shell. And very little remained of the ornithomimid. After the tyrannosaur had finished feasting on the better parts of the ornithomimid, it went off to sleep. Scavengers closed in. Within three hours they had stripped the ornithomimid to the bone. Other scavengers moved in. During the night, they feasted on the bones. And the next morning when the sun rose over the night fog that settled on the plain, all that marked the place where the ornithomimid had fallen were a * few large bones and footprints—thousands of them.₃

That morning found Tekla far from the cliffs. Her instincts had told her to run with the other grazing animals on the plain. So she did. She found herself near a group of about twenty triceratops. They moved slower than most of the other grazing animals, and they ate constantly. They were quite calm—much like a herd of cows on a hot day. From time to time, they lay down. During the hottest part of the day, they slept. Tekla slept with them. They seemed to half ignore and half accept * her. After resting with them for about an hour, she began to trot around. Some of them lifted their heads and looked at her for a moment, but then they returned to their afternoon sleep.₄

Tekla felt playful, but there wasn't much to play with. She sniffed a snake that was about seven meters long. The snake slowly began to slither away. Tekla stepped on the snake's tail. Instantly, the snake turned and struck at her. Instinctively, Tekla ducked her head. The snake struck the large plate on Tekla's head.₅ Before the snake could strike again, Tekla turned and ran * back to the sleeping triceratops. She nibbled on grass and strolled around the snoozing animals. She felt content. There were occasional sounds of animals fighting in the distance, but the grazing animals were calm. And so was Tekla.

1 un re pre tri dis

2 beetles related discovery crouched
glancing experiencing carnivores floated
herbivores occasionally extinct fierce

3
1. foliage
2. prance
3. resume
4. unison
5. scramble

4 treacherous crocodile period
metasequoia dignified ginkgo
Cretaceous similar dragonflies warmth
mammal grove history ruled inhabit
earth frequently business realize
flesh listened aware

Asleep on the Plain

The sky became dark as clouds of insects floated over the plain in the late afternoon. Some insects were flies that looked exactly like the flies you see today. Others were dragonflies. Though they were similar to today's dragonflies, they were much bigger. There were butterflies, fleas, and flying ants. There were grasshoppers and flying beetles. Tekla was covered with insects, but they didn't bother her very much. Occasionally, she felt a sharp bite. She would roll over so that some of the insects would fly away. The grass waved in the breeze.₁ In the distance was a grove of * trees.

Two types of trees in that grove are alive today. One is related to the redwood. It is called the metasequoia. Its foliage is like that of the redwood, except that its needles fall off in the fall. Until 1946, scientists had thought that the metasequoia had been extinct for over a hundred million years. However, the tree was discovered growing in a remote part of China. The other tree that grows today is the ginkgo. It has leaves shaped like fans, and it makes a good shade tree. Some of the trees in the grove might have looked * similar to trees you see today, but they were different and have been extinct for more than a hundred million years.₂

Tekla didn't know anything about her place in the history of the world. She lived in what we call the last part of the dinosaur age. The dinosaurs were on earth for more than one hundred fifty million years. The last part of the dinosaur age is called the Cretaceous period; the end of the Cretaceous period marked the end of the dinosaurs.₃ Tekla didn't know that there would be humans on Earth eighty million years after the end * of the Cretaceous period. She didn't know that the world would be ruled by a mammal, the human, who would control more power than the most fierce tyrannosaur that ever lived. She didn't know that animals like horses, cows, and elephants would someday inhabit Earth. What she did know was that the sun felt good, that the bite of some insects hurt, and that she was thirsty.₄

The other triceratops were thirsty, too. They awoke, resumed eating, and then began moving slowly toward the water hole that was about five kilometers away. Tekla tagged along, stopping frequently to look at * lizards or other animals. When they reached the water hole, the young triceratops splashed and pranced around in the shallow water. The adults went about the business of drinking in a more dignified way. Experiencing water for the first time, Tekla felt its warmth and listened to the sounds it made as she thrashed about.₅

The water hole was teeming with animals. Some were wading and drinking. Others crouched along the shore, drinking and glancing around to make sure that no predators were near.

Tekla didn't realize that the different types of animals around her were similar to animals of * today. There were those animals that ate the flesh of other animals—the carnivores. And there were those, like Tekla, that ate plants—the herbivores.₆ She wasn't aware that there were carnivores that made their home in the warm water of the water hole. She didn't know that one of those carnivores was a few meters from her. It was a crocodile hidden under a bed of floating weeds, with only its two eyes and the end of its snout above the surface of the water. Tekla didn't notice that the crocodile's tail was beginning to move, making the animal * slide forward in the water.₇

1   re   ly   tri   pre   dis

2   reopened   usually   motionless   charged
intelligent   thundered   experience
released   probably   bothered

3
1. alert
2. visible
3. secluded
4. gash
5. daggerlike

4   movement   capable   instead   unison
dangerous   scramble   crocodile   flee
instinctively   narrow   instincts   alert
shoulder   jaws   drastic   instantly

A Narrow Escape

The movement in the water sent off an instinctive alarm in Tekla. She turned toward the movement and lowered her head. Almost in unison the other triceratops stopped drinking and stood motionless. Some of the younger ones began to back out of the water, still facing Tekla.

Suddenly, a huge open mouth shot from under the water. The mouth was bigger than Tekla. Tekla quickly backed up, almost falling down. The huge crocodile jaws closed on her head. Instantly the jaws reopened. They had closed on Tekla's three horns, and the horns had punched holes in the roof of the * crocodile's mouth.₁ As soon as the crocodile released her, Tekla scrambled from the water hole. Within a few moments, she was calm again. She didn't feel the blood running from the front of her neck where the crocodile's lower teeth had dug in.

Tekla didn't react very much to the pain because she was a reptile, and pain doesn't serve reptiles the way it serves most intelligent animals. Intelligent animals learn more quickly. Pain helps them learn. When they do something and then feel pain, they soon learn that what they did leads to pain.₂ Humans probably react more to * pain than any other animal that has lived on Earth. On the other hand, pain didn't help triceratops learn, because they were not capable of learning very much. They had brains that were tiny compared to their overall size, and they were capable of learning very little. But triceratops had instincts that helped them get along in the world. Tekla's instincts told her how to walk, what to eat, when to feel frightened, when to run, when to fight, and when to mate.₃

The days went by and Tekla grew. Every day during her first year, she gained weight. When * she was one year old, she was about one-fourth the size of a full-grown triceratops; she weighed about two metric tons. She stood one and a half meters tall and measured two meters from the tip of her middle horn to the end of her long tail.

That first year went by quickly. Tekla did the same thing day after day. She ate. She became alert if the sound of a tyrannosaur was heard across the plain. She stood shoulder to shoulder with the other triceratops facing a tyrannosaur when one came near the herd. But tyrannosaurs never * bothered the herd.₄ Instead, they chose to run down lone dinosaurs as they tried to flee across the plain to the water hole. These attacks were not always successful, especially if the other dinosaur was a large, healthy adult.

Tekla's first year was not marked by drastic changes in seasons. One part of the year was drier than the others. Another part of the year was a little cooler with more rain; however, all seasons were fairly warm and wet with heavy clouds usually visible in the sky.

Shortly after Tekla's first birthday, she left the herd. Four adult female * triceratops were going back to the sand near the cliffs to lay their eggs. Tekla tagged along. When the adults got near the cliff, they split up, each going to a secluded spot. Tekla began to follow one of the females. She turned and attacked Tekla. She charged with her head down.₅ Tekla tried to get out of the way, but the middle horn caught her hind leg. She turned and began to run. The adult's horn had made a deep gash in her leg, and the leg seemed to drag when she ran.

Suddenly, Tekla sensed something more dangerous * than the female triceratops. She stopped and looked around, trying to locate the danger. Then she saw it. Standing above a grove of small trees, it looked like a green mountain. Its mouth was open in a half-smile, revealing two rows of daggerlike teeth. It was the biggest tyrannosaur Tekla had ever seen.

1

hesitation   pretended   differently   roamed

measured   prance   blindly   instantly

2

1. faked
2. viciously
3. vegetation
4. knee-deep
5. incredible

3

chorus   kangaroo   tangled   tremendous

smiling   defend   full-grown   behave

juvenile   grazing   confused   butted

though   adult   predator   plodded

drew   herbivore   occasion   unison

thundered   shoulder   bumped

4

Surviving the Attacks

The huge tyrannosaur hopped forward like a kangaroo. Then it began to walk toward Tekla. Tekla backed up, out of the path of the tyrannosaur. The great dinosaur forgot Tekla. It decided to go after the adult triceratops now in its path.

The tyrannosaur ran around to attack the triceratops from behind, but the triceratops turned around quickly. The tyrannosaur faked with its head several times, then quickly jumped to one side. Again the triceratops turned to face the predator, but as quickly as it turned, the tyrannosaur jumped to the other side. Before the triceratops could turn again, the * great smiling jaws of the tyrannosaur came down on its back. The sound of the breaking bones carried across the plain. The tyrannosaur struck again, this time from behind. The triceratops was still on its feet, but it could hardly move. The tyrannosaur moved to the side of the triceratops, butted it viciously until it fell over, and then struck again for the kill.

By now, Tekla was far from the cliffs, running as well as she could across the plain. Her instincts told her to return to the herd. There was safety in the herd.₁ Five or more triceratops * could defend themselves against a tyrannosaur; however, a single triceratops, though it was huge and had great horns, could not hope to survive a battle with a full-grown tyrannosaur.

By the time Tekla reached her fourth birthday, she was full-grown. She didn't behave much differently from the way she had behaved when she was a juvenile. She didn't, however, move around as much now. She plodded along with the herd as it roamed the plain, eating nearly all the time. Now Tekla ate more than a ton of vegetation a day. She measured nearly eight meters from the * tip of her nose to the end of her tail. She weighed nearly eight metric tons. Every time she stepped on the plain, she left a footprint that was several centimeters deep.₂

Her size had changed and so had some of her instincts. When Tekla had been a juvenile, her instincts had told her to hide in the face of danger. Now, her instincts told her to fight. When a tyrannosaur drew near the herd, Tekla took her place with the other triceratops, her head down and her large horns pointed at the predator. Perhaps twice a week some large * tyrannosaurs would come near, but none ever attacked the herd. Usually the tyrannosaur would prance and jump and make passes at the triceratops. Sometimes it pretended to charge the herd, hoping that one of the herbivores would break away from the group. But on each occasion, the triceratops herd stood its ground, and the tyrannosaur would soon leave to find a meal elsewhere.₃

Shortly after her fourth birthday, Tekla had her first battle with a tyrannosaur. It happened at the water hole. There were many animals along the edge of the hole, most of them grazing animals. Suddenly, a tyrannosaur * charged through a grove of trees toward the water hole. In unison, the animals stopped drinking. They stood alert for an instant, and then they ran. The triceratops thundered from the hole. Hundreds of birds took to the air with a chorus of wing flapping that could be heard for several kilometers. Small reptiles sped from the water hole.₄

The animals moved in two waves, one going left and one moving right, leaving a path for the charging tyrannosaur. Tekla and three other triceratops were knee-deep in the water. They were caught in the middle of the confused animals * that were all running blindly from the water hole. Before Tekla and the others could leave, they saw they were right in the path of the tyrannosaur.

Instinctively, the four triceratops stood shoulder to shoulder and faced the tyrannosaur. Without hesitation, the huge predator jumped to one side of the group and tried to bite the back of the closest triceratops. All the triceratops tried to turn and face the tyrannosaur, but they just bumped into each other. One of them, a young male, began to run from the water hole. Instantly, the tyrannosaur charged after him.₅

LESSON 52

1

sub

submerge

submit

substandard

subtract

2

moaning   semicircle   wildly   released

thrashing   infection   heaving   breathed

either   leisurely   experienced   flail

3

1. ribs

2. shrill

3. trample

4

strength   knocked   silent   injured

struck   flicking   message   normal

lowered   powerful   locomotive   seriously

finished   occasionally   scavengers

fallen   settled   meanwhile   incredible

5

The Tyrannosaur Attacks

Fight, Tekla's instincts told her. Fight. Without fear, Tekla charged after the tyrannosaur, who now had its jaws firmly planted in the male's back. The male was trying to turn to face the tyrannosaur, but the tyrannosaur had a firm hold on his back. Tekla lowered her head and charged with all her strength. Like all dinosaurs, her back legs were bigger and more powerful than her front legs, and she pushed so hard against the soft ground near the water hole that she made footprints almost half a meter deep.₁ She pushed with all her strength. Faster—move faster, * her instincts told her.

Her two large horns struck the tyrannosaur in the side. One broke the tyrannosaur's lowest rib. The other entered the side of its belly. Both horns went in their full length.

Tekla had hit the tyrannosaur so hard that the ground shook. The tyrannosaur released its grip on the young male, let out a shrill roar, and fell over, kicking wildly.₂ The two other triceratops charged from the water hole. Almost as quickly as the tyrannosaur had fallen over, it stood up again, wildly flailing its tail, and jumping around like a huge kangaroo. Tekla stood * her ground with her head down. As the tyrannosaur lowered its head to strike at Tekla's neck, she charged again, this time planting her two large horns in the tyrannosaur's soft belly. At the same time, the two triceratops that had been in the water hole charged forward—one on either side of the tyrannosaur. The tyrannosaur went down as the six horns tore into its sides with the force of a locomotive. Meanwhile, the injured male triceratops stood and watched. It tried to move forward, but it was seriously injured. It would die before the sun set.

The tyrannosaur * was on its back, roaring and thrashing its tail from side to side. The tail struck one of the triceratops and knocked it over. One of the other triceratops charged and struck the fallen tyrannosaur in the neck. Another charged and drove its horns into the predator's side.

Just when it seemed as if the tyrannosaur was finished, the giant animal rolled to one side and snapped at Tekla with frightening speed. Its huge jaws caught her front shoulder, right below her armor plate. The tyrannosaur released its grip when the other triceratops charged and struck it in the side * of the head.

Suddenly, the plain was silent. The tyrannosaur lay on its back, flicking its tail from time to time. The four triceratops stood in a semicircle facing their fallen enemy. The birds settled along the shore of the water hole and many dinosaurs returned, acting as if nothing had happened. Some of them walked near the fallen tyrannosaur without even looking at it. It was almost as if a message had gone out to all the animals that the danger had passed and things were back to normal.₃

The four triceratops stood over the tyrannosaur for about a * minute. Then Tekla and two others turned away and returned to the water hole. The injured male didn't follow. It stood there bleeding, its head down and its sides heaving every time it breathed. Long after Tekla and the other triceratops left the water hole and returned to grazing, the injured male stood there. At last it lay down as some of the smaller predators and scavengers moved in for the great feast that night.₄

The grass around the two fallen dinosaurs had been trampled when the sun came up the next morning. Only a few of the larger bones * of the tyrannosaur and the male triceratops marked the spot where the battle had taken place. The animals had forgotten yesterday's battle.

Tekla had several cracked bones and an infection, but she didn't remember the battle. She knew only that she should eat and rest.₅

1

sub

A	B
submarine	subtract
submerge	submit
	substitute
	sublet

2

required interest insurance
experienced accurately

3

1. stampeding
2. offspring
3. urge
4. concealed
5. scent

4

focus ancient occurred veered
occasion gallop sprinted tumbled
secluded mated strongest sixteenth
groves electric straight ginkgo buffalo
scrambled skeleton fought instinctive

5

The Battle to Survive

When Tekla was five, she mated with a large male triceratops. Three males had fought over her. Their instinctive fighting to see who would mate was insurance that only the strongest would produce offspring, and those offspring would inherit their parents' strength.[1]

In the spring, Tekla experienced some new instincts. She had a strong urge to be alone. If another triceratops drew near her, she would lower her head and move her horns from side to side, a sign that she was ready to attack. The other triceratops kept their distance. A few days after Tekla had experienced the urge * to be alone, the urge took on a new focus. Instinct told her, "Go to the cliffs. Go to the cliffs." And so, late one afternoon she left the herd and walked to the ancient beach near the cliffs. Her instincts told her to find a secluded spot and dig a deep hole. She dug the hole with her front feet. Then she walked around the hole three or four times, making sure that she was safe. "Hurry," her instincts told her. It was time to lay eggs.₂

She laid seven large eggs, then covered the hole and returned to * the herd. She had done everything that was required of a mother triceratops. She would never know her babies. She would have no interest in them. They were on their own, just as Tekla had been from the day she was born.

Every year for the next twelve years, Tekla returned to the sand beach to lay eggs. Every year after laying the eggs, she returned to the herd.₃ During those twelve years, she had one more fight with a tyrannosaur. She and five other triceratops killed a large female. Tekla left the battle with the tip of her left * horn broken off.

Tekla's last fight occurred shortly after her sixteenth birthday. She was grazing on the edge of the herd. The herd made a practice of grazing in the open, far from the groves of trees which could hide the predators. On this occasion, however, the herd had moved close to a grove of ginkgo trees. There was almost no breeze, so Tekla couldn't smell the danger that the grove concealed.₄

Suddenly, the herd stopped grazing; it was as if an electric shock had been sent through the herd. Then the triceratops began to run. Tekla hadn't caught the * scent of the predator, but she caught the panic of the herd. Like stampeding cattle, they began to gallop from the grove of trees. Almost as quickly as they began to stampede, one large tyrannosaur, and then another, sped from the grove. Part of the triceratops herd split, moving off to the right. The rest kept running straight ahead. Tekla also ran straight ahead, but she was far behind the other triceratops. Behind her was one large tyrannosaur that could easily outrun a triceratops.

And it did. As the other tyrannosaur ran after the triceratops that veered to the right, * this tyrannosaur sprinted after Tekla, overtaking her about three hundred meters from the grove of ginkgo trees. It tried to break her back with its powerful jaws, but the two animals were moving too fast for the tyrannosaur to direct its jaws accurately. It caught some of Tekla's flesh in its jaws as it fell on her back. Both animals tumbled to the ground with a terrible crash. Tekla scrambled to her feet, began to run away, and then suddenly stopped to face the predator.

Nobody is sure why grazing animals sometimes run from predators and at other times fight. * Sometimes water buffalo will run from lions, even though a water buffalo can easily kill a lion. The triceratops herd ran from two tyrannosaurs, although they could easily have killed both of them if they had stood their ground. Tekla had run because the other triceratops had run. Now, however, her instincts told her that she must fight.₅

1

pre re ly un dis sub

<u>A</u>   <u>B</u>

reconstruction	submerge
abruptly	remains
unsuccessful	carefully
seriously	removing

2

motionless   partner   surviving   weakened

3

1. pounced
2. preserved
3. silt
4. fossilized
5. buckles
6. paleontologist

4

paralyzed inflicted Wyoming sun-bleached
transforming chiseling sidestepped locusts
seeped scar wonder skeleton died
agreed replied attempt washed
ringing blinked through respond

5

Tekla's Last Battle

Tekla fought with all her might. She charged the tyrannosaur and planted her horns in its belly. She lifted her head and tossed the tyrannosaur to the side. The predator, seriously wounded, walked away from her and stood motionless for a moment, as Tekla waited with her head down. The tyrannosaur sidestepped Tekla's next charge and pounced on her back. It was all over for Tekla. She thrashed around, trying to roll over, but the huge carnivore held fast. Its jaws had come down like a mammoth vice on her spine, breaking the bones. Tekla felt dizzy. She tried to * move her hind legs, but they wouldn't respond. Her rear half was paralyzed. She turned her head and watched the predator, but she didn't attempt to fight any more. A warm feeling spread over her, as if the sun had become brighter and brighter. Things looked lighter to her. The plain in the distance seemed washed out, almost white. The noises of the plain became faint ringing sounds.

She didn't remember her early years on the plain, the hundreds of times she had roamed through the grass, the water hole. She simply blinked several times. Then she saw no more. * She felt very warm as the plain faded farther and farther away. Her huge head dropped to the ground, and she was dead.

The tyrannosaur didn't feed on her. It was bleeding from the deep wounds Tekla had inflicted.₁ It walked around Tekla several times. Then it stood motionless, with its mouth half open. The other tyrannosaur returned from an unsuccessful chase. It caught the smell of blood. Quickly, it hopped around Tekla. Then without any warning, it attacked the wounded tyrannosaur, closing its jaws around the huge animal's throat. Within a few moments, the weakened tyrannosaur was dead, lying * next to Tekla.

Later that afternoon, after the surviving tyrannosaur had eaten its fill and the smaller predators had moved in to finish off the fallen dinosaurs, a strange thing happened. A great cloud of locusts swept over the plain, eating everything in their path. The grazing animals, the scavengers, and even the predators moved quickly to the north, leaving the remains of Tekla and the tyrannosaur to the locusts. If it hadn't been for those locusts, very little might have remained of Tekla. As it turned out, however, her bones and the bones of the tyrannosaur were preserved. * They lay sun-bleached on the plain for more than fifty years.₂ Then a great flood came, and the place where Tekla had fallen became the bottom of a lake. Each year, more and more silt and sand covered the bones. After thousands of years, a solution of limestone had seeped into the bones, transforming them into solid rock. Tekla's bones were now fossilized.

Eighty million years passed. During that time, the lake dried up, the dinosaurs disappeared from Earth, and the crust of Earth buckled, forming new cliffs and mountains. Tekla's bones were near the edge of one of * those cliffs.₃

One day over eighty million years after Tekla's death, two paleontologists were digging for fossil remains in northern Wyoming. They were chiseling small bones from the face of a cliff. One of them chiseled around the bones of Tekla's tail. "I think we've found something," the paleontologist said to his partner. It took the paleontologists more than a month to remove the remains of Tekla and the tyrannosaur from the limestone cliff. The paleontologists carefully laid out each bone until they had reconstructed the skeletons of the two animals. They couldn't find the tip of Tekla's left horn. *

When they had completed the reconstruction of the two animals, one paleontologist said, "The triceratops has a broken back. It also has an old bone scar. I wonder if the tyrannosaur killed this triceratops."₄

"I don't know," the other paleontologist said. "The tyrannosaur has broken bones in its neck. I don't see how a triceratops could inflict that kind of wound. And there are no signs of horn wounds on the tyrannosaur's skeleton."

"Yes," the first paleontologist said as he looked at a row of fluffy clouds above a nearby mountain. "We'll never know what happened, I guess. * But I sure would have liked to have been there and seen just how those animals died."

"Me, too," the other paleontologist agreed. "But I guess we'll never know."₅

LESSON 55

| A | B | C | BONUS | = |

1

Word-Attack Skills ....0 points
Information Passage ....5 points
Reading Checkout..10 points
Homework..5 points

2

fantastic   variety   unbelievable

interested   world   sorting   kilometers

famous   bathtub   snack   ounce

3

1. champion
2. records
3. official

4

Setting Records

Most people are interested in champions. They want to know who is the best at doing different things. They are interested in the biggest, the oldest, the longest, and the most. They enjoy talking about champions and records, and they sometimes argue about who is the best at doing this or doing that. To settle arguments, people need an official, authoritative list of records. There is just such a list. It is *The Guinness Book of World Records,* a book that set a record of its own. It has become the fastest-selling book in the world.1

The Guinness Book of World Records is fascinating because it lists some of the most fantastic records ever set. Some of these are accidents of nature. Who was the tallest person, what was the largest animal, what was the oldest living thing? These were not records that anyone tried to set. These things just happened.

Some people are apparently so interested in being a champion that they aren't too concerned about what record they set, so long as they set a record or win first prize.2 Some of the records they have set are amazing. The Guinness book records them all.

Take sports—not just ordinary, everyday sports such as swimming, baseball, and track. Here are a few unusual sports records.

Catching a grape in the mouth: longest distance on level ground, grape thrown from 327 feet.

Bathtub racing: 36 miles (58 kilometers) in one hour, 22 minutes, 27 seconds.

Crawling (at least one knee always on the ground): longest distance, 31 ½ miles (50 kilometers).

Hoop rolling: 600 miles (968 kilometers) in 18 days.

Pogo-stick jumping: 64,649 jumps in 8 hours, 35 minutes.

Riding on horseback in full armor: 146 miles (235 kilometers) in 3 days, 3 hours, 40 minutes.[3]

There are also, if you're interested, records for balancing on one foot, custard-pie throwing, and a record for onion peeling that almost makes you cry!

Some of the records suggest interesting questions. The one for nonstop joke telling, for instance. It was set by someone who cracked jokes for eight hours straight. The question is: How many listeners were still laughing at the end of the eight hours?

1

ea

head
spread
bread
instead

2

ly

re
dis
sub
tri

3

university   intelligent   absolutely
replied   disgustedly

4

1. physics
2. fault
3. property
4. transform
5. detect

5

constantly   abruptly   producing   failure
researchers   devices   laboratory
mathematical   laser   escalator   irritating
focused   deliver   professors   attractive
involved   clothespins   conducted   series
detector   instruments   stranded   locomotive

Milly, the Joker

6

Although Dr. Milly Jacobson was only twenty-eight years old, she was a professor of physics at State University. She was tall, intelligent, attractive, and friendly. She was good at playing tennis, at bowling, and at shooting pool. She had one serious fault, however. She constantly played jokes on the other professors. And some of her jokes were very corny and quite irritating to those involved.[1]

For example, one day she came into her laboratory and said to Dr. Fred Frankle, "Freddy, what's one plus one?"

"Two," Fred Frankle replied.

"And what do the letters *t-o-o* spell?"

"Too," Fred Frankle * replied.

"And what's the last name of the person who wrote stories about Tom Sawyer?"

"Twain," Fred replied.

"Good," Milly said. "Now say all of the answers you gave."

Fred thought for a moment. He then said, "Two, too, twain."

"Very good," Milly said and began to laugh. "Tomorrow I'll teach you how to say *locomotive*."

Fred shook his head and said disgustedly, "Milly, don't you ever get tired of playing those corny jokes on people?"

"I'm sorry," Milly said, walking toward her laser machine. "I just can't help it." She began to laugh again. "Two, too, twain," she said * softly to herself. She abruptly stopped smiling and faced Fred. "Oh, by the way. Did you hear about the robbery near campus this morning?"

"No," he said.

"Two clothespins held up a pair of pants," Milly said and began to laugh again.

"Come on, Milly," Fred said. "We've got work to do."

Milly went to her desk and took out a folder containing charts. Next to each chart was a long mathematical formula. For the past year, Milly had been working with laser beams trying to discover some of the basic properties of metals like silver, lead, iron, and gold. *₂ She had conducted hundreds of experiments and had carefully recorded the results of each. For these experiments, she would place a bit of metal on a screen. Then she would turn a laser beam on the metal. Some laser beams are pure red light, and since they are absolutely pure, the beams do not spread out as they move from the laser gun to a nearby target. If a beam is one millimeter wide when it leaves the laser gun, it is one millimeter wide when it strikes the target. And when it strikes the target, it is capable of * producing so much heat that it can transform a piece of metal into gas. Milly was using different recording devices to measure how the gas form of silver was different from the gas form of lead.₃

In the last experiments she had run, she noticed something very strange. She had set the laser gun so it would deliver a series of very short bursts of light and focused it on bits of gold. This experiment had given a strange reading on the metal detector. The reading was unlike readings for lead, zinc, or any other metal.

She prepared another experiment * with gold. After placing a bit of gold on the target, she again set the laser gun so it would deliver a series of short bursts. She checked the other recording instruments. Then she turned to Fred Frankle, who was writing notes in a notebook. "Say," Milly said, "did you hear about the power failure in the administration building yesterday?"

"No," Fred replied.

Milly said, "The dean was stranded on the escalator for three hours." Milly began to laugh.

Fred shook his head. "Some day," he said, "you're going to be serious about something, and nobody will believe you. You're * like the little child who hollered 'wolf' too many times."₄

"I know," Milly said. "I should stop joking around, but it makes the day so much more fun."

1

ea

dealt

instead

wealth

thread

deaf

2

association   expression   reservation   cigars

3

1. researcher

2. physicist

3. jokester

4. bonds

4

conventions   exchange   surprised

exploding   performing   complicated

molecules   behavior   probably   cue

professors   responded   receiving

supposed   involved   earlier   daylights

opportunity   accompany   provide

5

Convention

Every year there are several large conventions for people who do research in physics, and every year Dr. Milly Jacobson went to one of those conventions. This year she planned to attend the convention of the International Association of Physicists. This convention allows researchers to exchange information about their latest projects, and provides an opportunity for a researcher in a branch of physics to talk to other researchers in that same branch. Milly's behavior at these conventions probably would surprise you. She played a number of jokes at home at State University, but when she went to a convention, she * became a full-time jokester.[1]

Before she left for the convention of the International Association of Physicists, she packed her handshake buzzer and her loaded cigars. She also took along her pride—a pool cue with an exploding tip that she invented herself. She had placed an exploding cap in the tip of a cue, so that when somebody tried to shoot a ball with the cue and the end of the cue would strike the ball—bang![2]

Milly was scheduled to present a paper on the experiments she had been performing with the laser beam and different metals. She * wasn't ready to report on the strange readings she was receiving when she used short bursts of laser light on gold. However, she had prepared a paper on some of the earlier work she had done with the laser beam. The paper was very involved and complicated. It dealt with the kinds of bonds that hold the molecules of metals together and how the bonds of different metals responded to the laser beam.[3]

The convention of the International Association of Physicists was held in New York City. Fred Frankle was to accompany Milly. She told him, "Don't worry about reservations, * Freddy. I've taken care of everything." Indeed she had.

Fred and Milly arrived at the airport; they went to the gate for the New York flight; they stood in line waiting for the agent at the gate to take their tickets and check them in for the flight.

When it was Milly's turn, she handed the agent two tickets, one for herself and one for Fred. The agent looked over the tickets. She then looked up and said, "Which one of you is Dr. Frankle?"

"I am," Fred replied.

"Well, I'm very sorry, sir," the agent said. "But this ticket * is not for the New York flight. It's for Bismarck, North Dakota."

"Bismarck!" Fred shouted. "I'm supposed to go to New York."

By now Milly was laughing so hard that tears were forming in her eyes. She reached in her purse and pulled out another ticket. "Here," she said, handing the ticket to the agent. "I think this is the right one." It was Fred's ticket to New York.[4]

"Milly," Fred said as he and Milly approached the gate. "One of these days I'm going to get really mad at you. You scared the daylights out of me. I could * just see myself going to Bismarck, North Dakota."

"Oh," Milly said laughing. "You should have seen the expression on your face. I wish I had a picture of it."

"Well, I just hope you behave yourself at the convention. Don't make a fool out of yourself like you did last year."[5]

"I'll be good," Milly replied. She was lying.

1

A	B
deaf	weather
deal	wheat
dealt	steal
death	pleasure

2

applauded   Virginia   physicist   Terrance

3

1. harmless
2. formal
3. delicately
4. prominent

4

warn   restaurant   snickered   serious   arrived
couple   collar   effects   buzzer   wonderful
embarrassing   association   audiences
stroked   ushers   researchers   gentlemen

Living It Up

Milly and Fred arrived in New York City shortly after seven in the evening. They took a bus directly to their hotel. In the lobby they met several physicists they knew. One was a very serious man named Dr. Osgood Terrance, who always spoke as if he were in front of a class of students.

"Well," he said, "Dr. Jacobson and Dr. Frankle. It certainly is a pleasure to see you again. I noticed from the program that Dr. Jacobson is delivering another paper. I'm certainly looking forward to it."₁

Milly, who was facing Dr. Terrance, pointed straight ahead and * said, "Did you see that? A man picked up somebody else's bag over there." When Dr. Terrance turned around, Milly pinned a large red-and-white button on the back of his collar. The button said KISS ME IN THE DARK.

Fred started to object, but Milly said, "Shhh. It's a harmless joke."

So the very formal Dr. Terrance chatted for a few moments and then walked across the lobby as people turned around and snickered.₂

After going to her room, Milly took her exploding cue stick and went to the hotel's pool room. She beat a couple of physicists * and a truck driver in a game of eight ball. Then she secretly loaded the tip of the cue stick with three caps, handed it to one of the physicists, and said, "Here, try this cue stick. I think you'll get a bang out of it."

He did. He was trying to make a very delicate shot. He stroked the stick back and forth several times. Then, very delicately, he hit the cue ball. BOOM. The physicist dropped the cue stick and jumped about a half meter off the floor. Everybody laughed, but the physicist who tried to make * the shot didn't look very happy.

Before going to bed, Milly shook hands with a very prominent physicist. Of course, she had her handshake buzzer in her hand. She pinned another red-and-white button on the back of a woman from California. Then she went to her room and retired for the night. She was having a wonderful time.3

The next morning at nine o'clock she gave her talk. About seventy people were in the audience. A professor from Virginia introduced her. "Dr. Jacobson," he began, "is one of the leading laser researchers today." He then listed some of the * papers Milly had written for publication and told something about her latest research.4

The people in the audience clapped, and Milly stood up. She said, "I am passing out a paper that summarizes what I have learned about the effects of laser beams on different metals." Three ushers passed out copies of the paper to everyone in the audience. "Please do not open the paper yet," Milly said, as the papers were being passed out. "We'll go through it together." The members of the audience held their copies and waited. Printed on the cover of each copy were these words: *
EVERYTHING I HAVE LEARNED ABOUT THE EFFECTS OF LASERS, BY DR. MILLY JACOBSON.

"OK," Milly said after all the papers had been passed out. "You can thumb through your copy now." As the members of the audience thumbed through the pages, they began to laugh. Every page was blank. A young physicist from Texas yelled out, "You've learned just as much about lasers as I have." Everybody laughed. Others in the audience made comments.

Then Milly delivered her real paper, and after going through it, she answered questions from the audience. She was very well received. The audience applauded for * over a minute and Milly smiled broadly.5

She was having a great time. Just as the audience was getting up to leave, Milly said, "Ladies and gentlemen, I would like to warn you against eating in this hotel's restaurant." Everybody stopped and looked at Milly. "They have some very embarrassing things going on there. Yesterday evening I looked at my table and saw the salad dressing."

"Oh, no," some of the people shouted. "That's corny." But Milly loved it.

1

A	B
pleasant	deal
please	dealt
dream	instead
health	creature

2

pre sub un re ly

3

college taught slightest
seriously pretended

4

1. impish
2. undergraduate
3. graduate student
4. doctor's degree
5. related to
6. incurable

5

apologized entertainers respond
advantage practical impish wrong
gathered faked conducted striking
attracted professional equals

6

The Same Old Routine

Milly had a ball during the remaining two days of the convention of the International Association of Physicists. She attended sessions during the day and was generally very serious, except when she shook hands with her handshake buzzer or pinned one of her red-and-white buttons on another physicist. In the evenings, however, she played one joke after another. By the end of the last evening of the convention, she had attracted a crowd of people who followed her around, waiting to see what her next joke would be. Most of the people in the crowd were physicists, but * some were people who found Milly more entertaining than the professional entertainers in the hotel. One reason they found Milly so funny was that, though she had an impish twinkle in her eye, she didn't look like the type of person who would play practical jokes.₁ For Milly, the convention was more fun than a circus. She had so much fun that she began to plan her tricks for the following year's convention of the International Association of Physicists.

Milly found it a little dull to return to the routine in her laboratory and her classroom. She taught two courses * —one for undergraduates who were taking their first college course in physics, and another for graduate students who were studying for their doctor's degree. She was pleasant and entertaining when she taught. She told stories that related to whatever the students were studying.

Milly made it a rule never to play practical jokes on her students. From time to time she would break the rule with her graduate students, but she never joked with undergraduates. She didn't want to take advantage of them because she felt they were not in a position to get even if she played a joke * on them. The other physicists, on the other hand, were Milly's equals. They could get mad at her or laugh at her or play a joke on her if they wished. And sometimes they did.₂ For example, after Milly returned from the convention, she had very strange results when she performed a laser experiment on a piece of zinc. The reason was that the piece of zinc was not pure zinc. Fred and one of the other physicists, Dr. Helen Mark, had treated the zinc with acid. As Milly conducted the experiment and recorded the results, Fred watched her, laughing * to himself.₃

Milly quickly figured out what was wrong, but she didn't give the slightest clue that she had. Instead, very seriously she performed several other experiments with the treated zinc. For one of these experiments, she placed a piece of the zinc in a box. What Fred didn't know was that Milly had also placed a large rubber snake in the box. The snake was on a large spring, so the snake would pop out of the box when the lid was opened.

Milly placed the box on the laser target and faked an experiment. Then she pretended to * open the box and look inside. Finally, she called Fred over and said, "Freddy, I can't understand what's happening with this zinc. Look inside that box; you're not going to believe what you see."

"OK," Fred said, smiling. He opened the box, and the snake flew out, striking him on the chin. He dropped the box lid and jumped in fright. His face turned quite red as he said, "We were just trying to teach you a lesson, but I think you're incurable."₄

Milly apologized for her joke; then she returned to her experiments. For some reason, she decided to * put a piece of gold in the box and see if the metal detector would still give strange readings. It did. Then she filled the box with dirt and shot a series of short laser bursts at it. The metal detector reacted the same as it had when there was no dirt in the box. Milly began to reason this way: If the box and the dirt don't affect the reading on the metal detector, the laser can be used to find gold when it is underground. If the beam goes in the direction of gold, the metal detector will * respond in that strange way. I can find gold with my laser.₅

LESSON 60

1
compare scientifically creature designed greyhound cosmopolitan measuring cheetah accurate capable distance spine-tailed falcons maximum marine

2
1. fascinated
2. attained
3. breed
4. surpass
5. achieved

3

Speed Records

For some reason, people are fascinated with records. We like to know the record size of fish that are caught, the record weight of animals, and record feats of strength. The question of record speeds is one of the more popular record topics.

Let's start with human records. The fastest recorded time for a person to run 100 meters is 9.79 seconds, which would be an average speed of 36.8 kilometers per hour.[1]

The human being is much slower in the water. The record time for swimming 100 meters is 46.7 seconds, which is only about 7 kilometers per hour. This speed is very slow when we compare it with that of the male killer whale.[2] This creature can swim about 55 kilometers per hour, but it is certainly not the fastest marine animal. The fastest fish to be scientifically clocked was a cosmopolitan sailfish, which attained a speed of 108 kilometers per hour. At this speed, the sailfish would swim 100 meters in about 3 seconds.[3]

Measuring the speed of land animals is much easier than measuring that of creatures in the water. The fastest racehorse achieved an average speed of about 45 miles (72 kilometers) per hour over a course approximately one-quarter of a mile (four-tenths of a kilometer) long. The fastest dog is the greyhound, which has been clocked at 41 miles (66 kilometers) per hour.

The fastest land animal in the world is probably the cheetah. Experts have not been able to accurately check the top speed of a healthy cheetah. Most agree, however, that it can run over 60 miles per hour (96 kilometers) over short distances.[4]

There are animals that are much faster than the cheetah—these animals fly. The spine-tailed swift has been clocked at 105 miles (168 kilometers) per hour. At this speed, the bird could fly about 100 meters in about two seconds. There are reports of other birds that can surpass the spine-tailed swift in speed, but none has been proven. Falcons, for example, are supposed to dive at a speed of 186 miles (300 kilometers) per hour. But the maximum speed ever recorded for these birds has been 81 miles (130 kilometers) per hour.[5]

Machines, of course, can go faster than any creature. The fastest car reached a speed of 763 miles (1220 kilometers) per hour; the fastest plane reached a speed of 4520 miles (7232 kilometers) per hour; and the fastest rocket flew at 158,000 miles (252,800 kilometers) per hour.

There is an incredible difference between the speed of the human being and that of some machines. The fastest person could run 100 meters in 9.79 seconds. The fastest airplane can travel that distance in about five-hundredths of a second!

LESSON 61

 1
treated   treasure   please
pleasure   retreat

 2
carefully   discovered   sprawling   garbage

3
1. sarcastic
2. apparatus
3. maintenance department
4. data
5. calculate
6. computer program
7. identify

 4
surrounds   repeating   experiment
recording   response   truckload   shovel
dandelions   vehicle   beautiful
conclusions   equipment   arrived   gravel
campus   developed   effect   hasty
phoned   machine   entire   types

 5

The Gold Detector

Milly Jacobson had discovered that the metal detector responded in a strange way to gold, even when there was dirt around the gold. She repeated the experiment with the piece of gold in the box of dirt, carefully recording the metal detector readings. She tested the gold to make sure it hadn't been treated. Then she got a garbage can, phoned a dirt-and-gravel company, and told the woman on the phone, "Deliver one truckload of dirt and one truckload of gravel to the physics laboratory at State University."

When the two truckloads arrived, Fred Frankle said, "Milly, what * are you up to now?"

"I think I've discovered something very important," Milly said.

"I'll just bet you have," Fred said sarcastically. He was sarcastic because he thought that Milly was setting up another one of her jokes.₁ He said, "I'll tell you, Milly. I don't think the dean is going to be very happy when he sees these two piles in front of the physics lab." The piles did look rather ugly. The State University campus was very beautiful, with large sprawling trees shading a lawn that was almost free of weeds and dandelions. The lawn was carefully edged * next to the sidewalks that connected the different buildings on the campus. And there they were—a huge pile of dirt and another of gravel—on the lawn in front of the physics lab, with some of the dirt and gravel spilling onto the sidewalk.

Milly looked at the piles, shook her head, and said, "I guess they'll be <u>mad</u>, but I think I'm on to something very big. I'll arrange to have this stuff removed when I'm done."

"Good luck," Fred said sarcastically.

Milly loaded the garbage can with dirt and hauled it into her lab. She dug down * and placed a very tiny bit of gold in the dirt. Then she covered the gold. Checking her equipment, she said to herself, "Now we'll see what happens with a very small piece of gold when a lot of dirt surrounds it."

The metal detector showed a weaker response than it had shown before, but the response was basically the same. It was a gold response.

Next, Milly took her laser apparatus outside. This was not an easy thing to do. The laser gun, weighing more than two hundred kilograms, was not designed to be moved. It took three students, * Milly, and Fred over half an hour to set the machine up outside, facing the two piles. During the entire time Fred kept repeating, "This better not be another joke."₂

Milly got a shovel from the maintenance department and dug down to the bottom of the dirt pile. She placed a fairly big piece of gold in one spot and a tiny piece about one meter to the side of the large piece. She covered the gold with dirt, aimed the gun at the pile, and fired short bursts at different parts of the pile. She repeated the experiment six * times, recording the readings from each part of the pile. Then she sat under one of the large sprawling trees near the piles and studied her results. The results showed that she could locate each piece of gold in the pile and that she could tell if one piece was bigger than another.₃

She repeated the experiment with the pile of gravel. "Perhaps gravel will have a different effect on the gold," she thought. It didn't. She placed bits of other types of metal in the gravel pile and repeated the experiment to see what effect these other metals would * have. They didn't affect the results. The metal detector responded to the bits of copper and iron that were close to the surface of the pile, but it didn't respond in the same way it did for gold, which could be identified in any part of the pile.

"Don't jump to any conclusions," Milly warned herself as she returned to the lab and examined the data again.₄ For over three hours Milly went over the data. She did a series of calculations on each experiment she had performed. She developed a computer program and used the computer to test her * results. It was almost seven in the evening when she realized that her conclusion had not been hasty.₅ She tossed a stack of papers in the air and screamed, "I can find gold." She ran out of the lab.

Three maintenance men were standing next to the piles in front of the lab. One of them began to ask Milly as she ran from the lab, "Do you know who dumped these piles of—"

"Gold," Milly shouted. She ran up to the top of the dirt pile. "I did it. I found gold."

One maintenance man turned to the other * and said, "She *must* be the one who had these piles dumped here."

1

less
soundless
motionless
meaningless
purposeless

2

sub   dis   un   tri   pre

3

geology   foundation   available   convince

additional   certainly   ain't   experimental

4

1. recreational vehicle
2. mounting
3. salary
4. request
5. recommend
6. grant

5

personally   pleasure   please   guide

suggested   shrugged   awarded   secretary

involve   machine   foothills   argued

equipment   objected   couple   double   hiring

6

Some Hasty Preparation

Milly was on the phone early the next day, and she stayed on the phone for most of the morning. She called a friend in the geology department at the University of California and asked her where she would suggest looking for gold. Her friend suggested the foothills near Sacramento, California. Then she called a recreational vehicle place in Sacramento and rented a four-wheel-drive pickup truck. She asked the man if he would recommend someone to guide her to the foothills and help her find gold. He gave her three names.

Milly called the first two, but they * were not available to guide her. The third said that he could guide if it didn't involve too much walking. "I'm a very old man. I'm all right for a couple of miles," he said, "but my feet and legs give out after that."

Milly asked him if he would be able to dig for some gold if she could locate it. "That depends," he replied. "There is digging and there is digging. If there ain't too many rocks and if the gold ain't too deep, I can do 'er."₁

Next Milly called the campus machine shop. "I have a * rush job. I need a mounting for my laser gun, so I can put it in the back of a pickup truck. I have the plans."

The man at the machine shop told her there was no way he could do the job before next Tuesday, but Milly argued and argued and argued. She told him she would pay him double if he could complete the job by the following morning. At last the man agreed.₂

After spending most of the morning on the phone, Milly went to the office of the physics department. She handed the secretary a pile * of forms. Each form was a request for money. One was for the truckload of dirt and the truckload of gravel. One was for a round-trip plane ticket to Sacramento, California. Others were for shipping and mounting the laser, renting the four-wheel-drive truck, hiring the guide, and for additional equipment Milly needed for her trip. The secretary thumbed through the stack of requests, looked up, and said flatly, "I'll have to get the dean's approval on these." She carried the forms into the dean's office.

After a moment, a voice said loudly, "What is all this?" Then * the dean rushed out, carrying the forms.

"Dr. Jacobson," he said angrily, "what do you think you're doing? Who is supposed to pay for these things? Certainly not your grant."

Milly's research with the laser was paid for by the Federal Science Foundation. The Foundation awarded her a grant, but the grant indicated how the money was to be spent. And the money was not to be spent on four-wheel-drive trucks or plane trips to California. "There's no way I can approve these expenses," the dean said.₃

"But you don't understand," Milly said. "It's very important. I think * I've found—"

"Oh, yes, I'll just bet it's important," the dean said sarcastically. "Just like it was important last year when you had to buy three dozen baby rabbits so you could plant them in Dr. Jenkins's lab and make him think his two experimental rabbits had given birth to all those babies."

"No, Dean," Milly objected. "This is different."

"I can see it's different," the dean said sharply. "Three dozen rabbits cost less than fifty dollars. Your latest trick is going to cost thousands."₄

Milly tried to convince the dean that she was not playing a joke, but he * wouldn't give her a chance to talk. At last, she became angry and said, "All right. You can take the expenses out of my salary. Just bill everything to me, but please approve the requests so I can leave tomorrow."

The dean didn't agree at first. He asked who would take over Milly's classes while she was gone. He argued that he wasn't sure how the university would go about taking the money from Milly's salary. In the end, however, he agreed and signed the requests. After signing the last one, he said, "Milly, I personally have a great deal * of respect for you in most things, but if this is another one of your jokes, I'm going to recommend they take your grant away from you."

Milly shrugged but didn't say anything.₅

1 sub dis un re tri pre

2 less hopeless fearless
pointless regardless hatless

3 outskirts introduced excuse
thoughtfully instead

4
1. hazy
2. arranged
3. scurried
4. indicate
5. approval

5 damaged trousers sprouted entertain
noticed actually ain't hesitation
recreational device landscape
indicated vehicle suspenders Troy
washtub glory dynamite special

Go for the Glory Hole

Milly was in Sacramento the following afternoon. The landscape was flat and the sun was hot. She tried to see the mountains to the east. Her map indicated the mountains were not far away, but a haze over the city blocked her view of the mountains. Milly arranged for a driver to bring her four-wheel-drive pickup from the recreational vehicle place to the airport. With the help of three airport maintenance men, she mounted the laser in the bed of the pickup. Then she checked the laser to make sure it hadn't been damaged during the trip. After * loading her gear into the truck, she drove to the address of her guide, whose name was Gregory Hicks. He lived in a small white house on the outskirts of Sacramento. She parked the pickup in his driveway and knocked on his door.₁

He looked exactly as she expected. Milly had discovered a long time before that people's voices usually don't indicate how people look. A man with a big husky voice could be small. A woman with an old-sounding voice could be young. But Milly figured Mr. Hicks would be an exception, and she was right. There he * was, standing in the doorway, dressed in baggy trousers and suspenders. A gray stubby beard sprouted from his chin; what hair he had on his head was white. He was not wearing shoes, simply gray socks with red toes. "Howdy," he said. "What can I do for you?"₂

Milly introduced herself, and Mr. Hicks invited her in. "You'll have to excuse the mess," he said, waving his arm. "I live by myself and I don't have much call to entertain people." The inside of the house was indeed a mess. Dirty clothes were draped over the backs of two well *-worn easy chairs. A dog was sleeping on the matching couch, next to an untidy pile of newspapers. There were dirty glasses and dishes scattered around the room.

"As you can see, it ain't much of a watchdog," Mr. Hicks said, pointing to the dog, who was now looking at Milly without moving its head from the couch. Mr. Hicks then scurried to the couch, tossed the pile of papers on the floor, slapped the dog gently on the rump and said, "Get on the floor where you belong, Doctor. Can't you see this young woman wants to sit down?"*₃

"No, no," Milly said very sincerely. "I've been sitting for hours. I'd much rather stand."

Mr. Hicks explained why he named the dog Doctor. "Thought it would grow up to be something special if I gave it a high-class name, but I guess that didn't work." Doctor was a large hound dog with drooping eyes and ears. It walked over to Milly, sniffed her left shoe, slowly looked up at her, and returned to its warm spot on the couch.

"Let's talk about tomorrow," Milly said. So that's what Milly and Mr. Hicks did for the next few hours.* Milly explained that she had developed a gold-finding device. Mr. Hicks laughed. When he did, Milly noticed that most of his teeth were missing.₄

"Sure," Mr. Hicks continued thoughtfully, "I must have seen twenty to thirty gold-finding devices in my day. I've seen divining rods. I've seen dynamite devices. I've seen 'em all. And one thing you can say for them: one works just about as good as the others. They don't work at all—no how."

Milly didn't try to convince Mr. Hicks that her device actually did work. Instead she went over the schedule for the * next morning. She took out her map and asked Mr. Hicks where he thought there would be some gold. "Well," he said, rubbing his beard. "You can go after bits and pieces or you can go after a glory hole. Mind you, I don't think you'll find a glory hole, but that don't mean you can't look for one." Mr. Hicks explained that there are bits of gold in some of the streams and that some people make a good living sifting through the sand and gravel of the stream bed for these bits. "With gold at about four hundred * dollars an ounce, you can make a pretty good living with a few bits of gold. But gold don't come from streams; streams just wash the gold from the rock in the mountains. That's where the real gold is—up in them mountains—and if you're lucky, you'll find you a pocket of gold chunks. Maybe that pocket is as big as a washtub. And it ain't nothing but gold. That's what you call a glory hole. When you find one of them glory holes, you never have to work another day in your life."

"Let's go for the glory * hole," Milly said without hesitation.₅

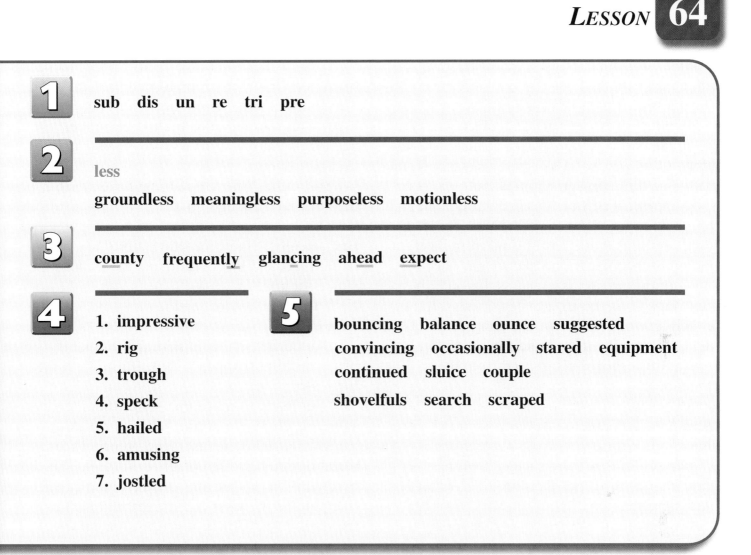

1 sub dis un re tri pre

2 less

groundless meaningless purposeless motionless

3 county frequently glancing ahead expect

4
1. impressive
2. rig
3. trough
4. speck
5. hailed
6. amusing
7. jostled

5
bouncing balance ounce suggested
convincing occasionally stared equipment
continued sluice couple
shovelfuls search scraped

6

In Search of Gold

At seven the next morning, Mr. Hicks and Milly were turning off a country road to follow a stream up into the foothills. The pickup moved along slowly, bouncing over rocks alongside the stream and sometimes going through parts of the shallow stream. Mr. Hicks was driving, while Milly sat next to him, and Doctor rode in the bed, sniffing the air. Milly looked out the back window frequently to make sure that her laser was not being jostled too much. "Never have seen a rig like that one before," Mr. Hicks said, glancing back at the laser. "Thought I'd * seen 'em all, but that one takes first prize. Sure looks impressive."

"Is there gold in this stream we're following?" Milly asked.

"Oh sure," Mr. Hicks said. "Might find half an ounce if you panned. Might get three times that much with a sluice."₁

Milly was about to ask what a sluice was when Hicks pointed ahead. "Lookie there. There's some fellers with a sluice."

Two men were working in a place where the streambed was quite narrow. They had built a long trough of wood. A pipe took water from farther up the river and dumped it at one * end of the trough. The water flowed through the trough and spilled out the other end. The men were dumping shovelfuls of sand from the bottom of the stream into the trough. They were sifting through the sand as the water in the trough flowed over it. After sifting through several shovelfuls of sand, the men scraped the old sand from the trough and replaced it with several fresh shovelfuls of sand from the streambed.₂

Mr. Hicks said, "Those boys will get themselves a couple of specks from that sluice."

High cliffs rose from each side of the narrow streambed, and the sluice * blocked the only place that the truck could pass. "We can't get around them," Mr. Hicks said, stopping the truck. He stepped out of the truck, and Doctor jumped from the pickup bed. "Hi, boys," he hailed. "Looks like we got us a problem. Can't get by your sluice."

"That's your problem," one of the men replied. "We're not about to take this rig down so you can get by."

"I can see your point," Mr. Hicks said. Milly was out of the truck now. She asked, "Won't they move their sluice so we can pass?" *

"Don't hardly think so," Mr. Hicks said as the men returned to working their sluice. "Take them maybe an hour to set that sluice up again after we pass. Can't hardly expect them to do that."₃

Milly walked up to the men. Neither looked up at her. One was scraping sand that had already been sifted from the sluice bed. The other man was standing ankle deep in the shallow stream, waiting to shovel fresh sand into the sluice.

Milly said, "Would you move the sluice if I help you find enough gold?"

The man standing in the water smiled * sarcastically, "Sure," he said flatly. "You help us find lots and lots of gold and we'll move the sluice for you."

"How much is lots and lots of gold?" Milly asked.

"An ounce," the man said and shook his head. Then he scooped a shovelful of sand into the sluice.

"Get ready to move that sluice then," Milly said. She climbed into the bed of the pickup truck, uncovered the laser, and prepared the metal detector and her other equipment. The two men, Mr. Hicks, and Doctor stared at her. She pointed the laser at the riverbank next to the truck * and slowly began to swing it around. "Don't stand in front of that beam," she said without looking at the men. She abruptly stopped moving the beam. "There," she said. "Mr. Hicks, dig in that spot where the beam is pointing, and you'll find a bit of gold that is probably a fourth of an ounce."

Mr. Hicks didn't move. Then he and the other two men began to laugh at the same time. Mr. Hicks slapped himself on the leg and said, "If that don't beat all." He continued laughing.

"I'm serious," Milly said. "The gold is probably * less than half a meter under the sand."

"I'll just bet it is," Mr. Hicks said in an amused tone. But he didn't move.₄

1

Mauna Kea Whitney height
impressive frozen compared
temperature serious Hawaii world
ascend Yosemite conterminous

2

1. sea level
2. peak
3. volcano
4. Himalayas
5. sheer
6. amazement

Many Mountains

The United States has many beautiful mountains, some of which tower more than 13,700 feet (4200 meters) above sea level. Mount Whitney, in California, is the tallest mountain in the conterminous forty-eight states. (The forty-eight conterminous states have a common boundary, and they made up the United States before Alaska and Hawaii became states.) Mount Whitney climbs to a height of 14,494 feet (4418 meters). Mount Rainier, in the state of Washington, stands 14,410 feet (4392 meters) above sea level and is the second-highest peak in the forty-eight conterminous states. The third-highest mountain in these states is Mount Shasta, in California. Mount Shasta stands 14,162 feet (4317 meters) above sea level. Both Mount Rainier and Mount Shasta are volcanoes that were active thousands of years ago.[1]

The highest mountain in North America is Mount McKinley. It lies between the cities of Anchorage and Fairbanks, in Alaska. It rises to a height of 20,320 feet (6194 meters) or almost four miles above sea level. Mount McKinley is very impressive, with massive ice flows and high cliffs. It is small, however, compared with the highest mountain on earth, Mount Everest. Mount Everest is in the Himalaya range of Asia, on the border between the countries of Tibet and Nepal. It is 29,028 feet (8848 meters), or more than five and a half miles high. At the top of the mountain the temperature is very low and there is very little oxygen. A few groups of climbers have reached the top of Everest, but several members of these parties have paid for the climb with frozen toes, frozen fingers, and serious illnesses.[2]

Although Everest stands higher above sea level than any other mountain in the world, it is not the mountain that is highest from base to summit. Mauna Kea, a mountain in Hawaii, rises to 13,796 feet (4205 meters) above sea level. However, measured from its true base under the water, Mauna Kea is 33,480 feet (10,203 meters) high, or more than six miles high. This measurement makes Mauna Kea 4451 feet (1357 meters) higher than Mount Everest.

The largest and tallest mountains are not necessarily the most beautiful. Some mountains that are famous for their beauty are less than 10,000 feet (about 3000 meters) high. One face of Half Dome, a mountain in Yosemite National Park in California, is only 2000 feet (610 meters) high. It is one of the most impressive mountains in the world, however, because it rises straight up from the floor of Yosemite Valley. From bottom to top, the sheer face of Half Dome is almost as straight as the walls of a building. Every year many experienced climbers scale Half Dome, and campers and tourists watch with amazement as the climbers ascend the sheer face.[3]

1 ly pre less dis

2 angrily pretended already
motionless cleared

3
1. irritated
2. antics
3. expression
4. scan
5. dismantled
6. manner

4 daydreaming caught examining
invitation pleasure located
through trough touched fours
waved embarrassed scenery
supposed clowning jostled chili

5

Convincing the Miners

Milly was becoming irritated. She had located a piece of gold, but Mr. Hicks didn't believe that she had.

"Mr. Hicks," Milly said angrily, "You're supposed to be working for me. Now take your shovel and dig down in the spot where the beam touched the ground."

"Yes, ma'am," Mr. Hicks said. He then pretended to move very fast toward the spot, but he was simply clowning around. The two men operating the sluice were laughing at his antics. Mr. Hicks began to dig. He dug out three or four shovelfuls of sand. "Tell me when to stop digging," he * said, "unless, of course, that nugget is in China."[1]

"Stand back," Milly said. "I'll tell you if the piece is in the sand you've already dug out." She turned the beam on the sand piled next to the hole that Mr. Hicks had dug. "Yes," she said. "It's in that pile, near the left side."

"Well, I'll sure find 'er," Mr. Hicks hollered in a comic manner. He got down on all fours and made a great show of sifting through the sand. Suddenly, his expression changed.₂ Very slowly he held up a very small stone. He spat on the * stone and rubbed it. For a moment he stared at it. Then he said, almost to himself, "I don't believe it." Then, more loudly, "I don't believe it." He stood up and faced the men who operated the sluice. "It's real," he shouted. "I don't know how she did it, but it's real gold, and it's a good one."

The two men stood motionless for a moment. Then one of them ran over to Hicks while the other walked. "Wow," the first man said after examining the nugget. "It's real."

The three men passed the nugget around saying such things * as "I don't know how she did it" and "It's real."

Milly felt pretty proud. She stood there in the bed of the truck looking at the men and feeling the clear morning breeze. The sun was bright and hot, but the air was still quite cool. Beyond the sluice, the streambed rose steeper and steeper into the mountain. For a moment, Milly forgot about the gold and enjoyed the beautiful scenery. She caught herself daydreaming and said, "Well, let's get on with it. We still have about three-fourths of an ounce to find."

Milly turned on the laser * beam and continued to scan the area near the truck. Suddenly, she stopped scanning and said, "There's another one, right there. It's bigger than the first one, but I think it's deeper."

Mr. Hicks began to run to the spot.₃ One of the men from the sluice beat him to the spot.

"Take a break," he said to Mr. Hicks. "I'll dig this one." He dug very fast. He stopped several times as Milly trained the beam on the pile of sand he had dug to see whether he had dug up the nugget.

After he had dug down about * a meter, she told him that the nugget was in the pile. "Near the very top of the pile," she said. And there it was, a little bigger than the first nugget.

Milly helped the men locate two more nuggets. The last one was the biggest. "There you are," Milly said to the men who operated the sluice. "Now would you please move the sluice so that we can pass?"

"We sure will," one man said. "And thank you. I mean thanks a lot. And if you ever want to come back this way, we'll let you pass any time. * And if you want to come back for lunch, we're having some chili, and we'd sure be pleased to share it with you."₄

Milly felt a little embarrassed—not knowing what to say. "Thank you for the invitation," she said politely. The men moved the water pipe from the sluice and dismantled the sluice trough. Mr. Hicks helped them. The men talked to Milly constantly as they worked. They asked questions about the laser. They told her about places up the bed that might have glory holes. They told her what a nice day it would be. They told her * about themselves. At last, a path was cleared for the truck.₅

Each man shook hands with Milly. "We sure wish you all the luck in the world," one man said as Milly got into the cab and Doctor jumped into the bed. Then the men waved after the truck as it jostled slowly alongside the streambed to the higher foothills.

1

basically   excited   adventure
uneven   disappeared   trained

2

1. adventurous
2. reliable
3. cascading
4. shimmering
5. grade
6. calculator
7. estimate

3

waterfalls   clouds   surface   beneath
brushed   repeated   blaster   procedure
interested   scientific   beautiful   dizzier
tried   terrific   dynamite   trailed
vertical   straight   series   deposit

4

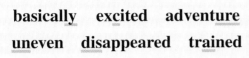

Will They Strike It Rich?

Milly, half turned around in her seat so she could watch the laser in the bed of the pickup, was becoming excited about the prospect of finding a glory hole. She really wasn't too interested in becoming rich. However, she was basically very adventurous, and this was a great adventure. She was first—the first person to discover how to find gold reliably with a scientific instrument. "This is really exciting," she thought, as the truck bounced and jostled alongside the bed of the stream. The grade was now becoming quite steep, and the stream, which had moved slowly in * the lower foothills, was now almost cascading down the side of the mountain. The land alongside the stream was becoming quite narrow and uneven, and the truck leaned first to one side and then to the next as Mr. Hicks steered it alongside the stream. At last he stopped and said, "Well, Dr. Jacobson, I think we're at the end of the line."[1]

Milly looked out the front window. Ahead, the streambed rose almost straight up, and the stream was a series of misty waterfalls. When Milly looked back, she became a little dizzy. The truck had been moving up * a very steep grade, and now Milly could see how steep it really was. Way, way below, she could see the place where the two men had the sluice. The stream was a slim shimmering ribbon that disappeared in a haze beyond the tiny speck that marked where the sluice was. "What a beautiful sight," Milly said. She took a deep breath and felt dizzier.

Mr. Hicks said, "The air's thin up here. Better take it easy at first if you ain't used to it."₂

"Good idea." Milly sat down next to the truck, which was leaning to the right * with the right wheels along the bank of the stream. Doctor walked over to her and wagged its tail three times. Then Doctor moved off to sniff for something to hunt.

"Do you think there are glory holes around here?" Milly asked.

"Sure there are," Mr. Hicks said. "Maybe not right in this spot, but those specks of gold in the stream didn't come down from the clouds. They came from up here someplace."

"Well, let's get with it," Milly said, standing up. She brushed the sand from the seat of her jeans. Then she climbed onto the bed of * the pickup and prepared the laser gun. She trained the gun on the rocks that were on the right side of the truck. Nothing. The laser didn't read a speck of gold. She turned the gun around and tried the rocks on the other side of the truck. Again, not a speck.

"There's nothing here," she said.

"Well then, we better start moving down because we ain't going to move up."₃

There wasn't enough space to turn the truck around, so Mr. Hicks began to back down. He backed down about fifty meters. Milly tried the rock on either side * of the truck. Nothing. Mr. Hicks backed down another fifty meters and Milly tried again. This procedure was repeated four more times, but the laser located only five bits of gold, none of which was very big.

The seventh time Mr. Hicks backed down, things were different.₄ The first spot where Milly pointed the laser gave a terrific reading. She moved the laser to the right. Another terrific reading. She moved it to the left, then up and down. Each time, the reading showed that there was a great deposit of gold. "It's there," Milly said. "It's more than a * glory hole." She took more readings. She had Mr. Hicks drive the truck forward. Then she pointed the laser to the same spots that showed the great deposit of gold. She did this so that she could see how big the deposit was and how far beneath the surface of the rock it was. She took a pocket calculator from her pack and did some calculations. At last she said, "That gold is two meters in the rock. I can't estimate how much gold there is, but there is a lot—really a lot."₅

Mr. Hicks got out of the * truck and walked toward the rock that would have to be removed before the deposit was reached. "Hmmm," he said, rubbing his hand over the almost vertical wall of rock. "The only way to get through this rock is with dynamite. Hmmm."

"Can we do it?" Milly asked.

"I brung along some dynamite," Mr. Hicks replied, "but I ain't no blaster. I've done some dynamiting, but . . ." His voice trailed off. Then Mr. Hicks faced Milly and said, "Well, let's give it a try."₆

1 ness weakness fitness newness boldness

2 interrupted wound explanation motionless

3
1. shorings
2. chisel
3. wick
4. impatient
5. initial
6. enlarged
7. assured

4
explained examination weakened
concealed blaster breathing shaking
tumbling closest kilogram shrugged
layer thunderous reared echo
scratched chiseled continued
struggled attached hazy

5 # Mr. Hicks, the Blaster

Mr. Hicks felt the cracks in the almost-vertical rock that concealed the glory hole. He spat on the rock and rubbed that spot. He stood back and looked at the wall of rock. Then he said, "Used to work with an old boy named Elmer Tooley. That old boy was a blaster to end all blasters. You'd tell old Elmer how much rock you wanted to drop, and he'd set charges of dynamite. Boom. And if you told him to drop three cubic meters, you'd have three cubic meters. If you told him to make a hole two meters * deep, you'd have a hole two meters deep."[1]

Milly was standing next to the truck. She said, "Well, that's interesting, but—"

Mr. Hicks interrupted, "But I ain't no Elmer Tooley. Fact is, nobody else is. That old boy could take on blasting jobs that nobody else would touch. I remember one time when there was this mine. And the shorings were weak. And old Elmer—"

"What are you trying to tell me?" Milly asked.

"I don't know if I can do 'er," Mr. Hicks said, shaking his head. "That's hard rock and it's steep. The wrong kind of blast might * make the whole side of the mountain come tumbling down."₂

Milly didn't respond. She looked at the rock and then back at Mr. Hicks. After a few moments, Mr. Hicks returned to his examination of the cracks in the rocks. Then he scratched his head and went to the truck. He returned with a chisel and a hammer. He chiseled four holes in the rock. Each hole was about two meters from the hole closest to it, and each hole was on a crack in the rock. Two of the holes were above the glory hole and two were below. *

Then Mr. Hicks pulled three sticks of dynamite from his pack. He said, "Now Elmer Tooley would set all four holes at the same time and he could tell to the kilogram how much rock would fall. But I ain't no Elmer Tooley, so I'm going to set them off one at a time. I just hope I don't set too much in any hole." Mr. Hicks shrugged and stuffed the three sticks of dynamite into the top hole on the right. He wound the wicks of the dynamite sticks together. Then he connected a longer wick to the wicks. * As he worked, he explained to Milly why he wasn't using blasting caps. Milly didn't follow his explanation, but Mr. Hicks assured her four times, "This should work out OK."₃

Then he said, "We're ready. You'd better get uphill out of the way of any falling rocks. I don't know what these rocks are going to do, so we'd better get the truck out of the way, too." Mr. Hicks rubbed his chin. He continued, "But if we have a slide and the truck is uphill, we'll never get it back down. I'd better drive it way downhill where it's * out of the way."

Mr. Hicks backed the truck downhill while Milly struggled uphill. After she had gone about one hundred fifty meters, she was breathing very hard, and she felt dizzy. She sat on a rock and waited for Mr. Hicks to return to the dynamite. She was becoming impatient as she watched him get out of the truck and slowly start the climb to the dynamite. Finally, he reached the blasting site. He waved to Milly, smiled, and lit a match on the seat of his pants. He lit the wick that he had attached to the shorter * wicks, and then he began to run uphill, holding his hat with one hand and calling, "Come on, Doctor, let's get out of here." When he was still about fifteen meters from Milly, the blast went off. It was a very sharp sound that hurt Milly's ears. The initial sound was followed by a deep, thunderous roar that echoed and reechoed from the surrounding mountains. A large puff of light blue smoke spouted from the rock and then fanned out, forming a hazy layer of smoke. Milly then heard the sound of tiny bits of stone landing like raindrops in * the streambed.

Milly and Mr. Hicks ran down to the blasting spot. Nothing. The blast had enlarged the hole that Mr. Hicks had made, but Milly could see no new cracks in the rock or signs that the rock was weakened.

"Maybe I should try four sticks in the next hole," Mr. Hicks said.₄

1   ness   sickness   baldness   happiness   sadness

2   tri   re   ly   un   sub

3   triangular   reechoed   suddenly
       neither   heading   revealed

4
1. glistening
2. scarcely
3. brilliance
4. flask

5   speechless   sparkling   crouched   sliding
       scrambled   downward   downhill
       stripped   jewelry   thickest   loose
       whoopie   terrible   cough   deposit
       aware   brilliant   golden
       showcase   caught   visible

6

The Glory Hole

Mr. Hicks set four sticks of dynamite in the lower hole on the left. Milly went uphill so that she would be out of the way if there was a rock slide. This time she held Doctor as Mr. Hicks lit the wick. Mr. Hicks scrambled up alongside the streambed, but before he reached Milly, a terrible blast, much louder than the first, shook the ground. But the rock looked almost as if nothing had happened. There was a large triangular chunk of rock missing next to the hole formed by the second blast, but the second blast apparently hadn't * done much more.

Again Milly went up hill and waited with Doctor as Mr. Hicks set the third blast, another four-stick blast. Again Mr. Hicks lit the wick and scrambled up alongside the streambed. Again, the mountains echoed and reechoed the sound of a great blast. When the smoke cleared this time, however, Milly noticed that part of the mountain was moving downward. It was sliding into the streambed.

"Oh, no," Mr. Hicks shouted above the crashing sound of the rock as it peeled from the surface of the mountain and slid into the streambed. "Shoot. There she goes."* Mr. Hicks took off his hat and threw it on the ground. He said how sorry he was that Elmer Tooley wasn't around to do the blasting.₁

A great cloud of dust filled the streambed below. The rock had stopped sliding and the mountain was suddenly quiet. After the dust had cleared some, Mr. Hicks and Milly went downhill to the blasting site. The dust was still so thick near the blasting site that Milly couldn't see where she was going. She began to cough.

"How much damage did that rock slide do?" Milly asked.

"I sure don't know," Mr. * Hicks said. "That blast stripped off a lot of rock, but it all depends on how it piled up. We may have to dig through loose rock for a week before we reach the deposit."₂

A sudden breeze came up when Milly and Mr. Hicks reached the pile of fresh rock in the streambed. As the breeze swept the dust away, Milly and Mr. Hicks looked in the direction of the blasting site, waiting for the dust to clear. Suddenly, Milly could see the spot. She stood there for some time, but she wasn't sure how long. Everything seemed to * stand still. She wasn't aware of the breeze or the mountains or Mr. Hicks, who was standing next to her with his mouth open. Her eyes were fixed on a huge glistening mass of rock, sparkling with a thousand sharp edges. Its color was gold, and it was so brilliant that Milly could scarcely believe what she was seeing. It was glistening from the side of the mountain like a giant golden eye, with more brilliance than a jewel in a jewelry showcase. Still staring at the sight, Milly moved her head to one side and a thousand edges * of gold caught the sun and danced with sparkles.₃

Suddenly, Milly was aware that Mr. Hicks was talking. "Glory," he said slowly. "Glory," he repeated. "Now I know why they call them glory holes. I've never seen one before. Never seen nothin' like that in all my born days. Never."

"Neither have I," Milly replied. She was almost speechless, still staring at the huge gold deposit visible on the side of the cliff. The deposit was shaped like a large flask turned on its side. It was at least one meter wide in its thickest place.₄

"Here I am," Mr. * Hicks was saying, "sixty-eight years old and standing here looking at a glory hole. It's the most beautiful day there ever was, in the most beautiful place in the whole world, and I'm looking at the most beautiful sight that anyone could hope to look at." He was talking faster now and starting to walk across the loose rock toward the glory hole. "And who would think it? Me. Gregory Hicks—who some folks think isn't worth his salt—would get to see something like this. Would you believe it?" Now he was almost shouting. "Well, dance me around * the floor three times. This is my day. Whoopie! My day," he shouted.₅

He jumped up and down and began to talk and yell and sing. He ran over to the glory hole and kissed the rock. Then he grabbed Doctor and kissed the dog. Doctor ran uphill and crouched down with its tail between its legs, as if to say, "Has my master lost his mind?"

Milly began to laugh. Then she realized that there were tears in her eyes. She was laughing and crying at the same time.

1
amazing   average   full-grown   photographs
centimeters   Chamberlain   Abdul-Jabbar
Kareem   pituitary   Iranian   straight
doorway   remember   newborn   kilograms

2
1. coordinated
2. exaggerated
3. glands
4. abnormal

Human Height Records

People come in all sizes and shapes, but some of the record sizes and shapes are amazing. Professional basketball players sometimes stand a head taller than the average person. The average full-grown adult male in North America stands about 179 centimeters tall. Wilt Chamberlain, who set more National Basketball Association records than any other basketball player, is 7 feet 3 inches tall (221 centimeters). Another tall professional player was Kareem Abdul-Jabbar, who is 7 feet 2 inches tall (218 centimeters). Although these men are referred to as giants, they are simply very tall people who are very well coordinated.[1]

Sometimes claims of height are exaggerated. The greatest exaggeration came from a professor who submitted photographs of an Iranian man 10 feet 5 inches tall (318 centimeters). When the man was later measured at a hospital, he was only 7 feet 2 inches tall (218 centimeters).

Sometimes, when glands in the body do not function properly, a person will experience unusual growth patterns. An improper function of a gland in the brain called the pituitary gland can change an average-sized person into one who is abnormally small or abnormally large. The following people had pituitary gland problems.[2]

Zeng Jinlian of China is the tallest woman on record; she is 8 feet 1 ³/₄ inches tall. The tallest man on record was Robert Wadlow from Illinois. He continued to grow until his death at the age of twenty-two. By then he was 8 feet 11 inches tall. To get some idea of how tall that is, compare it to an average doorway.

The top of this doorway would come to the middle of Robert's chest. The ceiling in most houses is 8 feet. Robert would not have been able to stand up straight in the average room.[3]

At the other extreme are people who are very small. The smallest full-grown adult was Gul Mohammad of Delhi, India, who was only 22 1/2 inches tall. The most he ever weighed was 37 1/2 pounds. To get an idea of how small Gul was, remember that it is not uncommon for newborn babies to be the same length as he was.

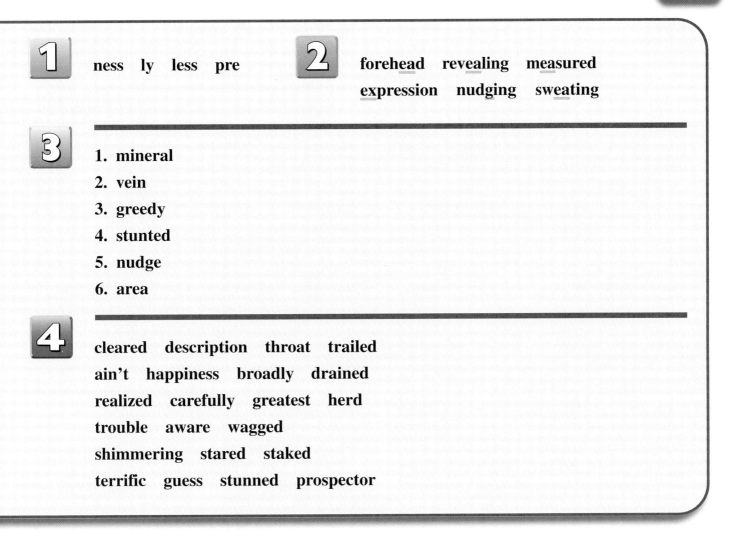

1 ness ly less pre

2 forehead revealing measured
expression nudging sweating

3
1. mineral
2. vein
3. greedy
4. stunted
5. nudge
6. area

4
cleared description throat trailed
ain't happiness broadly drained
realized carefully greatest herd
trouble aware wagged
shimmering stared staked
terrific guess stunned prospector

5

Marking Off the Claim

The blast had been nearly perfect. It had peeled off a layer of rock about ten meters thick, revealing the glory hole. Mr. Hicks danced and jumped and shouted for a few minutes. Then he said, "That's a terrific blasting job. Fact is, I don't think Elmer Tooley could have done much better—faster maybe, but not better."

Suddenly, Mr. Hicks slapped himself on the forehead and said, "Oh, no. I never thought of that."

"What?" Milly asked.

"The claim," Mr. Hicks replied. "I never did seriously think that you'd find any gold, so I just wasn't thinking about a * claim. But . . ." his voice trailed off and he stared at the vein of shimmering gold visible on the side of the cliff. "But,—" he continued slowly, "I guess that we shouldn't have much trouble."

He explained to Milly how claims work. When people discover a good find on public land, they can reserve twenty acres for their claim. If they discover a vein, they can claim more than twenty acres. Mr. Hicks said, "But I think we can get by with twenty acres. We just have to be careful about marking it off so that we'll be sure to get * all the gold. Why be greedy?" He smiled. Doctor wagged its tail.₁

Marking off the claim took most of the day. The biggest problem, Mr. Hicks explained, was to make sure the claim was well staked off so he could mark it correctly on his map. "Many prospectors have lost their claims because they didn't mark the map carefully," Mr. Hicks explained. "Twenty acres is not a big area, and at the recording office, they give you a claim according to your description of the claim. They don't come out and look at your claim. They just record the information * you give them. If you don't mark the claim just right on the map, you may have no claim at all."₂

Mr. Hicks took a large roll of string from the pickup. He measured the distance from the stream to the cliff. Then he measured off about three hundred meters along the cliff. The afternoon sun was hot. Milly sat near the stream under a stunted tree. Doctor was resting next to her, nudging her from time to time. Each time the dog nudged her, she patted it on the head, and it wagged its tail two or three times. *

At last, Mr. Hicks said, "I think I've got it marked on the map." He showed the map to Milly. Mr. Hicks explained that he marked the claim so that the glory hole was right in the middle of the twenty acres. "This claim ain't too hard to mark," Mr. Hicks said, "because the cliff is easy to see on the map."

Before leaving the claim, Mr. Hicks and Milly made large piles of stones at each corner of the claim. Mr. Hicks drove a stake into the pile that was closest to the glory hole. He wrote a note * that said, "Twenty acres claimed by Milly Jacobson for gold and other minerals." Then Mr. Hicks wrote the date and

his address in Sacramento. He stuffed the note into a tin can and placed it on top of the stake.₃

"Well, that does it," Mr. Hicks said, sweating freely. His shirt was wet and sweat was dripping down his face. "Yep, that does it."

Before leaving the claim, Milly and Mr. Hicks picked up the loose chunks of gold and put them in a large cloth sack. "My, my," Mr. Hicks said when the bag was almost filled. "I have * never seen more gold in one place before in my entire life."

As Milly and Mr. Hicks drove back down alongside the streambed, past the place where the sluice had been, and back to the highway that led to Sacramento, the sun was setting. Milly felt very tired—drained. She had trouble keeping her eyes open as the hum of the truck engine seemed to lull her to sleep. Suddenly, she became aware of Mr. Hicks saying, "Well, here we are." Milly opened her eyes and realized that the truck was parked in front of Mr. Hicks's house.

Milly took * a piece of paper from her shoulder bag. As she wrote, she said, "I want you to file the claim in the following way. I want one-third of the claim to go to my university, one-third to go to the state of California, and one-third to go to you." She handed Mr. Hicks the note.

Mr. Hicks stared at Milly with a stunned expression.₄ "You mean—" he said and stopped to clear his throat. "You mean you'd give me part of your claim after I made fun of you—after I gave you such a . . ."

Milly * smiled and said, "I never would have found it without you."

"But," Mr. Hicks said, "there's nothing left for you. You gave your whole claim away."

"Oh, there's plenty for me," Milly said, smiling very broadly. "I had about the greatest time I ever had in my life."₅

1 amazingly   villages   population
basically   vegetation

2
1. reduced
2. resident
3. capable
4. deceive
5. effective

3 rhinoceros   elephant   impala   extinct
lion   predators   leopard   antelope
wounded   buffalo   African   favorite
designed   series   destroyed   temple
stalks   heroes   species   welcomed
equipped   thicket   delicate

Dangerous African Animals Part 1

Today many species of African animals are in danger of becoming extinct. The lion, which used to hunt in many parts of Africa, is now found in fewer places. Other African animals have followed the same pattern. The African elephant, the African Cape buffalo, the rhinoceros, and the leopard—all have been reduced in numbers. All could become extinct.

Not long ago there were so many wild animals in some parts of Africa that the people living in those areas were in great danger. Big game hunters were welcomed in villages where wild animals had been killing the residents.

Today * we think of the big game hunter as one who kills for the sport of it. But around 1900, when the population of Africa was growing and the people were trying to build farms, some big game hunters were heroes. They went to places where elephants had destroyed crops that farmers had planted. They hunted down the elephants and shot them. They went to places where lions were killing people, and they hunted down the lions.[1]

When the sport of big game hunting in Africa was popular, there were many arguments about which of the big game animals was the * most dangerous. The animals that were most frequently argued about were the elephant, the lion, the rhinoceros, the Cape buffalo, and the leopard.₂ Which animal do you think would be the most dangerous to hunt? After reading the rest of the parts in this series, you may change your mind.

Before we look at some facts about which is the most dangerous African animal, we should discuss some points about all African animals. Basically there are two types of animals in Africa—grazing animals and predators.₃ The same two types lived millions of years ago when triceratops and tyrannosaurs roamed * the plain. Even the most innocent-looking grazing animal in Africa is equipped to survive. A delicate-looking antelope is quite capable of killing a person. The impala is a delicate-looking animal that survives by fast moves and high kicks. When a startled impala leaps, it gives two kicks. The first kick hurls the impala into the air. That kick has enough force to shoot the impala up over three meters high, and the second kick has as much force as the first. The impala is capable of delivering a kick powerful enough to punch holes into any enemy * chasing directly behind it.

The fight for survival has made all African animals tough. Their looks may deceive you, but just remember that without effective defenses they wouldn't survive in a place filled with predators and other dangers. Some animals run very fast. Some are very strong and can fight off their enemies. Those that are designed to kill other animals are very good killers.₄

Let's look at the big game animals one at a time and see just how dangerous each one would be to hunt. We'll begin with the biggest grazing animal, the African elephant. It stands three * meters tall and weighs as much as five and one-half metric tons. It has huge tusks that may be two meters long. These tusks are very, very hard. It can run amazingly fast for its size—perhaps fifty kilometers an hour. And it is so strong that it could roll over a car as easily as you could overturn a chair.₅

One more thing about the African elephant: it is extremely smart. A wounded elephant will use many tricks to trap its hunter. Perhaps its favorite trick is to leave a very clear trail into an area of dense * bush, such as a thorn thicket. When the hunter enters the thicket, the elephant attacks. Because the vegetation is very dense, the hunter cannot see the elephant. With its head down, the elephant charges, knocking down the bush in front of it. This vegetation, which may be five meters tall, hits and flattens the hunter. The hunter does not have a chance to take aim at the elephant.₆

So the elephant can be very dangerous to hunt. But the elephant is not the most dangerous African animal. In the next part we will see why.

1 un pre ness less ly

2 extremely crouched weapons
situation claws

3
1. retreat
2. evolution
3. strides
4. bounding
5. hurtle
6. enormous

4 positions clever overhanging tusks
designed capable biting reports
thicket strength dense weight
actual incredibly tremendous keen
strangling growling effective pride

5 # Dangerous African Animals Part 2

The only animal that will make the African elephant retreat is the ant. Indeed, any animal retreats when millions of biting and stinging ants attack. An elephant can kill a lion or a Cape buffalo or step on a leopard and crush it. But the elephant is not the most dangerous animal for a person to hunt. Why? Because an elephant is big, and it makes an easy target. The elephant is dangerous when a hunter tracks it into a dense thicket, but then any animal can be dangerous in this situation. All animals use clever tricks to kill their * hunters and the elephant is no different. It has keen senses—good eyes, ears, and a sense of smell—but it makes a very big target. An elephant cannot lie down in the tall grass of the plain and hide from the hunter the way a leopard can.₁

The hunter who cannot hit a target as big as an elephant should not be a hunter. The hunter may have to use a very powerful rifle, but one well-placed shot will kill an elephant. A bullet that hits the front of the skull will not kill an elephant and probably * won't hurt it, because the front of the elephant's skull is very thick. But the side of its skull (the temple) is very thin, so a bullet in the temple will kill it. Also, a bullet hitting its neck or between its tusks will kill it.

Let's look at another dangerous animal, the lion. Through millions of years of <u>evolution</u> the lion has developed into an expert predator. The lion cannot run long distances, because after going a few hundred meters it runs out of breath. But for short dashes it is extremely fast. Starting from a crouched position, the * lion can be running at the rate of fifty kilometers per hour after taking only a few strides. It can run a hundred meters in about four seconds. A lion is incredibly strong. And it can lie flat in tall grass or hide fairly well in a small thicket.₂

The lion can be very dangerous to hunt. Let's say that a hunter is walking across the plain and a two-hundred-kilogram lion is in the brush a hundred meters away. Suddenly the lion charges the hunter. It takes the hunter a second to realize what is happening. Soon the * lion, moving at top speed, is only about eighty meters away. The hunter raises a rifle and tries to aim at the form bounding toward the hunter through the shoulder-high grass. By now the lion is forty meters away. The hunter fires a shot and misses. Quickly the hunter takes aim again. The lion seems to be a bigger target than it actually is because its mane makes its head look twice its actual size. The lion is ten meters away and is leaping toward the hunter. In panic the hunter shoots again. Even if the bullet hits its * mark, the hunter

might be killed. The lion, two hundred kilograms of muscle and bone moving at fifty kilometers per hour, could hurtle into the hunter with enough force to kill the hunter.₃

The lion has long claws that can cut like knives, and it has enormous teeth that can crush. Even more important than these weapons is the lion's tremendous strength. According to reports, a lion can leap over a three-meter fence while carrying an animal of one hundred fifty kilograms in its jaws. The lion's neck muscles are so strong that it can toss a hundred-kilogram * wart hog as if it were tossing a rag doll.₄ Just one cuff from a lion's paw could break your neck or crush your ribs, but the lion is designed to kill animals that are far more powerful than humans. The lion can kill these animals in an instant. For instance, the lion can bring down a powerful antelope by grabbing the animal at the neck, biting its throat, and strangling it.

Yes, the lion is probably more dangerous to hunt than the elephant, but the lion is not the most dangerous African animal. The lion lives in a group * of lions called a pride. A lion is very lazy and usually sleeps about twenty hours a day. A hunter can often find a lion snoozing with others in its pride. Although the lion can hide in the grass, it gives away its position by roaring and growling. Even when the lion retreats into the brush, the hunter can often locate its position by throwing rocks into the brush. The lion's response—growling— will give its position away. The lion is smart, it can kill, and it is dangerous to the hunter; but the lion is not Africa's *most* dangerous * animal.₅

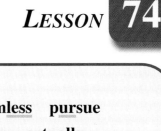

1 sub dis ness re tri

2 leathery harmless pursue
draw selection actually

3
1. ill-tempered
2. matted
3. glance
4. confused
5. strategy
6. tick

4 ruled cousin thickets weapons ivory
suddenly eyesight neither impossible
probably dodging frequently
remarkable conclusion ridge instead
incredibly fault snout discussed
pounding bony gored trampled

5 # Dangerous African Animals Part 3

We have discussed the African elephant and the lion. Both can be very dangerous to the hunter, but neither one is the most dangerous African animal. Let's look at the rhinoceros. It is mean, ill-tempered, and huge. An adult rhinoceros may weigh three and one-half metric tons. Although it cannot move as fast as the elephant, its top speed is about thirty-five kilometers per hour.[1] But it will attack anything—even an elephant. The rhinoceros has two large horns on its snout. These are strange horns because they are not made of ivory as the elephant's tusks * are. They are made of *hair.* The hair is matted together, forming horns so hard that a rhinoceros could easily punch a hole in the side of a car.

The rhinoceros is probably the least dangerous of the African animals—at least for the hunter. The rhinoceros has very poor eyesight but a good sense of smell and of hearing. It uses tickbirds for its eyes. These birds ride around on its back and sides, picking ticks from the folds of its leathery hide. The tickbirds have very good eyes—when something moves nearby, the tickbirds take off, giving an * alarm call. When the tickbirds fly away, the rhinoceros knows that danger is near.₂

The rhinoceros has many other faults. It will charge at anything. Once the rhinoceros puts its head down and begins to charge, it heads straight forward. During such a charge, the hunter might be able to step to one side, and the rhinoceros would go <u>pounding</u> right past the hunter. The rhinoceros would then turn and again charge blindly with its head down. The hunter could keep dodging the rhinoceros until the rhinoceros got tired of the game.

Don't draw the conclusion, however, that the rhinoceros * is a harmless animal. If the hunter wounds the rhinoceros, it will trot off into the bush and hide, waiting for the hunter. It may wait until the hunter is in a place that makes it impossible to dodge the rhinoceros.₃ The rhinoceros may wait until the hunter is only four meters away—then charge. It doesn't make an easy target with its head down. If a bullet hits the rhinoceros on its bony skull with its huge horns, the bullet will glance off. But if a rhinoceros hits the hunter, that hunter will be dead within seconds. The victim * will be knocked down, gored by the rhinoceros's horns, and trampled. Although the rhinoceros may not be the most dangerous animal, it is still very dangerous.

We have ruled out the elephant, the lion, and the rhinoceros as the most dangerous African animal. The two animals that remain are the Cape buffalo and the leopard. At the beginning of this series you probably didn't pick either of these animals, but they are very dangerous to hunt. Consider the Cape buffalo. It is big and fast, and it probably has the best senses of any African animal. Its eyesight and sense * of smell are incredibly keen, and its hearing is remarkable. With these senses the Cape buffalo can keep far away from any hunter who is trying to pursue it. It can spot a hunter at a remarkable distance and avoid the hunter for days. The Cape buffalo can do a lot more than stay away from the hunter; it can kill.₄

People frequently confuse the African Cape buffalo with its cousin, the Indian water buffalo. The African Cape buffalo looks quite a bit like its Indian cousin, but the African Cape buffalo has larger horns that form a ridge across * its forehead and then arch back and out. Each horn is about one-half meter long. The African Cape buffalo is also bigger and more powerful than its Indian cousin. It can easily kill a lion. The African Cape buffalo's usual strategy is to pretend it is running from the lion. The lion will run after the buffalo. The buffalo will allow the lion to catch up, so that the lion is running alongside the buffalo. Just as the lion is ready to make its leap onto the buffalo's back, the buffalo suddenly slows down and swings its head down * and toward the lion. The buffalo's horn goes into the lion's body.₅

The African Cape buffalo is a remarkable animal. We will examine it further in part 4.

1

New Orleans false poisonous cobra
deaf mamba wading Australia
moccasin heaviest India anaconda
squeezing true swamps assortment

2

1. trance
2. venom
3. potent
4. aggressive
5. coiling
6. comparison

3

Snakes

Some stories told about snakes are true, but many are false.

Take the question of speed. The black mamba of Africa is the fastest snake, but reports that it can move faster than a horse are untrue. Experts believe that this poisonous snake, which grows to 14 feet (4.3 meters), can glide for a short distance at about 15 miles (24 kilometers) per hour, or about as fast as most people can run. Because of its size and speed, it is also capable of slithering over walls as high as 10 feet (3 meters).[1]

The longest and heaviest snakes are not poisonous. They are constrictor snakes that kill their victims by coiling around them and crushing them.

One of the longest snakes ever found was a South American anaconda that was 37 ½ feet long (over 11 meters), or the length of two full-sized cars parked end to end. The monster weighed about 1100 pounds (500 kilograms) and was able to crush its prey with a force of more than 30 tons (17 metric tons).

The most poisonous snakes of the ocean and the land are found near Australia.

The most poisonous of all snakes is the sea snake, which lives on reefs off Australia. When it strikes a victim, it spits out enough venom or poison to kill five hundred sheep. Sometimes it is very aggressive. Skin divers near the reefs must be very careful, because nothing can save the life of a diver bitten by a sea snake.[2]

The most poisonous land snake is the fierce tiger snake, which lives on islands near Australia. One bite from this snake contains enough venom to kill more than a thousand sheep.

Snakebite is a serious problem in India, where about twenty-five thousand people die from it each year. The most common poisonous snake in India is the cobra, which also happens to be the longest poisonous snake. One king cobra was 19 feet long (5 ½ meters).

The cobra is also the subject of a snake story that is false. A snake charmer's music is said to put the cobra into a trance. But, like other snakes, the cobra is almost deaf. When the snake's head sways to the music of a snake charmer's flute, it is not responding to the music but to the movement of the musical instrument.[3]

In comparison to the snakes of India, Australia, and Africa, the varieties found in North America are mostly harmless. Not many people die of snakebites in North America. There are swamps near New Orleans, however, where a visitor can find an assortment of poisonous snakes. Among these are the water moccasin and the copperhead, two snakes that nobody would want to meet on a Sunday picnic. Fortunately, not many people go wading in these swamps.[4]

1
able
curable
movable
believable
preventable
understandable

2
selection   instead   expertly
heavier   experienced   nearly

3

1. range
2. efficient
3. instantly
4. advantage
5. determined
6. rescue
7. relation
8. particularly

4

license   smarter   claws   extremely
nature   unusually   probably   decided
difference   effectively   wounded
well-designed   hooves   professional
heart   lose   impala   wrestling   incredible

5 ## Dangerous African Animals Part 4

In part 3 of this story we discussed why the Cape buffalo is very dangerous. The hunter will have great trouble getting within range of the buffalo because of its very keen senses.

Also, the Cape buffalo is an efficient killer, far more efficient than the rhinoceros. The Cape buffalo will charge, but unlike the rhinoceros, it will be careful about when it charges. It will move much faster than the rhinoceros, so the hunter will not be able to dodge it. The Cape buffalo can change direction very quickly, and it uses its horns, its skull, and its hooves * effectively.₁

Another fact about the Cape buffalo is that it is hard to kill. Cape buffalos have reportedly charged up to one hundred meters with a bullet in the heart. Unless the shot is expertly placed, a bullet in the chest usually will not kill the buffalo instantly. And if the bullet does not kill the Cape buffalo instantly, the hunter may be the first one to die.

Experienced big game hunters agree that the Cape buffalo is a most dangerous animal when wounded. Some professional big game hunters have lost their licenses to hunt because they have failed to * track wounded buffalos into the brush. A professional hunter must kill an animal—not wound it. If the animal is wounded, the professional hunter must track it into the brush and kill it, but some hunters have decided that they would rather lose their licenses than go into the brush after a wounded Cape buffalo. The buffalo in the brush has a great advantage. It can hide and wait, just like the rhinoceros. The difference is that the buffalo is smarter and harder to kill than the rhinoceros, and probably it is more determined to kill the hunter. The hunter * must be extremely careful when tracking a wounded buffalo, because when the buffalo charges, it is probably too late for the hunter to stop it.₂

The Cape buffalo is dangerous indeed, but the smallest big game animal, the leopard, is the *most* dangerous animal to hunt. How could the leopard be more dangerous than an elephant, a lion, a rhinoceros, or a Cape buffalo? A leopard may not weigh more than seventy-five kilograms. It is not much larger than a full-grown police dog, and it certainly doesn't look very dangerous. Actually, it looks like an overgrown house cat * with spots and a long tail.

Look again, and you will see one of nature's best-designed predators. Anybody who has ever tried to rescue a kitten from a tree knows how much damage this small pet can do with its claws. If you took a house cat and made it ten times heavier, you would have a powerful predator, but it would not be as powerful as the leopard. The leopard has more strength in relation to its size than nearly any other animal.₃ With little effort a leopard can carry a full-grown impala up the side of * a tree to an overhanging branch. The leopard moves up a tree with its prey as easily as if it is carrying something that weighs no more than an overcoat.

Besides being almost as strong as a lion, a leopard can kill a hunter nearly as quickly and easily as a lion can. Although a leopard can't crush someone with its charge, it can leap on the hunter and, holding on with its teeth and front claws, tear into the hunter's body with its rapidly moving back claws. The attack is quick and efficient. Even if the hunter wards off * the leopard's jaws, the leopard's claws—particularly its back claws—can kill the hunter in a few seconds.₄

There have been reports of a leopard killing two persons in less than three seconds. The leopard moves with lightning speed and incredible strength. Like the lion, the leopard is designed to kill animals that are far more powerful than people. So don't believe those old jungle movies that show people wrestling with leopards. A wrestling match between a hunter and a leopard would be over quick as a wink, and the winner would probably be the leopard.

1 able   readable   predictable
workable   believable

2 brightly   mentioned   deadly   lunge

3
1. downed
2. disadvantage
3. created
4. filtering

4 actually   splattered   clearly   consider
frequently   abruptly   intelligence
crouched   sailing   bravery   scarcely
instantly   baboon   favorite   stray
warning   invisible   spotted   listening
growls   thrown   stretched
straight   appreciate   designed

5 # Dangerous African Animals Part 5

Like the lion, the leopard is a lazy animal. It spends most of the day sleeping in its favorite spot—on the limb of a tree. It doesn't like the open plain, and it doesn't often stray from the trees. The leopard will move onto the plain to hunt, but after it has downed an antelope or a baboon, it will return to the shade of the forest. And that brings up another reason that the leopard is dangerous to hunt. The hunter who goes after the leopard will have to go into the forest where the hunter is at * a great disadvantage. When the leopard stands out in the open, it seems to be very brightly marked. When it is in the shade-splattered forest, however, a leopard is almost invisible. Its tan-and-black-spotted coat looks just like the spots of light and dark created by the sun's rays filtering through the trees. The only thing that gives the leopard away is its tail. It has a habit of letting its tail hang down from the limb of a tree. Often its tail is the only part that is visible.₁

When the leopard is on the ground * in some brush, it is very difficult for a hunter to find. A hunter can locate a lion in the brush by throwing stones and listening for the lion's growls. However, the leopard won't growl; silently it will lie there, flat against the ground. Some of the stones thrown by the hunter may actually hit the leopard, but it won't move, and it won't make a sound. With its ears back and its eyes fixed straight ahead, the leopard will wait for the right moment to leap out.₂

A leopard in a tree usually will not bother a hunter unless * the leopard is wounded. The hunter may walk right under the tree, but the leopard won't attack unless the hunter happens to look up. If the hunter looks up, the leopard will attack instantly. The leopard, with its very keen eyesight, watches the movement of anything that may be dangerous. It considers people dangerous. As soon as a leopard feels it has been seen, it will attack.

We mentioned how deadly the leopard can be. When a leopard attacks, it is very difficult for the hunter to stop the leopard. Like the lion, the leopard can move from a crouched * position to full speed in only a few steps. It easily can jump seven meters from a crouched position. Its legs are like springs, and with one powerful lunge it flies at the hunter.₃

Let's consider a hunter who is moving through the jungle. The hunter looks around, knowing that leopards are near. Suddenly the hunter spots a form in a tree that is eight meters ahead. At that instant, with no warning, the form leaps at the hunter. The hunter scarcely has time to raise the rifle and take aim. The hunter must shoot now—but consider the target. * When a leopard is sailing through the air, its body is stretched and its front legs are straight out on either side of its head. The target, the leopard's head, is only about one-third of a meter across. There will be no chance for a second shot before the leopard reaches the hunter.₄

So the leopard is clearly the most dangerous African animal to hunt. The leopard is extremely powerful, very smart, and difficult to find. It is quick, and it makes a difficult target. The hunter usually will have less than two seconds to respond to an attack.

When * you see leopards in a zoo pacing back and forth and panting, it's hard to appreciate how dangerous they are. If you could see one in its natural home, you would see what a well-designed predator it is. Nature gave the leopard great bravery and a lot of intelligence. Though a leopard will attack almost any animal, it will not attack at any time, the way a rhinoceros will. It will choose the right time and the right place for the attack.₅

1   able   pre   ness   ly   re

---

2   pleasant   exhausted   creature   survival

3

1. magnificent
2. puny
3. required
4. concerned
5. apparent
6. intruder
7. referred

4

poison   outsmart   topics   usually

incredibly   protection   series

involves   through   defending   including

although   contrast   though   snooze

invade   listen   healthy   develop   efficient

5   Dangerous African Animals Part 6

Some of the things you've read in this series may have bothered you. Killing and death are not pleasant topics. We don't like to think about people being killed by wild animals. But the animals that we have discussed are designed to survive, and their survival involves defending themselves against other animals, including human beings. The magnificent African elephant—that incredibly large and powerful animal—will protect itself and the other elephants in its herd against any animals that threaten it—including people. The lion and the leopard kill to survive. If they don't kill, they don't eat, and if * they don't eat, they don't live. Every part of them has been designed to help them kill, but they do it only to eat and to protect themselves.₁

People, in contrast to the animals we have referred to, are rather puny. If people were required to fight as the other animals are, they wouldn't survive three seconds against a healthy leopard or lion. But people don't fight the way other animals do. They hunt the leopard and win, but they don't give the leopard a fair chance. Each hunter goes into the forest with several dogs. Although a leopard could * kill *any* dog quick as a wink, the leopard usually runs if there is more than one dog. Usually the leopard climbs a tree, and the howling of the dogs tells the hunter where the leopard is. Now the hunter can stand twenty meters away, take careful aim, and kill the leopard with no great danger. People have chased the leopards and the lions from their homes by using drums and fires and trucks and poison. With trucks the hunter has chased the Cape buffalo—running it until it is exhausted and can run no more. Then the hunter has * shot that beautiful creature that was doing nothing more than trying to escape.₂

Ask yourself, do any of these African animals kill for the sake of killing? Does the leopard mount the heads of the animals it kills so it can show how brave it is? No, usually the leopard is concerned only with eating or finding a cool spot high in a tree away from the bugs where it can have a nice snooze. The only animal that attacks for no *apparent* reason is the rhinoceros, which is only trying to keep intruders out of the area that it * considers its own. The rhinoceros attacks those who invade its home.₃

Now look at what hunters have done over the past years. They have shown they can outsmart even the smartest African animals. They have shown they can develop weapons that are more effective killers than the horns of the Cape buffalo or the teeth of the lion. The hunters have also shown that often they may have killed just for the sake of killing. And consider what they have killed. The African animals that we have discussed are magnificent creatures that treat people as they would treat any other * intruders. Each has survived because it is the best at what it does. The leopard is the most capable predator in the world. The lion is the most effective killer on the plain. The Cape buffalo is one of the most efficient grazing animals in the world. Each of these animals has a place in nature. But people have changed all that. They have taken away the places—with farms and fences and guns. And they have killed these animals—in many cases with no good reason.₄

When you consider that there are only about two thousand leopards remaining in * Africa, where once there were tens of thousands, it seems a shame that this world may lose such a beautiful creature—brave, smart, and efficient. The same is true of the elephant, the rhinoceros, the lion, and the Cape buffalo. People have killed these animals by the hundreds of thousands. Yet, in a fair contest with these animals, the hunter would not fare well. Even with a gun, the hunter may not win the contest, particularly if the contest is with the African Cape buffalo or with the most dangerous of all African animals—the leopard.₅

1

less   ness   dis   ly   re   un

2

managed   directly   physicists   paused
experience   revising   disbelief   weakness

3

1. reaction
2. presentation
3. duplicated
4. coincidence
5. nagged
6. bombardment

4

permission   experimental   occasionally
tasteless   delivered   Chicago   slumped
computer   memorized   procedures   awakened
stretched   pizza   scheduled   wearing
laboratory   various   data   amazement

5

Milly Prepares Her Paper

Milly Jacobson returned to State University still wearing the dusty jeans and other clothes she had worn in the mountains. She had gone directly to the airport from Mr. Hicks's home and had managed to get on a late-night flight. The plane landed at four in the morning, and Milly went directly to her laboratory in the physics building. She noticed, on her way into the building, that the piles had been removed from the lawn. She turned on the desk lamp in her lab, sat down, stacked her records on one side of the desk, turned on her * computer, and typed the title of her paper: "The Reaction of Gold to Laser Bombardment."

She paused for a moment before beginning to type the paper. She thought about how the other physicists would react when she presented her paper at the International Convention of Physicists. That was Milly's plan, but she had to work fast, for the convention in Chicago was only three weeks away.₁ Milly had to complete the paper and then get permission to present it. The program for the convention had already been set for months. Milly would have to talk somebody into letting her make * her presentation at one of the sessions. But first, she had to complete the paper.

She typed for about two hours. Occasionally she referred to her notes, but she had memorized most of the data. The first part of her paper described the experimental procedures. She told how she tested the various metals and how they reacted to short <u>laser</u> blasts. Before Milly could begin the second part of her paper—which was to tell about her field experience with the laser gear—she fell asleep in the lab, sitting at her computer. Waking up in the middle of the * morning, she noticed that several people were working in the lab. She greeted them, slumped over her computer, and went to sleep again.

Around noon Fred Frankle awakened her by gently shaking her shoulder. "Come on, Milly. If you want to sleep, you should go home and go to bed."

"I don't want to sleep," Milly said. "I want to write. But I'm so tired." She stretched and yawned, stood up, and stretched again. "I'm awake now. I'll just have a cup of coffee and I'll be fine."

Milly typed all afternoon. She called a pizza place and had a * small pizza delivered to the lab. Eating and typing at the same time, she completed the first draft of the paper before she finished the pizza. Then she began revising the paper; she crossed out sentences; she rewrote parts; she read the paper over carefully; and just to be sure, she reread it once more.

At nine at night, the paper was completed. By nine the next morning, the paper had been retyped and duplicated by a typist that Milly hired. Milly had offered the typist three hundred dollars if he typed the paper before noon of the following day. *₂

Next Milly called the program chairperson for the International Convention of Physicists and explained that she had a very important paper to present.

"That's a nice coincidence," the chairperson said. "We find that one of our scheduled presenters can't be with us for the convention. His wife is going to have a baby and he wants to stay home."

"That's great," Milly said.

Now Milly waited. She was dying to tell somebody about her discovery, but she wanted to surprise everybody when she presented her paper at the convention. She realized that she was sort of a show-off, but * she also realized that she had made an important discovery and that she deserved the chance to show off.₃

There were several times during the next three weeks that she almost told Fred about her experiments. For three days after she returned he nagged her, trying to find out what she did in California. Each time, Milly responded, "I was doing a field study." But each time, she wanted to tell him. She wanted to see his eyes become large with amazement and his mouth fall open with disbelief. But she made herself keep the secret. To keep it was * getting more difficult each day.₄

1

parents   inherited   skeleton   scarce
millions   diet   vitamins   proteins
minerals   nutrients   stunned
enormous   generation   influences

2

1. ancient
2. nutrition
3. genetic
4. starvation
5. plentiful

3

Are People Getting Taller?

Some people think that the human race is taller than it used to be. Is it?

No. Even though some groups of people today are taller than their parents and grandparents were, the whole human race is not growing taller.

Height is a genetic, or inherited, characteristic.[1] That means that the possibility of being a tall person or a short one is something that you are born with. This possibility is passed on to you from your parents, grandparents, great-grandparents, and so on. Each person's genetic inheritance goes back many, many generations.

Inheritance sets a limit on growth. If you come from many generations of tall people, you may grow to be very tall too. But if you come from many generations of short people, you will probably be short.

Inheritance is only part of what determines how tall you will become. One of the things that most influences how you grow and develop is nutrition: the amount, kind, and quality of food you eat.[2] If two people have the same growth potential, the person who always has enough good food to eat will grow taller and stronger than the person who hasn't.

Although genetics might permit you to be tall, a starvation diet would not give your body the proteins, vitamins, minerals, and other nutrients it needs to grow tall.

Good food is not always easy, or even possible, to get. At many times and in many places during the history of the human race, there have been long periods of starvation. People who lived during those periods were smaller than they would have been if they had lived when food was plentiful.

Some ancient skeletons of adults are very small, and at one time people thought that all ancient people were small. Not all of them were. Some skeletons have shown that many ancient people were as tall as tall people of today.

Today there are still many places in the world where people don't get enough good food to eat. These people are a lot shorter than they would have been if they had always had enough to eat.

1   weather persuaded audience angrily

2
1. hassle
2. peeved
3. acoustics
4. moderator
5. podium

3

discussion interrupted exploding
seriously performance entertaining
conference quickness thoughtless
originally curtain wandering delayed
introducing apparently trouble
stumbling quieted scheduled entire
equipment phony embarrassed
scene irritated bombardment

4

Milly's Arrival

The weather in Chicago was rainy when Milly's plane arrived two hours late. She was a little irritated because it seemed that the entire trip had become a hassle. The dean didn't want her to go. He had told her that she was scheduled to go to only one conference that year, not two. After some discussion, Milly persuaded the dean to allow her to go. Then Fred became angry with Milly. He had told her, "Sometimes you're too much! First you go into the mountains for days, and then you take off for another convention." She had tried to * explain to him that it was important for her to go to the convention, but he had still seemed peeved with her. Then Milly had a great deal of trouble trying to ship her laser equipment to the meeting. She wanted to put it on display for the physicists. And on top of everything, bad weather delayed the plane.

But now Milly was in a cab on her way to the convention hall, and she was beginning to feel better. She loved conventions. She hadn't prepared any jokes for this convention—no exploding cigars or exploding cue sticks, no red * -and-white pins. She had a handshake buzzer in her suitcase, but she wasn't seriously thinking about using it.[1]

When she walked into the hotel lobby, one physicist said, "Oh no, there she is. Watch your step around Dr. Jacobson."

Four physicists came over and began to joke around with Milly. One said, "We all heard about your last <u>performance</u>. Are you going to put on a better show at this convention?"

Milly smiled and answered, "It will be different. I plan to give a very important paper."

"It's a joke, right?" one of the physicists asked. "I can see * that phony-serious expression on your face. A very important paper," he said sarcastically. "I'll just bet it's important."

"No, really," she said. "This is serious."

"Listen, we've heard about how serious you are. Like setting off smoke bombs and—"

Another physicist interrupted. "And what about that paper you passed out at the last convention? That was pretty serious."

"Believe me," she said. "This time I'm really serious."

"Listen," one of them said and patted her on the shoulder. "We'll be there. I wouldn't miss your paper for anything."[2]

Milly met other physicists before the meeting and most of them * reacted the same way the first group had reacted. It seemed that everybody expected her to play a superjoke on the group. As one physicist said, "We need you, Milly. We take ourselves so seriously that we sometimes forget that we're just a bunch of people stumbling around trying to find out new things. We need you to remind us about what we are. Give a good talk."[3]

The meeting room where Milly had originally been scheduled to talk held about fifty people. But apparently the word got out that she was going to put on an entertaining show, because * more than two hundred physicists showed up and the meeting room had to be changed. The new room, a large conference hall that had more than four hundred seats, was on the first floor of the convention center. By the time everybody got settled in the new room and Milly set up her laser behind the curtain, it was already fifteen minutes after the meeting had been scheduled to begin.

Milly waited another half-hour as a physicist from Michigan gave a talk on acoustics. Milly tried to become interested in the speech, but her mind kept wandering back to * the glory hole. She remembered that scene when the smoke cleared and she stared at the glory hole for the first time. Milly's thoughts were in the middle of that scene when she realized that the audience was applauding. The paper was completed, and it was now Milly's turn to present hers.[4]

The woman who moderated the panel stood before the podium introducing Milly. "The title of Dr. Jacobson's paper is 'The Reaction of Gold to Laser Bombardment.' " Several people in the audience began to laugh.

Someone yelled, "Get ready for the put-on of your life." Then everybody began * to laugh.

The moderator looked embarrassed. She said, "Well, without further delay, I give you Dr. Milly Jacobson."

Great cheers went up from the group. It

sounded more like a football game than a physics convention. "Go, Milly," some of the physicists yelled.

At last the audience quieted. Milly held her hands out and said, "Some of you are expecting a joke, but the paper I'm about to deliver is no joke. It is very serious."

At that, the audience again broke into waves of laughter.[5]

1 participants imagined expression announced

2
1. summary
2. modified
3. formulas
4. confirm
5. interruption
6. routine

3
audience   friendliness   disbelief

substance   measurement   explained

applause   snickers   decided   indicated

calculations   identify   equipment

apparently   serious   concrete   nugget

moment   exit   mathematical   data

aisle   volunteer   dozen   scan

4 # The Presentation Begins

The audience wouldn't let Milly talk. Every time she tried to say something, the people began to laugh and shout. At last the moderator for the meeting stood up and said, "Ladies and gentlemen, let's try to give Dr. Jacobson a chance to present her paper."

"Yes, be quiet," somebody yelled from the audience.

Milly said, "Well, let me try to give you a quick summary of what I discovered. I discovered that I can identify gold—even when it is underground—by using a modified metal detector and short bursts of laser light."

There were a few snickers from * the audience, but most of the participants were quiet and smiling. Their expressions indicated that they were waiting for the big joke. Milly presented the details of her experiments, showing slides of the different metal-detector readings and presenting mathematics formulas and calculations that explained the difference in the readings between gold and other metals.

Then Milly said, "And to confirm these findings, I took the laser equipment to the mountains near Sacramento, California." She showed the slide of herself with Mr. Hicks standing next to the pickup truck.

"That's great," somebody from the audience yelled, and everybody began to * laugh.₁

A young woman near the back of the audience said, "I've got a question."

"Yes," Milly responded.

"Where did you find that guy in the picture? He looks like he's right out of some old movie."

Everybody laughed. Milly explained how she had located Mr. Hicks. Again, everybody laughed. Some people were laughing so hard they had tears in their eyes.

Milly was beginning to realize that her entire paper sounded like a big joke. For a moment she imagined how she would react to the paper if she were in the audience. What would she think if she * saw that picture of Milly and Hicks next to a dirty pickup truck with a laser gun mounted in the bed? What would she think if somebody told her that gold could be identified with a laser gun? She decided that she'd probably laugh, too.₂

"Please, let me go through the rest of my paper, and then I'll answer questions." The audience remained quiet until Milly told about the glory hole.

Then somebody from the third row yelled, "Come on, Milly. This is too much."

"Everything I have told you is the truth," Milly said, but not many people heard * her above the laughter of the group. Three interruptions later, Milly finished her talk. Apparently nobody in the audience took it seriously. Even the moderator was laughing.

Milly opened the curtain, showing her laser gun. Everybody clapped and cheered, but the audience's response was not serious. One physicist yelled, "Don't shoot, Milly—we'll be good."

Milly walked to the side of the stage where she had a large shoulder bag. She reached into the bag and pulled out a large nugget, bigger than an orange. People in the audience cheered and whistled.₃

Milly said, "I'd like to put on a * demonstration to show you that the data I have reported is real." She pointed to the wall to her left. "That wall is concrete," Milly said. "If somebody in the audience would volunteer to take this gold nugget and—"

"I'll take it," somebody yelled, and everybody laughed again.

Milly repeated, "If somebody will take it and hold it in different spots on the other side of this wall, I'll demonstrate that I can locate it."

"I'll volunteer," the moderator said. Milly handed the nugget to her. As the moderator headed down the aisle, she was met with applause and laughter. * She smiled and nodded to the members of the audience as she walked down the side aisle to the back of the room and out one of the exits.

Then Milly said, "Will somebody near the rear of the hall tell me when she's got the nugget in place?"

About six physicists walked out of the meeting room. After a moment or two, they returned. "She's ready," one of them announced.

Milly adjusted her laser gun and pointed it at the left wall. She said, "I'll start in the rear and move forward."

She aimed the gun at the far * end of the wall and began to scan it with short laser bursts. Each burst left a small dark mark on the painted wall. Soon the smell of burning paint filled the room.

"Oh, no!" somebody yelled. "It's the old smoke bomb routine."

About a dozen physicists stood up and left the room.₄

1   ly   ness   re   less

2   ceiling   steady   rear   precisely

3
1. typical
2. adequate
3. reinforced
4. ducts
5. distinguish
6. proceed

4

piece   hurried   collection   foolish

lengths   detection   reappeared

excitedly   exactly   demonstration

treated   damaged   thoughtless   zinc

ignore   touched   entire   electrical

scanned   moderator   system   iron

smokey   identify   agreement   spray

5

Demonstrations

Milly tried to ignore the comments from the audience as she scanned the left wall with the laser gun. The wall near the rear of the room looked as if somebody had used a can of black spray paint to paint zigzag lines over it. More people were leaving the room, which was now becoming quite smokey.₁

Milly began to scan the middle of the wall. Suddenly the needle on the metal detector gave its typical gold reading. "There," Milly said, holding the laser beam steady. It was pointing to a spot near the bottom of the wall, about halfway * between the front and the back of the meeting hall. "Would somebody mark that spot?" Somebody did. Then the moderator was called back into the room. "Where did you place the nugget?" Milly asked.

"I'll show you exactly," she said through the smoke. She stood with her back against the rear wall of the hall. Then she began to walk forward placing the heel of her foot against the toe of her other foot. She marked off fifty foot-lengths. She bent down and touched the exact spot marked on the wall.

"Put-on," somebody yelled. "She's part of the * gag."

"No," Milly said. "She is not, and it is not a gag."

One physicist stood up and said, "I feel a little foolish asking a serious question, but how do we know you couldn't do that with any metal, given that you have adequate detection equipment?"[2]

"Let's do it again," Milly said. "This time, I'll give somebody four <u>smaller</u> bits of metal—one gold and three zinc."

"Why not some other metals, too?" somebody asked.

"Because the wall is made of reinforced concrete," Milly said. "It has iron reinforcing bars in it, copper wires for the electrical system, and steel heating * ducts. If you wish, I can locate these metals. However, I can't identify them precisely. I can only distinguish between gold and not gold." Milly walked to her shoulder bag and brought out four bits, each smaller than a dime. She handed the bits to the moderator and said, "Please place them somewhere near the back or middle of the wall. I don't want to mess up the entire wall."[3]

A few moments passed as the moderator left the room with three other physicists who went with her to place the metal pieces. When they reappeared at the * rear exit door, the moderator said, "They're set."

Milly turned on the gun and began scanning the wall. She stopped near the back ceiling. "There," she said. "That's a bit of zinc."

"Exactly right!" the moderator said.

A man who had helped the moderator set the pieces said, "That's right. I set it there."

Milly moved the laser gun and stopped again. The audience was quiet now. "There's another bit of zinc," Milly announced.

"Wrong," a woman said. "It's a dime. I taped it there."

"As I told you," Milly explained, "I can only distinguish between gold and not gold." *[4]

Milly moved the gun again. She scanned for about thirty seconds. By now she was almost to the middle of the room. Suddenly she stopped. "And there is the gold."

"Right," the moderator said. The others nodded their heads in agreement.

"This is fantastic," one of them said.

"Hey, wait a minute," somebody in the audience said. "Do you mean this demonstration is on the level?"

"As far as I know it is," the moderator said. "We placed those pieces."

"Hey," a man from the audience said. "I want to place that gold piece myself. OK?"

"Sure," Milly said. The * man hurried out of the room. Fifty or sixty people from the audience followed. After he returned to the conference hall and announced that the piece was placed on the other side of the wall, Milly scanned the wall with her gun. She stopped near the ceiling in the back. "There," she said. "It's about six inches from the ceiling."

"I can't believe it!" the physicist who placed the piece said. "It's not a put-on."

Members of the audience began to talk excitedly among themselves. "Do it again," somebody from the audience said. "This time with more than one * piece."

"All right," Milly said. "And I'll be able to tell you the size of each piece."

"Not that I don't trust you," the physicist said, "but that gold you used may be treated. I have a gold ring and I'm sure that other people in the audience have things made of gold. Let's use those. They won't be damaged, will they?"

"No," Milly answered, and the man proceeded to collect several things made of gold from members of the audience.[5]

1 dis sub pre ly less ness

2 gathered mentioned already comfortably

3
1. rectangular
2. technical
3. subsided
4. refused

4
articles seriously importance
disbelief prepared substitute necklace
probably applauding thundering
scanned distinguish trained
scheduled deposit special platinum
fault group worth million aisles
heard earlier brilliance

5

Milly's Reward

A large group from the audience left the conference hall to see where the different gold articles were placed on the other side of the concrete wall. A crowd gathered around the rear exits. "OK," somebody yelled from the rear of the hall, and Milly trained the laser beam on the rear part of the wall.

Suddenly she stopped the beam and said, "At that spot on the other side of the wall is a gold object that is fairly large. It is probably a pocket watch."

"Correct," a woman from the rear of the hall shouted. Some members of * the audience applauded, this time seriously.

Again Milly moved the beam, and again she stopped. "Right there is a small gold object that is quite long. Could it be a gold necklace?"[1]

"Yes," said voices from the rear of the conference hall. More applause followed. Milly bowed and smiled.

She scanned the wall for another moment, stopping near the floor about two-thirds of the way toward the rear wall. "That," she said, "must be a gold ring."

"Yes," a chorus of voices shouted, followed by thundering applause. Then members of the audience crowded down the aisles with their hands * raised, shouting out questions.

"Hey," Milly shouted back, "why don't you sit down, and I'll try to answer your questions."

The questions came for the next hour. Another meeting had been scheduled in the conference hall, but Milly's group refused to leave. When people who were going to the next meeting heard what was happening in Milly's meeting, they stayed to listen and ask questions. Soon the hall was packed, with people standing in the aisles and crowding around the rear exit doors.

After members of the audience had asked a number of technical questions about the laser equipment and * how it worked, a woman said, "Earlier you mentioned that, using the laser, you had discovered a glory hole. How much was the gold worth that you found?"

Milly said, "I would estimate that the deposit was worth close to one hundred million dollars."₂

The audience was silent for a moment. Then a voice asked, "What do you plan to do with all that money?"

Milly explained that part of the claim would go to her university, part would go to the state of California, and part would go to Mr. Hicks. "What about you?" somebody asked. "Don't you get * anything from the gold find?"

Milly smiled and didn't say anything for a moment. Then she replied, "I already got my share. Ever since I was a little girl, I wanted to do something special, something that would be really important and would help other people. I'll never be able to explain the feeling to you, but when the dust cleared and we saw the glory hole for the first time, reflecting its brilliance in the sunlight, I got a large part of my reward. And I got the rest of it today, when I presented my paper to you. * I live comfortably, and I have a very good job. I'm not hungry for gold or for the things that gold can buy. The real gold for me is the discovery I made, and it's all the reward I need."₃

The audience applauded. "I think you've lost your mind," somebody from the back of the hall shouted after the applause had subsided.

"Maybe I have," Milly said. "But I'll tell you one thing: I'm very happy. And if I ever happen to change my mind, I can always go back to Sacramento with my laser and find another glory hole. * I'll bet there are quite a few others that haven't been found yet."

Somebody from the audience said, "That may be, Milly, but now that the secret of the laser is out, other people will be able to use lasers to search for gold. If you don't act fast, those glory holes will be found before you can return."

Milly said, "You're probably right, but there are so many things about our world that we don't understand. Who knows, maybe I'll discover some way to find silver or platinum."

That day at the International Convention of Physicists was probably the * biggest day in Milly's life, but it didn't change her very much. Today she is still working in her lab at State University and playing jokes on the other physicists.

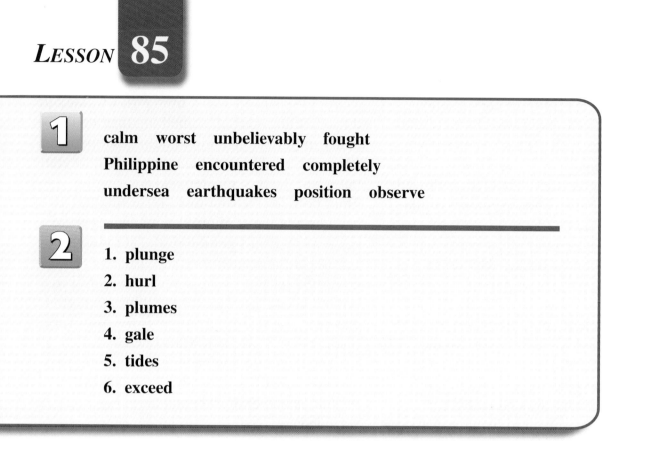

1 calm   worst   unbelievably   fought
Philippine   encountered   completely
undersea   earthquakes   position   observe

2
1. plunge
2. hurl
3. plumes
4. gale
5. tides
6. exceed

3

Ocean Waves and Tides

When you observe the ocean on a calm day, you can't really imagine what it looks like when it is angry. Even when the wind blows and the waves plunge against rocks and hurl plumes of spray into the air, you may think that you're looking at the sea when it is at its worst. But, occasionally, the sea can become even more wild. For example, in 1933, a ship on its way from the Philippine Islands to California encountered a gale with winds of more than 75 miles (about 120 kilometers) per hour. As the ship fought the gale, the waves rose higher. One soared 112 feet (about 34 meters). That's as high as an eleven-story building.

Undersea earthquakes sometimes cause waves that exceed the height of those caused by high winds. The reason that waves caused by earthquakes become higher is that they move faster.[1] Suddenly, part of the ocean floor drops. The wave that results moves out from the earthquake, forming a ring on the surface of the water. This ring is a wave. As this wave starts to move, it is not very high, perhaps only half a meter or so. Unlike wind-pushed waves, however, this kind of wave moves very fast. Some of these waves have traveled at a speed of about 500 miles (800 kilometers) per hour.

When this kind of wave comes near the shore, it begins to grow in height. The bottom part of the wave begins to drag along the ocean floor. The top part of the wave then begins to fall forward. More water keeps moving and climbing over the water that has slowed down. The result of this pileup is a great wave.[2] Sometimes the wave will grow to a height of about 96 feet (30 meters). The Alaska earthquake in 1964 caused a wave that measured 220 feet (66 meters). That is the height of a twenty-two-story building.

One of the most unusual things that happens in the ocean—the tides—occurs every day. Tides are caused by the pull of the sun and the moon. The part of the earth that is closest to the sun or moon is pulled the most.

When both the sun and moon are in the same part of the sky, the tides are the strongest.[3]

A bay between the state of Maine in the United States and the Canadian provinces of New Brunswick and Nova Scotia has the strongest tide in the world. The greatest difference between the high and low tides for a twenty-four-hour period is about 52 feet (15 meters). The tide is not this great on every day of the year—only when the sun and moon are in the right positions.

1

A	B
tial	special
cial	partial
	facial
	social
	potential

2

able less ly re un

3

garage complaining referred untangled

4

1. inhabitants
2. insist
3. invent
4. unconvincing

5

refrigerator uncertain respond
outskirts occasional houseful
scarcely rarely accident putter
Einstein break Edison defend
salesperson Lark admitted shove
gloves solar exactly machine
redden draped pour mumble
persist Agnes scraped

6

A Houseful of Inventions

Agnes Lark was an elderly woman. And while she wasn't exactly poor, she didn't have much money. Agnes lived in a small house on the outskirts of Redmond with her cat, Einstein, and her dog, Edison. Although the house had four rooms, the three inhabitants had to eat and sleep in the kitchen. The rest of the house and the garage were filled with junk. If anybody referred to the junk as "junk," Agnes would become angry. Her eyes would seem to pop out and her face would redden. "Junk?" she would say. "Don't refer to my inventions as junk!" *

Actually, Agnes didn't have many occasions to defend her junk, because she rarely had visitors. In fact, aside from an occasional door-to-door salesperson or youngster selling candy, nobody came to Agnes's house.₁

The daily routine in Agnes's house started at six in the morning. Einstein was the first to wake up. The cat would then wake up Agnes by standing on her back as she snored on a couch in the corner of the kitchen.

"Go away," Agnes would mumble, giving the cat an unconvincing shove.

Einstein would respond with a half-purr, half-meow, and the cat * would jump down to the floor. The cat would continue to meow while Agnes untangled herself from her blanket, stumbled to the refrigerator, and poured a bowl of milk.₂

Edison slept (usually with his paws on either side of his nose and his long ears draped over his paws) until the refrigerator opened. Then the old hound opened his red-rimmed eyes, stood up, and walked slowly to Agnes.

"I suppose you want something to eat, too," Agnes would complain, and Edison would respond with a few tired wags of his tail.

After the animals were fed and put outside, * Agnes began to work on one of her inventions. She usually worked on it until long after the sun had set and the animals were asleep. Now and then Agnes took a break during the day to walk to the store or putter in her garden, but she always returned to her work. The only problem with Agnes's inventions was that they weren't really inventions. It's true that she put together new things, but none of them did what they were supposed to do. Over the past forty years, she had invented three hundred new gadgets, and not one worked * as it should have. Her high-speed corn picker didn't work, and it now stood in the hall as a coatrack. (It didn't even make a very good coatrack.)₃

Her automatic shoe-tying machine didn't tie shoes. It scraped skin from your ankle if you tried to use it, and it didn't even do a good job of that. (Agnes had thought of using it as a toast scraper, but the machine tore toast into small bits.) Agnes's egg cracker didn't simply crack eggs, it splattered them all over the room. Her shoe-shiner was a pretty good shoe-cutter. * Her electric fork gave some hair-raising shocks. Her portable telephone was so heavy that two strong men could barely lift it, and her solar furnace didn't make enough heat to melt ice cubes.

But Agnes went on. Forty years ago, she had told herself that she would be an inventor, and now it was too late to admit that she hadn't succeeded. If she admitted that her inventions didn't work, then she had wasted forty years of her life. That's probably why she insisted on referring to all her junk as "inventions."₄

It's a good thing that Agnes had * persisted in trying to become an inventor. If she had given up years ago, she would never have invented the dop machine. Of course, Agnes invented the dop machine by accident, but it was a *real* invention because it worked. And it worked so well that it could have changed the history of the world.₅

1

A	B
tial	official
cial	confidential
	special
	initial
	social

2

rainbow   arranged   caused   remain

3

1. crest

2. penetrate

3. electromagnetic

4

sunburn   suffering   dangerous   machines

shooting   produces   actually   waves

visible   materials   radio   violet   Biv

indigo   ultraviolet   X rays   travel

although   plate   billions

5

From Radio Waves to X Rays

To understand how Agnes invented the dop machine, you have to understand something about waves. These waves aren't the kind you see at the beach but the type that make up the light of a rainbow or an X-ray picture. These are electromagnetic waves. The waves that you see at the beach measure more than one meter from the crest of one wave to the crest of the next. Electromagnetic waves have the same shape as waves at the beach but they are much smaller. Some electromagnetic waves are only a millimeter from crest to crest. Electromagnetic waves travel through * space at the speed of light.

Each type of electromagnetic wave is a particular size. When you change the length of the wave, you create another type of electromagnetic wave. Let's see what happens when we start with the longest electromagnetic wave and shorten the distance from the crest of one wave to the crest of the next. The longest waves are radio waves. Let's say that a radio wave measures ten centimeters from the crest of one wave to the crest of the next. When we shorten the distance so that there is only one centimeter from crest to * crest, the radio wave turns into a heat wave. It no longer produces a radio signal. It now produces heat. This is the kind of wave that is used in microwave ovens to cook things very fast.

When we make the heat wave shorter, the wave turns into a light wave.₁ And as we change the length of the <u>light</u> wave, the color changes. The longest light wave is red. The shortest light wave is violet. When you look at a rainbow, you're actually looking at the different wave lengths of light, arranged from the longest to the shortest waves. * Red is always at the outside of the rainbow and violet is always at the inside.₂ If you want to remember the order of the colors in the rainbow, think of the name Roy G. Biv. Each letter stands for a color:

R stands for red.
O stands for orange.
Y stands for yellow.
G stands for green.
B stands for blue.
I stands for indigo (which is purple-blue).
V stands for violet (which is purple).

The most important point to remember about the rainbow is that the color with the longest wave is red and that if the * wave is made longer than red, it turns into a heat wave. Violet light has the shortest wave. If we take a violet light wave and make it a little shorter, it turns into an ultraviolet wave. The waves in ultraviolet light are so small that one thousand of them stacked together would be as thin as a sheet of paper.₃

Sunburn is caused by ultraviolet waves. People may not feel burned when they leave the sun; however, later that day their body will feel hot and very tender because it is suffering from a burn caused by ultraviolet waves. *

When we make an ultraviolet wave very small, it becomes an X ray. Now it is an extremely dangerous wave. If we are continually hit by X-ray waves, we will die. People who work around X-ray machines must stand behind a lead plate when the machine is shooting out X-ray waves.₄ X rays cannot go through lead, but the waves are so short that they can penetrate most other materials.

An X ray is a hundred times shorter than a wave of violet light and billions of times shorter than a radio wave. The X ray is not the shortest wave there is. Agnes * Lark invented a machine that picked up waves much shorter than X rays.₅

LESSON 88

1

special produce paused
frightened partial burr

2

1. failure
2. indeed
3. whir
4. tug
5. panic
6. prickly

3

noise screwdriver overpowering
noticed screen hairs aloud calmly
experienced hooked gadget visible
electromagnetic television particular
ultraviolet gamma microwave smokey
apparatus kitchen plastic-handled
flattened glued unhealthy desired

4

Agnes's First Dop

Last time you learned that the longest electromagnetic waves are radio waves. And you learned that as radio waves become shorter, they change into heat waves. As heat waves become shorter, they become light waves. Each color of visible light has a particular wave length. Red light has the longest wave length. Violet light has the shortest wave length. (The name Roy G. Biv helps us remember the order of colors from longest to shortest wave lengths.)

Waves that are shorter than light waves are ultraviolet waves. And waves still shorter than these are X rays.

The shortest waves known are * gamma waves—or at least this was true before Agnes Lark invented the dop machine. Gamma waves are so small that a pile of one million of them would not be as thick as a sheet of paper.[1]

Agnes didn't know much about these waves. In fact, Agnes didn't exactly know what she was trying to invent. She started out trying to make a device that would turn on the microwave oven when the garage door opened. Such a gadget had already been invented, so Agnes decided to make a garage door that could be opened with a CB radio. * This invention didn't work out too well because any CB radio within twenty kilometers could open Agnes's garage. Every time somebody said, "Ten-four good buddy" or "Have you seen Smokey today?" the garage door would pop open.₂

Agnes tried to fix the garage door so that it would work only for one special sound. To make this sound, she hooked up a small electric motor with some parts from a microwave oven.

She then connected this apparatus to her CB radio and turned on the motor. To her surprise, however, no special noise came over the CB set. Agnes * didn't become upset, because she'd learned to expect failure. Instead, she went calmly to her tool kit to find a screwdriver. She thought that she might be able to produce the desired noise if she made the electric motor turn faster.₃

Agnes selected a long, plastic-handled screwdriver from her tool box and was carrying it back to the kitchen where the apparatus was hooked up. As she walked past her television set, she felt a small tug on the hand holding the screwdriver. Something was pulling her arm toward the television set. It was not an overpowering pull, but * it was strong enough for Agnes to notice it. She paused for a moment, listening to the quiet whir of the electric motor in the kitchen and feeling the gentle tug on her arm.

"What have we here?" she asked herself, allowing her hand to move closer and closer to the television set. The force became stronger until, like a magnet, it pulled the screwdriver to the screen with a loud clunk!₄ For a moment, Agnes was frightened. Her hand, still holding the screwdriver, was stuck to the television screen. Her skirt was flattened against the screen, and she could * feel the small hairs on her arm leaning toward the set. Agnes tried to pull her hand away, but all she did was move the entire television set. "This is indeed strange," she said aloud.

And then, quite suddenly, Agnes experienced her first dop. It came to her like a message, but not in words. It was more like a very strong feeling. The feeling was, "I have a burr in my fur and it hurts." For an instant, Agnes felt as if she were not herself, but someone or something else. That instant was followed by a feeling of * panic. Agnes felt trapped, glued to the television while strange things were happening to her.₅ She dragged the television set over to the kitchen table and turned off the electric motor. As the motor turned more and more slowly, the tug of the television set died away. Agnes pulled her hand from the set and dropped the screwdriver. She opened and closed her hand several times to see if it had been injured. She rubbed her arm. But there was no pain and no sign of injury.

"That was strange," Agnes said, glancing down at the screwdriver. Next to the * screwdriver was the cat Einstein trying to bite something in its fur. In a flash, Agnes knew what was in the cat's fur, and she knew where it was. It was a burr, a prickly burr, just below the cat's right shoulder. Even before she picked the cat up, she knew.₆

1 pre   re   less   able

2 predicting   diseases   reliving   radiation

4 frightening   worthless   apparatus
pleading   twice   perspire   tulip
glanced   inventions   during   severe
experienced   adventure   argued   famous
combination   diagnosing   electromagnetic
solo   invaded   scratching   succeeded
downward   antenna   mushy   rectangle

3
1. slanting
2. gamble
3. palm
4. consciousness
5. indifferently
6. scolded
7. anxiety

5

Cats, Dogs—and People, Too

On the day that Agnes experienced her first dop, she had a lot to think about. During most of the afternoon, she argued with herself about whether she should try the dop experiment again. There were two sides to the argument.

One side insisted that the machine might allow Agnes to read the thoughts of animals. She could become very rich with such an invention. She might become famous by joining a circus as an animal trainer or by diagnosing diseases in animals.

The other side of the argument warned her that the electromagnetic waves created by the machine could * be dangerous. Perhaps they would cause severe radiation burns or make one go mad.₁ She really didn't know anything about these new waves.

Shortly before supper, when the light was slanting through the kitchen window casting a bright rectangle on the wall, Agnes picked up the screwdriver. She had decided to try the experiment. After all, she had lived a good, long life, and she wasn't going to live forever. It was worth the gamble. Nevertheless, as she picked up the screwdriver, her hand was shaking. Her palms were sweating, and a voice inside was pleading, "I don't want to * die. I'm afraid."₂

Agnes tried to ignore her anxiety. She put down the screwdriver, took several deep breaths, and looked down at Einstein. "Well," she said, in a voice that sounded stiff, "it won't get any easier by waiting."

In her mind, she kept reliving that moment in which she had received the message about the burr. It hadn't been a thought and it hadn't been words. It was as if she had become Einstein for a moment and was able to experience what the cat was feeling. It was as if some other being had invaded her mind. It * was like becoming two beings at the same time: Agnes/Einstein.

As Agnes turned on the apparatus, she stood staring first at Einstein and then at Edison. The dog was in the corner, scratching behind his ear. "This is it," Agnes said. The television set was on; the apparatus was running. All that remained was to pick up the screwdriver.

"You worthless old thing," Agnes scolded herself. "Don't you have any spirit of adventure left? Pick up that screwdriver and get on with it." She did. She stood about a meter from the television set and closed her eyes. Slowly * she allowed her hand to be pulled to the screen. Her heart was pounding wildly. She began having second thoughts about her decision. (Maybe twice a day is too much. Tomorrow might be better.) Clunk! Her hand was stuck to the screen. But there were no thoughts, no other beings invading Agnes's consciousness.₃

She opened her eyes and glanced around the room. Edison was biting a flea on his back, but Agnes received no messages. The cat was staring somewhat indifferently at Agnes, but there were still no messages. "Perhaps the field isn't working," Agnes thought. To test the strength * of the field, she tried to pull her hand from the set. All she succeeded in doing, however, was to rotate the screwdriver so that the handle was directed downward.₄

What Agnes didn't know was that the screwdriver acted something like a radio or TV antenna. As it turned, it picked up messages from different directions. Suddenly, Agnes received a message. It was a very strong feeling—an urge—a great hunger to eat dog food. Agnes felt her mouth watering as her mind pictured a nice big bowl of mushy dog food. "Yum," she said to herself.

Without realizing * it, Agnes rotated the screwdriver a bit and received a new message: "But where is three sixty-one Tulip Lane? The way these streets zig and zag they ought to pay a taxi driver double just to come out here." Agnes felt very angry and had an urge to drive faster.

Again she rotated the screwdriver. Suddenly, she experienced great anxiety. She was on her first solo flight and she was preparing to land the plane. She was talking to herself. "First trim the plane, then glide slowly, no more than ten degrees down. Keep the wings level." Agnes began * to perspire.

She reached over and turned off the apparatus. Slowly, the thoughts of Dottie Collins, an eighteen-year-old woman flying directly over Agnes's house, began to fade away.₅

1

San Diego gorillas chimpanzees evidence
orangutans century language institute
captivity cords investigators occasions
mirror communicate incredibly gripping

2

1. intriguing
2. image
3. capacity
4. personality
5. accurate
6. focused

Great Apes

The great apes are the gorillas, the chimpanzees, and the orangutans. They are the three animals that are most like human beings. Both the likenesses and differences between people and the apes are very interesting.

A full-grown chimpanzee may weigh 180 pounds (82 kilograms), or a little more than the average adult male. Chimpanzees have a very powerful grip and can exert tremendous force when they pull.[1] A male chimpanzee at the Bronx Zoo that weighed 165 pounds (75 kilograms) set a record with a right-handed pull of 847 pounds (385 kilograms). A human male of the same weight has the capacity to pull about 210 pounds (95 kilograms). A female chimpanzee at the Bronx Zoo once achieved a right-handed pull of 1260 pounds (572 kilograms) when she was very angry. Her pull was almost six times the pull of an average human male.

People live longer than the great apes. The average person in the United States lives about seventy years. In captivity, some chimpanzees have lived forty years. The oldest great ape whose age is accurately known was an orangutan. It lived for 59 years.[2]

People may outlive the great apes, but in a contest of weight a great ape would be the winner—the gorilla. The heaviest gorilla ever in captivity was at the San Diego Zoo. This huge male stood 5 feet 7 3/4 inches (172 centimeters) tall, measured 78 inches (198 centimeters) around the chest, and weighed more than 683 pounds (310 kilograms).

People would clearly win an intelligence contest with the great apes, but the question of ape intelligence has intrigued scientists for more than a century. One question that is particularly fascinating is whether or not any of the great apes have the ability to learn language. At the Institute for Primate Studies at the University of Oklahoma, scientists work with chimpanzees to see if they can learn to speak and understand language. Their prize subject was Washoe. Because chimpanzees do not have the kind of vocal cords that would allow them to produce the sounds people can produce, the investigators taught Washoe to use sign language.[3] She learned the signs for many, many words. Investigators then observed Washoe to see if she would put signs together to express ideas that they had not taught her. The first time Washoe was presented with a mirror, she looked at the image and made the sign for her own name, showing that she recognized herself in the mirror. On many other occasions, Washoe used signs to express new ideas.

Not all scientists agree that chimpanzees are intelligent enough to use language, but those who have worked with Washoe think that she provides strong evidence that they are capable of using language.

1 porch uncertainties social
apparently ceremonies

2 received possibilities roam message
limitless demonstrate usually attached
experimented displayed focused
conducted immediately traveling
imaginative accurate millionaire
crazy summarized effective rocker
personality diagram schemes aimed

3
1. incurred
2. associated
3. productive
4. transmit
5. screens
6. patent
7. assuming

Display of Personalities

Agnes usually went to sleep early. But on the night that she first experimented with her dop machine, she sat on her front-porch rocker, drinking root beer until long after midnight. She finally summarized her experiences by saying, "That crazy machine displays personalities." And that's how it got the name, dop: *d*isplay *of* *p*ersonalities. It displayed more than thoughts. It transmitted the feelings that were associated with thoughts. "Dop," Agnes said over and over to herself. "I have invented a dop machine."₁

She realized, of course, that the machine was important; however, she wasn't certain how important it was * or how it could be used productively. "I don't mind being unsuccessful at inventing," she concluded. "But I never wanted to invent something that could be harmful."

In keeping with her uncertainties about the dop machine, Agnes told no one about it for three months. During that period, she conducted a number of experiments.₂ This is what she discovered:

1. When the dop machine was attached to a second TV screen, it was capable of transmitting feelings of people on TV.

2. The machine could also be hooked up to a telephone.

3. Two coat hangers wired together at right angles provided the * best antenna—much more powerful than the screwdriver, and more accurate in locating different targets.

4. The dop rays were not dangerous to one's health. (During some days, Agnes spent as many as five hours on the machine.)

5. The dop rays were capable of traveling through any substance that Agnes had tried, including lead. (Lead screens out most other rays, <u>including</u> gamma and X rays.)

6. If there were a great many people in the area at which the dop was aimed, no dops would be transmitted. (When Agnes focused on the audience of a TV show, no dops were received. When she * focused on the guest star, however, she received strong dops.)₃

Inventors must be imaginative. They must be able to look at all sorts of untried possibilities and let their imaginations roam. Agnes frequently found her imagination turning to the idea of fame and fortune. When the master of ceremonies of a quiz show presented questions, Agnes always knew the answer because the master of ceremonies knew the answer. And the dop machine transmitted the answer to Agnes. Agnes's imagination saw fantastic possibilities of entering quiz shows and winning thousands—*millions* of dollars!

She might become the most famous quiz show * participant in the history of television.

Or, she could become a famous gambler. At blackjack, for instance, how easy it would be to read the minds of the other players and know what cards they had. At a horse race she could learn which horse felt the strongest and bet on that one. The possibilities were almost limitless (and very attractive).₄

In the end, however, Agnes rejected these schemes. It seemed a shame to let those foolproof, money-making possibilities go by, but Agnes wanted to be recognized as an inventor, not as a gambler or a millionaire. Therefore, it * was only a question of time before Agnes contacted a patent attorney to see about getting a patent for her machine. Yet, when Agnes took her invention to the attorney, she began to have second thoughts.₅

The attorney spoke in a very businesslike manner as she asked, "What, exactly, is this machine designed to do?"

"It's a personality display machine," Agnes explained. "I can demonstrate how it works, and that should tell you more than I could with words."

"I don't really think that will be necessary," the attorney said. "I think that a diagram of the machine and a * simple explanation of what it does will be quite adequate for our purposes."

"I don't have a diagram," Agnes answered, "but I *can* explain how it works."

Agnes began to explain, but before long she realized how crazy she sounded. Here she was, a little old lady who had never invented anything successful before, talking about displaying personalities through waves that she couldn't describe. "I can appreciate how this must sound to you," she said smiling and shrugging. "But it really does do what I say."₆

"I'm sure it does," the attorney replied sharply. "But Miss Lark, let's discuss practical * matters for a moment. My initial fee, after adequate diagrams of the machine are provided, will be six hundred dollars. This amount will pay for a patent search to find out if someone else has already patented such a machine. And, if yours is the first such machine, the six hundred dollars will pay for filing a patent in your name. Assuming that we don't hit any great snags, no additional fee will be incurred. However, the six hundred dollars must be paid in advance. I'll be blunt. Do you have the money?"[7]

"No, not right now, but I think—" *

The attorney held up her hand. "I think that you should either look for another attorney or contact me when you have the money. Good day." The woman's smile faded and Agnes felt very embarrassed.

1

experience   rewarded   nightmares   obviously

2

weeping   calmed   chuckled   hallway

guard   laughter   microphone   dismal

shuffled   fantastic   suspect   detective

guilty   address   inspector   drawer

court   cabinets   museum

subjects   security   Cypress

3

1. superb
2. attentive
3. humiliating
4. approach
5. lingered
6. process

4

Agnes Gets a Superb Idea

Agnes was quite upset about her visit to the patent attorney. "That was the most humiliating experience," she said to herself. "I'll show them. I'll go to Las Vegas and play blackjack. I'll win more money than anyone ever has in the history of Las Vegas."[1]

By the next day, Agnes had calmed down and decided on another approach. She would demonstrate her invention to a local science society that met at a nearby museum each Wednesday. Agnes didn't realize that this plan would lead to an experience even more humiliating than her meeting with the patent attorney. She took * her apparatus to the meeting, but she wasn't allowed in.

"I'm sorry," a young man at the door of the museum said. "This meeting is for members only."[2]

Agnes wasn't going to take no for an answer, so as the first two members arrived, she tried to interest them in a demonstration of her machine. She quickly explained the apparatus and then pleaded, "Would you try it out? It really works."

"Is it safe?" the younger of the two members asked. The other chuckled and said, "We're not very good subjects. Why don't you try someone on the fourth floor? * They have much better subjects up there."

Both of the members began to laugh and Agnes felt herself becoming embarrassed and angry. "It works! Why won't you listen?" she found herself saying in a loud voice as they turned away.

The next club member to come to the meeting listened very attentively as Agnes explained to her how the machine worked. "If you will just allow me to demonstrate it, you'll be *well rewarded.*"

"I'm sorry. I don't have time," the woman said, and walked into the meeting. Agnes heard her ask someone inside, "Who is that strange person in * the hallway?"

"I don't know," someone replied. "But maybe we ought to get a security guard and have her thrown out."₃

"You don't have to have me thrown out," Agnes shouted into the room. "I'm leaving!"

"She must have read our thoughts with that machine of hers," someone said, and everyone laughed. The sound of that laughter lingered in Agnes's mind for hours. She felt like weeping. They wouldn't listen; they didn't understand. What's worse, they didn't want to understand.₄

That night Agnes had a nightmare in which she was running on a wheel much like those found in hamster * cages. In one hand, she held a microphone through which she kept yelling, "But if you'll let me stop, I'll show

that the machine works." The problem was that the microphone wasn't attached to anything. And there was no one around to hear her pleas.

When Agnes awoke in the morning, she had a splitting headache. She tried to shake the dismal thoughts and the pain from her head, but she couldn't. She shuffled to the door in her slippers, picked up the newspaper, and looked at the headline on the first page. "Suspect in Jewelry Robbery Questioned," it read. * Suddenly she felt everything stop.

Almost before the idea was formed in her head, Agnes knew that it was a good one—a superb one, a *fantastic one.* "I'll be a detective," Agnes said out loud. "Nobody can stop me from doing that. I can do something that is good, and . . ."

It was a nice day—the nicest morning that Agnes had seen in a long time. There would be no more trying to talk to attorneys or anyone else. Agnes was going to do great things.₅

Agnes was getting ideas faster than she could process them. At the same * time, she was trying to pour milk for Einstein, get dressed, call the police station, and look at the newspaper to see if the robbery suspect was going to be on television. "Hello," Agnes said as the phone at the police station was picked up. "This is Miss Lark, and if you would let me talk to your jewel robbery suspect, I could tell you whether he's guilty."

"We have enough trouble around here as it is," the police officer said, "so stop joking around, lady."

Agnes said, "All right. Just tell me the address of the jail at which * they're holding the suspect."

"Fifteenth and Cypress. Now get off the phone and don't call back."

"Thank you," Agnes said. She dashed to the wall in back of her TV set, where she'd hung a large map of the city. She stuck a pin on the corner of Fifteenth and Cypress, then rotated the hangers, turned on the dop machine, and tried to make contact with the suspect. The first message came immediately:

"Hurry up and pick the doughnut you want. I don't have all day. You're not the only police inspector on coffee break."₆

Agnes turned the antenna slightly. * "Where are we supposed to store this stuff? These district attorneys fill half a file drawer every time they go to court, but we ran out of file cabinets three months ago and the cases keep on coming in. The district attorney expects us. . . ."

Agnes moved the antenna again. This time the message was: "I better watch my step. I'm supposed to be polite to the cranks that call in but I can take only so much."₇

Agnes was getting close. That was the officer who'd answered her phone call. Now all she had to do was find the suspect * and read his thoughts.

1 convince perfumed concerned special

2 bracelets innocent scent unusual
descriptions urge approximately
suspect skillful focused janitors
lying jewels velvet spangled
extension obviously assured
Rialto district populated

3
1. fidget
2. momentary
3. acquainted
4. adjustment

Contacting the Suspect

It was almost eight o'clock in the evening before Agnes made contact with the suspect in the jail. At the time, she was holding a cold chicken leg in one hand and fidgeting with the coat-hanger antenna with the other. (She had become quite skillful with the dop machine.) She had been making small adjustments in the antenna for several hours but still couldn't locate the suspect. Agnes could tell from the dops she was picking up that the machine was still focused on the police station, but she seemed to make contact with everyone except the suspect. Agnes * had become acquainted with four police officers, two people in the crime lab, five secretaries, two janitors, and a young woman who sold sandwiches and doughnuts.

As Agnes was about to take a bite from the cold chicken leg, she made contact with something unusual. Apparently, the dop machine was focused on a phone line in the police station. "Eddie," one voice said, "don't say anything. Do you get my message?" The message that came through the dop machine was that Eddie was guilty.

"It's a bum rap," Eddie replied. "I didn't do a thing. They're just giving me trouble!" *[1]

Agnes could feel that Eddie was lying and that he didn't trust the other man. Eddie was also hoping that the police were listening in on the call, because he wanted to convince them that he didn't know about the jewels. *The jewels!* Agnes had made contact.

"Sure, Eddie," the other man said. "Of course it's a bum rap. But don't talk to anybody. Don't say anything. I'll get you out before tomorrow morning."

The man Eddie called had been involved in some of Eddie's other jobs, and he was afraid that Eddie would tell the police about him. That's * all he was concerned about—Eddie talking. And all Eddie was concerned about was trying to convince the police that he didn't know anything about the stolen jewels.₂

Suddenly Agnes picked up the image of a large velvet box that had a perfumed scent. Inside were rings and bracelets, all spangled with diamonds. Agnes had a momentary urge to possess those jewels. But then Eddie pushed the thought of the jewels from his and Agnes's minds.

"They're just out to lay a bum rap on me and I'm innocent," Eddie repeated to the man he had called. Then the conversation * was over. Agnes quickly marked the position of the antenna and then began to move it slightly, trying to follow Eddie. For some reason, however, she couldn't.

Before Agnes went to bed that night, she attached a wire from the antenna to her big toe. After she'd been asleep for an hour or so, a phone conversation awakened her. Agnes shared the anger of a young woman who'd been picked up for speeding. The woman was asking a friend to come and get her out of jail.₃

The next phone call was at six in the morning. Agnes awoke sharing * the anger of a man who was trying to reach his lawyer but kept getting a wrong number.

At 9:15, Agnes experienced another call between Eddie and the man he had phoned the evening before. The man assured Eddie, "I'll have you out before dinner tonight."

This time, when Eddie talked to the man, Agnes got a strong feeling of where the jewels were hidden. They were in a dry cleaning place not far from the Rialto Movie Theater. The jewels were in a red velvet box, which was in a large bag of clothes that had been sent to * the cleaners. The bag was checked under the name of Ruth Costello.₄

"I've got it!" Agnes said, jumping up. Einstein had been sitting in her lap and leaped clear as Agnes came out of the chair. "I'll go to the dry cleaning place and pick up the jewels."

Then Agnes realized that she wasn't sure of the cleaner's exact location. It was near the Rialto Theater, but so were dozens of shops. The Rialto was just west of the downtown district in a heavily populated area, and the streets were lined with businesses of all descriptions. Probably several of them * were dry cleaning establishments.

1   un   re   ly   able   ness

2 sweeping   direction   plastered   beneath

3 importance   approached   sternly
convincingly   arranged   search   assure
railroad   addition   striking   clothes
half-price   bargain-hunting   hey   ripping
stuff   ticket   background
carrying   uniforms   indicated

4
1. abruptly
2. rehearse
3. scrawl
4. bulge
5. mission

5

Finding the Cleaners

Agnes took a cab to the Rialto Theater. When she got there, the clock in front of the savings and loan building down the street was striking eleven. An usher was sweeping the area in front of the Rialto's ticket window. "Excuse me," Agnes said to the usher. "Is there a dry cleaning place near here?"

The usher stopped sweeping, leaned against his broom, and shrugged. "I don't know," he said smiling, "I don't get my clothes cleaned."[1]

"Well, thanks anyway," Agnes said, and began to walk away.

The usher began sweeping again but abruptly stopped and said, "Hey, I * just remembered. The theater has our uniforms cleaned at one of those two places on the next block. There are two shops there almost next door to each other." He pointed to show Agnes the direction.₂

Agnes thanked him and walked in the direction he'd indicated. As she moved along the street, she began to rehearse what she'd say when she went into the first shop. To get the bag, Agnes would have to tell a lie and she wasn't very good at lying.

The first cleaning place was a small shop with a large window. Signs were plastered all over * it. The largest read, "Dresses half-price, through June 1."

The words "June 1" had been crossed out and "July 4" was scrawled beneath them. Agnes found herself reading with interest and then sternly reminded herself that she wasn't bargain-hunting. Her mission was of much greater importance.₃

She took a deep breath, rehearsed her lie once more, and walked inside. A young woman was behind the counter. Agnes approached her and said, "I have a problem. I'm supposed to pick up Ruth Costello's clothes, but I seem to have lost the ticket."

"You do have a problem," the * young woman said. "No ticket, no clothes."₄

"Please," Agnes said. "I've got to have those clothes. It's really important. Can't I pay you a little extra and maybe—"

"I meant what I said," the young woman answered. "You can't just walk in off the street and tell me you're supposed to pick up someone else's clothes. How do I know that you're for real?"

"Oh, I assure you that I wouldn't do that," Agnes said, trying to lie convincingly.

"Besides," the young woman went on, "we don't check things by names. We have them arranged by number. I'd have to * know the number, or else I'd have to sift through a big stack of stuff."₅

"The number," Agnes said to herself. She began to search her memory of the dops with Eddie. Had there been a number?

Agnes called up a mental picture of the box. There it was—in a bag checked under the name Ruth Costello. The bag was white with a red tag around its neck. The tag looked something like a railroad ticket with black numbers on a red background. There was a big letter and then some smaller numbers. The letter was A. The first * numbers were 135, and then there were others.₆

Agnes looked at the young woman. "I believe that the bag began with the letter A, then 135."

"Really?" the woman asked. "And what was the rest of it?"

"I can't remember," Agnes said.

"I can't find it from that number. You'd have to tell me the last part."

"The last part," Agnes said to herself, and again searched her memory. She could now see a small t. And the numbers immediately before it were 56.

"The rest is 56 followed by a T," Agnes said.

"All right," the * young woman said, smiling. "Maybe I *can* help you out." She went into the back room and came out carrying a large bag. "You know I can't turn it over unless you can tell me what's in it."

Agnes knew that in addition to the jewel box there were clothes inside, but she couldn't describe those clothes because Eddie hadn't thought about them while Agnes was sharing his thoughts.

"Well?" the young woman asked. "What's inside the bag?"

Agnes pressed her lips together and tried to think of an answer. She could see the bulge of the jewel box at * the bottom of the bag.₇

1
earthquakes   volcanos   hurricanes
Indonesia   period   crater
explosion   hydrogen   destructive
unstable   tremors   damage

2
1. climate
2. erupted
3. lava
4. coastal
5. dwellings
6. staggering

Volcanos and Earthquakes

The earth appears to be solid and lasting, but powerful forces are at work beneath it. These forces sometimes result in volcanos and earthquakes. A volcano is an outpouring of hot molten rock called lava through a weak point in the earth's surface. A volcano's first stage is called an eruption and is usually a great explosion. Following the explosion comes the river of lava.[1]

In 1815 a volcanic eruption in Indonesia continued for two days. During that time, the opening at the top of the volcano spread until it measured 7 miles (11 kilometers) from one side to the other.

In 1883 another eruption occurred in Indonesia. It began with an explosion estimated to be twenty-six times as powerful as the most destructive hydrogen bomb ever tested. It threw rocks 33 miles (54 kilometers) into the air and caused a giant wave to roll over 163 villages, killing more than 36,000 people. The sound of the eruption was so powerful that four hours later it was heard almost 3000 miles (5000 kilometers) away.[2]

Earthquakes are caused by sudden shifts in parts of the earth. Earthquakes frequently occur in coastal areas where mountains rise next to deep seas. The great difference between the depth of the sea and the height of the mountains makes such an area unstable. For this reason California is the part of the United States most liable to experience serious earthquakes.[3]

Earthquakes can cause immense loss of life and property. In China in 1556 an earthquake killed an estimated 830,000 persons. In Japan in 1923 another earthquake resulted in the death of more than 140,000 people and the destruction of 500,000 dwellings.

The most powerful earthquake in recent years was the Alaskan earthquake of 1964.

However, the Lisbon earthquake of 1755 may have been the most powerful, but there were no instruments then to measure its strength. Scientists believe it was one hundred times stronger than the largest nuclear device ever exploded. It was so powerful that it disturbed lakes in far-off Norway.

About 500,000 earthquakes occur every year, but of these only some 100,000 can be felt by people living in the area where they occur, and of these only about 1000 do any damage.[4]

1

stall ain't partial
change awkward briskly

2

patience managed glanced swerve
vision initiation blur laugh lousy
establishment outweighed counter
doorway dared scurried bumped
intersection attempted blurry
half-crouched revolving proof

3

1. confidential
2. surge
3. sensed
4. hulk
5. determination
6. skirt around
7. convey
8. disguise

4

Agnes Gets the Jewels

The young woman asked Agnes again, "What's in the bag? I can't wait all day."

"You see," Agnes said, trying to stall for time, "I'm not sure about the things that are in the bag because my friend didn't tell me."

"Look," the young woman said. "I can't turn this bag over to you unless you can give me proof that you're supposed to have it."[1]

"All right," Agnes said, and leaned over the counter. "I can tell you one thing that's in the bag, but this is highly confidential. There is a jewel box in the bottom of the * bag. Inside that box are some of the finest imitation jewels in the world."

"Imitation jewels in a cleaning bag?" The young woman shook her head. She began to laugh. She reached down in the bag and pulled out the box. "Well, I'll be," she said, staring at the box. "There *is* a jewel box in here." She opened the box and looked at the jewels. "But you're wrong about one thing," she continued. "These aren't the finest imitation jewels in the world."

Agnes felt her heart pound faster. The young woman continued, "These are lousy imitations. They're too showy. * Nobody would think that these things are real. Some of those stones are as big as ice cubes."₂

The young woman laughed and closed the jewel box. "OK, I'm convinced. The bill for this cleaning is $9.83."

Agnes gave the young woman ten dollars, told her to keep the change, and walked briskly from the dry cleaning establishment. As she was walking through the door, she almost ran into a man, and Agnes experienced a surge of panic. She instantly sensed that this man was connected with Eddie. Suddenly she realized who the man was—the man on the phone. * And she realized why he was here—to get the jewels. Agnes tried not to look at him, because there was something about him that conveyed meanness—the kind of meanness that was disguised with patience and cunning. For an instant their eyes met. "Excuse me," Agnes said, stepping to one side.

The man walked through the doorway past Agnes as if she didn't exist. Once outside, Agnes began to walk as fast as she dared.₃

"Where's a taxi?" she said to herself. The streets were becoming crowded with people. It was nearing noon. As Agnes scurried down the street, * she glanced back after every eight or ten steps to make sure that nobody was chasing her. "Where's a taxi?" she said aloud. She was almost a full block from the store now.

"Hey, watch where you're going," somebody shouted. Agnes had walked into a woman.

"I'm sorry," Agnes said, and she tried to dodge through the growing crowds. She glanced back and saw a large form running down the street—a huge hulk that moved without much grace but with great power and determination. "Oh, no," Agnes said, and she began to run. She bumped into people who were * knotted at an intersection. She managed to skirt around them, but she was forced into the street.₄

Screech—crash.

Agnes had stepped right in front of a car that attempted to swerve out of her way. Unfortunately, the car hit another car in the oncoming lane. "This is terrible," Agnes said, and then she began to run again. There were so many people on the sidewalk that Agnes, almost without thinking, began to run down the middle of the street. People were laughing and pointing at her. Drivers were yelling, but Agnes barely heard them.

She was becoming tired. She * wasn't a very fast runner at best—not at her age. And now she was out of breath. It felt as if her arms and legs were filled with heavy sand. They seemed to be moving in slow motion, and her lungs felt as if they would burst. Agnes couldn't catch her breath, and her vision was starting to blur. The hulk was catching up. There he was behind Agnes, running down the middle of the street, now less than half a block behind.₅

"I'll never make it," Agnes realized. She slowed to an awkward stumble. "If you can't run, * hide," some part of her mind said above the uproar of her burning breathing. Agnes stumbled between two parked cars and again tried to hide in the stream of people on the sidewalk. But the hulk was getting closer.

Almost without thinking, Agnes ducked into a doorway and then through a revolving door. She was inside the lobby of a large office building.₆

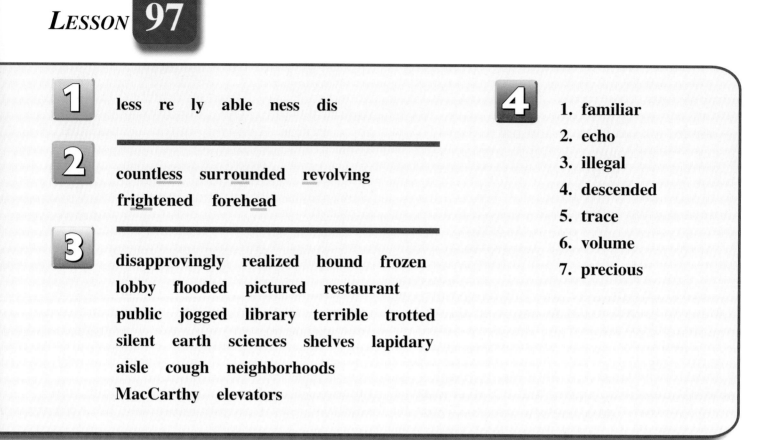

1 less re ly able ness dis

2 countless surrounded revolving
frightened forehead

3 disapprovingly realized hound frozen
lobby flooded pictured restaurant
public jogged library terrible trotted
silent earth sciences shelves lapidary
aisle cough neighborhoods
MacCarthy elevators

4
1. familiar
2. echo
3. illegal
4. descended
5. trace
6. volume
7. precious

A Rock Hound's Hiding Place

Agnes stood frozen in the lobby of the office building. Where could she hide? The lobby was large and almost empty, except for some elevators.

Suddenly the doors to the elevators opened and a seemingly countless crowd of people filled the lobby. Agnes found herself moving with them toward the door. As she was leaving the building, she saw the hulk coming through a revolving door and pushing his way through the crowd.[1]

"Move," Agnes said to herself. "Just keep moving." She was now outside the building, and the hulk was inside. Agnes pictured what would happen if the hulk * ever caught up with her. He would crush her like a child's toy; then he would take back the jewels.

Agnes realized that it might be a good idea to hide the bag somewhere, but she couldn't think of a likely spot. There was a restaurant to her left. Could she hide the bag in there? What about the bookstore next to the restaurant? But how would she hide the bag?₂

Across the street was a large building—the public library. Agnes hadn't been quite sure where she was up to now, because she hadn't been trying to reach a * particular place, merely trying to get away.

Agnes knew that people often return to safe, familiar places when they are frightened. And the library was just such a place, one in which Agnes had spent many pleasant hours. She already felt better as she jogged across the street and up the front steps of the library. She trotted through the large lobby, and her feet seemed to make a terrible echoing sound in the silent halls. Several people looked disapprovingly at her.₃

Agnes went into one of the smaller rooms to the right of the main reading room. The sign * over the door said, "Earth Sciences." Inside, twenty long tables were arranged in two rows. On all sides of the tables were shelves of books. Only two people were in the room, one studying a huge volume, the other apparently asleep. Agnes quickly walked down one of the aisles of bookshelves. The sign on the end of the aisle said, "Lapidary." Lapidary is the art of cutting precious stones. What better place to hide the bag?

At the end of the aisle Agnes stopped. The sound of her breathing seemed to echo through the room. "Stop puffing like that," she * told herself. She rubbed her hand over her sweating brow, then pulled about ten books from one of the shelves above eye level. She piled the books on the floor and stood on them to look inside the hole that she'd made. Yes, indeed, there was room for the bag inside the hole.₄

Agnes stuffed the bag into the hole, shoved the books back into place, and then walked slowly along the row of shelves into the open area of the Earth Sciences library. The same two people were at the tables. Outside the door two young people who looked * like students were talking.

Agnes walked through the hall and down the wide front steps of the library. She felt as if she were on display as she descended the steps, so she put her hands in front of her face and pretended to cough. When she reached the bottom of the steps, she realized that somebody was looking at her. Quickly, she looked up.

"Taxi?" the driver said.

"Yes, thanks," Agnes said, walking toward the dirty green cab parked illegally in front of the library. "Yes," she repeated under her breath four or five more times.

As the cab * moved through the downtown traffic and then through less crowded neighborhoods, Agnes kept looking out of the back window of the car. It wasn't until she stood on her own front porch that she felt safe. She sat down with Edison on one side and Einstein in her lap.₅ "Oh, it's good to be home," Agnes said to her pets. "Yes," she said over and over again.

Later, after rinsing her face with cold water and drinking a glass of root beer, Agnes called the police station. She recognized the voice of the officer who answered the phone. It belonged * to Ray MacCarthy, the officer who had talked to her earlier.

"Officer MacCarthy," Agnes said, "I can help you prove that Eddie is guilty of that jewel robbery."

There was a brief pause during which Agnes could hear MacCarthy say to somebody, "Trace this call."

Agnes didn't want the call to be traced, so she hung up.₆

instructions   special   slightly   innocent

attached   sliver   exactly   evidence
outskirts   convince   imprisonment
trace   impossible   thoughts
dismantled   sore   banana   aisle
unusual   attractive   cooperative
focused   activity   Ramsey   confessed
buzzing   touch   solve   robbery   detective
crazy   possibility   impatient

1. rigged
2. futile
3. respected
4. retrieve
5. guaranteed
6. responsible

The Police Cooperate

Agnes was impatient. She wanted to tell the police about the jewels, but she didn't want her calls traced. So during the night she rigged up another phone line from her house to the main cable that ran nearby. Now, when she telephoned, it would be impossible for anybody to trace the call.

As Agnes dialed the police station again, she realized how tired she was. She'd had very little sleep lately, and her legs ached from yesterday's chase.

"Hello, Officer MacCarthy," Agnes said, moving the antenna of her dop machine slightly so that she could talk to MacCarthy on * the phone and at the same time read his thoughts from the dop machine. Now the dop contact was strong.1

Agnes said, "Attempting to trace this call will be futile. This phone is attached to a main cable. Furthermore, if you even think of tracing it, I'll hang up. Please understand that I can read your thoughts at any moment."

"I'm very glad for you," MacCarthy said. "Now tell me what I can do for you."

"Just listen," Agnes said. "I'll help you prove that Eddie is guilty."

"So prove it," MacCarthy said flatly.

"First," Agnes said, "let me convince * you that I can read your every thought. Think of something unusual, and I'll tell you what you're thinking."

At the time MacCarthy was thinking that he was hungry, even though he'd already eaten breakfast and that the banana in his lunch bag didn't look very good—it had big brown spots on it.

Agnes told MacCarthy what he'd been thinking, and MacCarthy responded, "Well, I'll be."₂

Then Agnes said, "Do exactly as I say, and you'll have all the evidence against Eddie that you need. Go to the Earth Sciences room of the main library, third aisle on * the left. At the end of the aisle, on the sixth shelf from the bottom, is the book *Lapidary for Fun.* Pull out the book and you'll see a dry cleaning bag. The jewels are inside that bag."

Agnes repeated the instructions as MacCarthy wrote them down. Agnes then said, "I'll be in touch with you after you retrieve the jewels. Hurry."

"OK," MacCarthy said.₃

Later that afternoon Agnes focused the dop machine on the police station and discovered that the place was buzzing with activity. The jewels had been found. Agnes called MacCarthy.

"I see that you have the * jewels," she said. "Now find out the name of the huge man who was at the Speedy Dry Cleaning place on State Street, one block north of the Rialto."

"I don't have to look that up. That's Ramsey the Crusher; he owns part of that cleaning business. What's he got to do with this?"₄

"Pick him up," Agnes said. "He's in on this with Eddie. Then tell Eddie that Ramsey confessed. Eddie will tell you everything you want to know."

"How do you know all this stuff?" MacCarthy asked.

For a moment Agnes didn't know how to respond. At last * she said, "I have unusual powers. I call them dop powers." Agnes went on to explain what *dop* stood for. Then she said, "In the future I hope you'll be more cooperative when working with me. Also, my fee is one hundred dollars per day. If I don't solve the case, I'll return the money. My work is fully guaranteed."₅

"We'll be glad to cooperate. Just tell us what to do, uh, uh. . . ." MacCarthy's voice trailed off.

"Just call me Dop," Agnes said. "Dr. Dop."

"OK, Dr. Dop."

Agnes Lark still lives on the outskirts of Redmond with her cat, * Einstein, and her dog, Edison. She still works at inventing different things. And she still has a house full of junk. But her life changed somewhat after she broke the big jewel robbery. Now Agnes has plenty of money, and she is a respected detective who operates from her home. She focuses the dop machine on suspects, and before long she knows who is guilty and who is innocent. Agnes feels very good about what she does. During her first six months as a detective, she was responsible for five innocent prisoners being set free and for the imprisonment of * more than a dozen guilty criminals. "Not bad for an old lady who people thought was crazy," she tells herself.₆

Agnes considered the possibility of telling the truth about her invention and perhaps giving it to the police. But after thinking about it, she decided that the machine could be far too dangerous in the wrong hands. According to Agnes's will, all her inventions will be dismantled and sold as junk when she dies. But the way she has it figured, all those dop waves may have given her other powers. She says to herself once in a while, "I * may just live forever."₇

1 nocturnal   intelligent   nighttime   disappeared

2 chimpanzees   lizards   nerves   replaced
messages   existence   keener
information   mammals   reptile   cranial
tongue   rotating   similarities
complicated   demonstrate   Mesozoic
tyrannosaur   triceratops   meant
developing   concluded   dinosaurs   wired

3
1. adjust
2. modeled
3. combine
4. impression
5. conclusion

4 Mammals and Reptiles

Mammals such as chimpanzees, horses, cows, dogs, and mice are capable of learning much more than reptiles and other cold-blooded animals like fish and frogs. One theory of why mammals acquired more powerful brains is quite interesting. Before beginning the story, however, we have to understand some things about the reptile brain. In some ways a reptile brain is the same as that of a bird or a horse or even a human being. For one thing there are twelve nerves leading from the brain to the body. These are called cranial nerves. Each nerve has a role. Particular *

cranial nerves, for example, move the tongue in a lizard or a chimpanzee. Other specific nerves move the eyes.[1]

Although there are some similarities between the brains of reptiles and the brains of mammals, there are important differences. A reptile brain is small and doesn't weigh as much as the brain of a mammal of the same body size. Also, the eye is actually an important part of the reptile's brain. This theory can be modeled by rotating the eyes of a lizard—up is now down and left is now right. When the lizard tries to strike at an * insect that is high on his left side, the lizard will strike down and to its right side. What's more, the lizard will never learn to adjust. The reason is that the reptile is wired in a fixed way. The eye is part of the wiring.[2]

Many people think that mammals first appeared in the Mesozoic era when great reptiles like the tyrannosaur and the triceratops ruled. Early mammals had the reptile eye. However, they could not compete with the reptiles during the daytime. So these mammals became nocturnal, or nighttime, animals. At night they could not use their reptile * eye because it was a daylight eye. Finally, mammals no longer had the reptile eye.[3]

Some scientists believe that the early mammals adjusted to the darkness by developing senses other than sight. They developed ears, which are body parts that are not well developed in reptiles. Reptiles are nearly deaf. Mammals also developed a sense of smell much keener than that of reptiles. The brain of the early mammal had to change so that it could use the information that came to it from its nose and ears.[4] The nose and the ears were not part of the mammal's brain, * which meant that the mammal's brain had to have a new kind of wiring system. While the reptile's brain responds directly to impressions on its eye, the mammal's brain had to combine impressions from the ear with impressions from the nose. Perhaps the mammal's ear told the mammal that a heavy form was moving in front of it. The mammal's nose indicated that the form was a bird. The mammal's brain combined the information about where the animal was with how the animal smelled, and concluded: "There is a bird ahead of me." This conclusion could never be drawn by * a reptile.[5]

Some people think that after millions of years passed and the great dinosaurs disappeared from the earth, some mammals began to change into daytime animals. For the mammals to operate in the daytime, however, they needed daytime eyes again. And somehow, these eyes developed. But they were not like reptile eyes; instead, they became wired into the brain the way the ears and nose were wired into the brain. Messages from the eye went to the brain. There they were combined with messages from the ears and from the nose. The brain that performed this job was far, * far more complicated than the brain of the reptile.[6]

It is interesting to think that the night existence of the early mammals may have set the stage for them to develop brains capable of learning a great deal. They could no longer use the reptile eye. What's more, they needed other senses to locate objects in the dark—smell and hearing. Since the mammal had to use information from more than one sense organ, the mammal needed a brain that could combine the information from the various sense organs. That kind of brain is far more complicated than the brain * of a reptile.[7]

1
Egyptians   psychologist   experience
ancient   succeed   various   meant
undertaking   future   struggle
confidence   rapidly   aggressive
hostile   foretold   expression

2
1. theory
2. rejected
3. interpretation
4. symbol
5. nonsense
6. represent

3

Dreams

Dreams are thought pictures, or stories, that pass through the mind during sleep. Very little was known about dreams until the late 1950s. There is still much about dreams that scientists do not understand.

There have been theories and beliefs about dreams since very ancient times. One belief was that a dream predicted what was going to happen. The ancient Egyptians believed that dreams foretold the future. Dreams that predict are also mentioned in the Bible. Another very old belief was that the soul left the body during sleep and that dreams were things that happened to the soul while it was wandering in another world.₁

In the 1800s, people who studied dreams made up lists of dream symbols. Everything that happened in a dream was supposed to be a symbol that stood for something else. For example, falling in a dream represented failure. Climbing meant an attempt to succeed. Dream books that give the supposed meanings of dreams are still sold. They tell of dreams that mean good or bad luck, and foretell certain events. Scientists have rejected such interpretations as nonsense.₂

Today, many scientists think that dreams in some way reflect real experiences. Although dreams are still not clearly understood, they probably have something to do with how people feel about themselves and their lives. Some scientists think that people express feelings in dreams that they cannot express while they are awake. Such feelings might be fear or love or hate.

There have been some interesting discoveries recently about dreams. Scientists can now tell when a person is dreaming. They also know what changes take place in the body during a dream.

REM, or rapid eye movement, was first observed and studied in the late 1950s. When you dream, your eyes begin to move rapidly from side to side. Your heart begins to beat faster, and other signs of body activity increase.[3]

Dreaming seems to be necessary for people. If a person is awakened every time rapid eye movement shows that a dream is beginning, that person will become upset, restless, and angry. By letting us express and get rid of strong or unpleasant feelings in a harmless way while we are asleep, dreams may help keep us emotionally healthy.

1

perfectly   choice   situation
responded   feature

2

Baluchitherium   powerful   interesting
positions   creatures   thousands   full-size
strange-looking   grazing   survived
opossum   predators   developed   attempted
porpoises   weighing   tongue   kingdom
horsepower   lizards   adequate   whales

3

1. occupied
2. complicated
3. avoid
4. marvelous
5. beneficial
6. incredible

The Spread of Mammals

Some scientists tell us that when the great reptiles ruled the earth, they were in the sky, in the sea, and on the land. They came in all forms, from tiny lizards to animals that could easily look into third-story windows of today's buildings.₁

For reasons that are not perfectly clear, the great reptiles of the Mesozoic era died off, leaving the sky, the sea, and the land open to new animals. Thousands of new birds and mammals appeared. We would consider many of the early mammals strange-looking. They

were as different from each other as the reptiles * they replaced. Some were huge, much larger than the African elephant, which is the largest living land animal. *Baluchitherium,* the largest land mammal that ever lived, stood more than five meters tall at the shoulder and weighed almost twenty metric tons. That's more than three full-sized elephants weigh.₂

Like the great reptiles, not all mammals survived. Some types died off. Some changed. And some live today in much the same way they lived during the Mesozoic era. The opossum, for example, lives at night, does not use its eyes very much, and has a fairly small brain. The reason * it has a small brain is that the opossum doesn't need a larger brain. The brain that it had in the Mesozoic era was adequate.

The brains changed most in animals that changed the way they lived. The horse became a daytime animal, changing in size from an animal no bigger than a fox to the full-sized horse of today.₃ Its brain also changed so that it could survive in the open among predators that hunted it. As grazing animals like the horse developed larger brains, they learned more tricks to avoid their hunters.

One theory is that predators * or hunters needed even bigger and more complicated brains than the hunted. Unless predators were smarter than grazing animals, they would not be able to catch their prey, and they would starve to death. Therefore, predators developed larger and more powerful brains, even larger than those of grazing animals.₄

Among the most interesting predators are those land mammals that became sea animals. Many of them live today as whales and porpoises. Their legs became flippers and tails. Their bodies took the shape of fish. Although they changed in many ways, they kept the mammal brain.

A killer whale's brain weighs * more than the brain of a human being. This does not mean that the killer whale is smarter than a person. The killer whale is a very large animal, weighing as much as an elephant. To handle messages in a body this large, the killer whale's brain must be quite large.₅

Whales are among the most amazing creatures in the animal kingdom. In addition to being smart, some are incredibly large. The largest animal that has ever existed on Earth is the blue whale. To get an idea of its size, let's compare the blue whale to an African elephant. * A blue whale is about as large at birth as a full-grown African elephant! A full-grown whale may be over thirty meters long and may weigh 175 metric tons. Its heart weighs more than half a metric ton, and its tongue weighs almost four metric tons. When it travels at top speed, which is over thirty-five kilometers an hour, it develops 520 horsepower. Indeed, the blue whale is one of the most marvelous creatures in the animal kingdom.₆

 1

un less re pre sub dis

2

conference advertised beneficial
displayed marvelous

 3

motionless supermarkets convince
occasionally college consumers
approached particularly appliance
refrigerator self-defrosting problem
demonstrated employed wasting
supplying continued graduated
choosy loosens fret special

 4

1. tantrums   5. campaign
2. valves   6. commission
3. favor   7. manufacturer
4. charm

5

Super Salesperson

Joe Kappas had a special talent, which was that he could talk anybody into anything. When he was still a child, he could talk his parents into letting him do just about anything he wanted to do. He wouldn't fret and cry and throw tantrums the way some kids do. Instead he would sell his parents on the idea that he wanted them to buy. By the time he was a teenager, he had become a marvelous salesperson. For example, one time when he was in high school, he wanted to use the family car, but his dad had told * him that he couldn't. Joe waited a few moments and then approached his father. "Dad," Joe said, "My friend Pete really knows car engines, and he says that the valves in your engine are starting to stick. He says that if they get really stuck, it will cost over a hundred dollars to fix them." Joe then held up a can of valve oil. He continued, "Pete says that if you put this valve oil in your engine, you can prevent the valves from sticking."₁

"Well, let's put it in," his dad remarked.

"OK," Joe said, smiling. "There's just one * thing, Dad. You should only put the oil in when the engine is warmed up. You should drive the car for at least one hour after you put the oil in. That way you can make sure that the oil loosens up the valves."

"That's a problem," his dad said. "I'm going to be at home for the rest of the day. But I guess I can do it tomorrow."

"Good idea," Joe said and started to leave the room. He stopped abruptly and turned around. "I've got an idea," he said. "If you want me to, I could put * that oil in today. I don't have anything really important to do, and I'd be willing to do it, particularly if it will save you over a hundred dollars."

"Well, thanks a lot, Joe," his dad said. Joe used the car all afternoon, and his father thought that Joe was doing him a great favor.₂

Joe demonstrated his talent for fast thinking and fast talking throughout high school and college. He had more friends than anybody else in his town. Occasionally people would get mad at him, but they couldn't stay mad very long. In college Joe didn't work very * hard, but he studied enough to learn about advertising and about managing a business. In his last year of college he got the top grade for putting together an advertising campaign.₃

After Joe graduated, he decided to get some sales experience by working in a store. He chose a big store that paid good commissions, and he got a job selling appliances. "Why don't you take a management job?" some of his friends asked. "Why do you want to sell?"

Joe replied, "As a salesperson, I'll make a commission on every appliance I sell. I believe that I can sell * enough appliances to make a lot of money."₄

And Joe did make money selling appliances. Everyone who stopped to look at the stoves or refrigerators or toasters ended up buying something. Joe convinced one woman that a toaster with a special electric eye would always produce perfect toast. One couple, who had a practically new stove at home, bought a model with a self-cleaning oven after Joe reminded them that oven cleaning is a nasty job and pointed out how much time they'd save. He also sold a lot of self-defrosting refrigerators—usually the most expensive models.₅

Joe * made more money in commissions than any other salesperson in the store. But Joe felt that he was wasting his talent selling appliances. He thought that he could sell bigger things to more people. So in less than a year he moved to another job, selling soap. He didn't sell to the consumers—the people who use the soap. He sold to supermarkets, which is not an easy job. All soap manufacturers want to get their brands into the supermarkets. And each manufacturer finds it beneficial to have its soap displayed on as many shelves as possible. There is only * so much shelf space in a supermarket, however. So the buyers for the supermarkets are very choosy about which manufacturers they deal with. If you go into the buying office for a supermarket chain, you will usually see several salespeople waiting to see the buyer, all ready to convince the buyer that their product is the best. All will tell the buyer that there is a great demand for their brand, that their brand is advertised, and that the customers will be mad if they don't find that brand in the supermarket. Then the salesperson will offer the buyer a * deal. If the buyer orders so many carloads of the brand, the price will be reduced by quite a bit.

That's how most other salespeople worked, but Joe Kappas was smart enough to know that he had to think of a new approach.[6]

1

announcement   discussions
puncture   arrangement

2

shrugged   wholesale   attention   submarine
corporation   invitations   opportunity
statement   professional   badminton
struggled   possibilities   reliable   prevailing

3

1. motive
2. auction
3. gimmick
4. invoice
5. receipt
6. lading

4

Soap Auction

Joe Kappas had an idea for selling soap to supermarket buyers. First he made arrangements for a great party. He sent out invitations to the buyers for all the major supermarket chains. He hired some professional football players to come to the party, because he knew that the buyers would like to meet professional football players.₁

As it turned out, over half of the buyers he invited attended the party, which began shortly before noon with a light lunch. It was an outdoor party at an exclusive country club. Joe made sure that the buyers had a good time. They * played tennis or badminton, or went swimming in the pool. They told jokes, talked to each other, and laughed a lot.

At about two o'clock Joe climbed up on the diving board at the swimming pool to make an announcement. "May I have your attention?" he shouted. Slowly the talk and laughter died down. "Ladies and gentlemen," Joe said, "I brought you here to sell you soap. It's that simple. I hope you're having a good time, and I don't want you to feel that you have to buy soap. But my major motive in bringing you here was to * sell to you."₂

Somebody yelled, "I'm here to party, not to buy." Everybody laughed.

"So don't buy," Joe said. "But if you don't somebody is going to get one whale of a deal. There is a railroad siding less than three miles from here, and on that siding are seventeen railroad cars, each loaded with Senso soap.

Right now Senso Soap Company owns that soap, but by tonight *every bit of that soap will be auctioned off.* I don't care how much each carload goes for—all the soap will be sold."₃

"What kind of gimmick is this?" one buyer asked. *

"There's no gimmick," Joe said. "We're going to have an auction—one carload at a time. Those who bid may get the bargain of a lifetime. They may save their companies thousands of dollars. And your bosses are always glad when that happens, isn't that right?"

Buyers shouted comments, but Joe ignored them. He held up his hands and said, "Carload one is now up for auction. I'm not going to try to sell you on the product because you know that Senso is a good, reliable soap. So what am I bid for carload one?"

"One dollar," one of * the buyers shouted.

"Good," Joe said above the laughter. "We have a bid of one dollar. Will anybody bid two dollars?"

"I'll give you five," a tall woman buyer shouted, holding up a five dollar bill.

Joe said, "We have five dollars for a full carload of Senso soap. As you know, that carload is worth $84,000 on the wholesale market. Do I hear any more bids?"

The buyers looked at each other and looked at Joe but nobody else bid. "Going once . . . going twice . . . sold to the woman with the five dollar bill." Joe shrugged and smiled. As * the buyer walked up to the diving board, the other buyers clapped and laughed. Joe took the five dollar bill and handed the buyer some papers. "Here's the bill of lading, here's the invoice, and here's the receipt. You just purchased one carload of Senso soap."₄

"Hey, is this for real?" one of the other buyers asked.

The buyer who had purchased the carload of soap was looking over the papers that Joe had handed her. At last she said, "I can't believe it. This is a real bill of lading."

"As I told you at the beginning," Joe said, * "all seventeen carloads will be sold this afternoon. They can go for five dollars or for two dollars. It makes no difference to me. But they're all going to be sold today. The next carload is carload two. Does anybody want to start the bidding?"

People were shouting out numbers so rapidly that the bidding, which started at five dollars, was up to over $2000 within a few seconds. Carload two sold for $40,000, less than half of its value on the wholesale market.₅

When Joe turned over the bill of lading and the invoice to the buyer who purchased * that carload, he said, "Well, you didn't buy it for five dollars, but you saved your company more than forty thousand dollars with your wise purchase."

Buyers were running to the telephones, calling their offices to get permission to bid on carloads. But Joe didn't wait for them. "Carload three is now up for auction," he announced. Carload three sold for $62,000. Joe shrugged. "Ladies and gentlemen, I see that some of you are not bidding. I hope that all of you have understanding bosses, because some of them may be curious about why you passed up the opportunity to * save your firm thousands of dollars. Maybe you're not thinking of the promotion possibilities. Consider this fact: Your stores could price Senso soap at a great savings, which means that you could attract customers to your stores. And you know that once those customers come into the market, they'll buy more than soap. But that's up to you."₆

The auction went on.

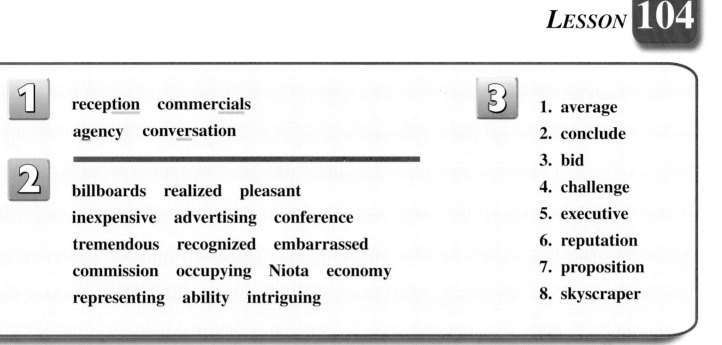

1 reception commercials
agency conversation

2 billboards realized pleasant
inexpensive advertising conference
tremendous recognized embarrassed
commission occupying Niota economy
representing ability intriguing

3
1. average
2. conclude
3. bid
4. challenge
5. executive
6. reputation
7. proposition
8. skyscraper

4 # From Senso to Niotas

By four thirty in the afternoon, Joe had auctioned off all seventeen carloads of Senso soap. They brought an average price of $68,000. All the buyers who purchased a carload felt that they had made very good deals, and they had. But Joe also made a very good deal. He didn't make any money on the sales, but he didn't lose any money either. And he achieved three very important goals. First, he forced nine major supermarket chains to sell Senso soap. Second, he made sure that the buyers would never forget the name Joe Kappas. Now he would have * an edge on all the other salespeople because the buyers would remember the auction and the fun they had.₁ Finally, Joe succeeded in making some of the buyers look good to their bosses. When a buyer goes to the boss and says that she purchased $84,000 worth of soap for $68,000, the boss is going to conclude that the buyer is a pretty smart person.

During the next year, Joe did not have to sit in reception rooms waiting to see buyers. Even the buyers who didn't bid at the auction welcomed him. Some of them were embarrassed after their * bosses had bawled them out for passing up the opportunity to purchase Senso soap at the auction. Within a year Senso soap went from the fifth-best-selling brand to the number one brand in the area that Joe serviced.₂

However, Joe didn't want to sell soap for the rest of his life. He wanted a new challenge. He thought that he was probably the best salesperson in the world, and he wanted to prove it by doing bigger and better things. And as it happened, he became involved in one of the biggest deals a salesperson could hope to * find. One day, Joe received a call from an executive of a large advertising agency. (An advertising agency works for different companies. The agency makes up magazine ads, television commercials, billboards, and other display pieces that help sell products.) The advertising executive who called Joe said, "You have quite a reputation in sales, and I think we have a proposition that will interest you."[3]

A meeting was set up for Joe at the advertising agency. The agency was very large, occupying two full floors in a downtown skyscraper. The offices were very plush. A secretary with a pleasant smile met * Joe and led him into a large conference room. On the walls were pictures of a small economy car. Three people were seated at the conference table, while two others stood near the door, carrying on a lively conversation. One man shook hands with Joe and introduced himself as the person Joe had talked to on the phone. After everyone was introduced, the man said, "Sit down, Joe, and I'll explain the deal."

The deal seemed very intriguing to Joe. The advertising agency was representing a Japanese manufacturer that built an automobile called the Niota. "Here's our problem," the executive * explained. "We can't seem to come up with a hot idea for promoting this product. It's a good car, just like a lot of the other imports. It's well built, it gets good gas mileage, and it's inexpensive. But we don't have a big advertising budget. And there are

only six dealers in the country who handle this car. We've got to figure out a way to increase the number of distributors, and somehow we've got to reach the people with a small advertising budget. Frankly, we're fresh out of ideas. That's why we brought you in. We figured that * a guy with your sales ability may be able to give us some ideas."[4]

"And what do I get out of it?" Joe inquired.

"I want to give you a chance to make a lot of money," the executive replied. "But I don't have much money to work with. So here's what I'll do. Last year, three thousand Niotas were sold in this country. If we use your ideas, we'll give you a commission of twenty-five dollars on every Niota over three thousand that is sold during the year. In other words, you don't receive any commission for the * first three thousand, but for every car sold after that, you will make twenty-five dollars—if we use your ideas."

"You have made a deal," Joe announced. "Draw up the papers, and I'll have my lawyer look them over. Give me all the information you have on the Niota, and give me one to drive. I'm not going to sell a product before I know that product."

And that's how Joe embarked on the biggest deal of his life.[5]

1

hypnosis mesmerism wailing
investigator Hamelin entertainment
flinch Sigmund suggestible trance
Freud predictable Vienna fascinating

2

1. feat
2. rigid
3. expectations
4. anesthetic
5. extracted
6. considering

3

Hypnosis

Hypnosis is a condition in which a person goes into a trance. People who are hypnotized are often not conscious of what is happening. However, they do things that are suggested by others. They may also see things that are not actually present.

The power of ancient "witches" and "magicians" over others may be explained by hypnosis. The Pied Piper of Hamelin may have used hypnosis to lure that town's children into following him.[1]

People didn't study hypnosis until the eighteenth century, when Franz Mesmer developed a technique now called "mesmerism," which could put people into a trance. Early investigators thought that hypnosis was some kind of "magnetism." They believed that the trances were caused by a magnetic force present in certain trees and rocks. People who were mesmerized would cling to "magnetized" rocks and trees for hours, wailing and weeping. After coming out of the trance, they would report that they were cured of serious illnesses.[2]

In the 1800s, hypnosis became a popular form of entertainment. Traveling hypnotists could hypnotize members of an audience and cause them to do strange things. "You can feel nothing in your hand," the stage hypnotist would suggest to a subject. Then, to the amazement of the crowd, the hypnotist would stick a needle in the subject's hand, apparently without causing pain.

In another popular feat the hypnotist would tell the subject, "Your body is as stiff as a board." The subject's body would become rigid. The hypnotist would then suspend the person between two chairs, leaving the subject supported only by the neck and heels.

In addition to being used as entertainment, hypnosis was used as an anesthetic on people who were having teeth extracted. Hypnosis was also used to bring back memories of painful events that a patient couldn't consciously recall. The famous psychiatrist Sigmund Freud used hypnosis in this way during his early years of work in Vienna.[3]

Research into hypnosis continues today. It is now known that the behavior of a hypnotized person depends both on the situation in which the hypnosis takes place and on the expectations of the subject. Someone who is hypnotized in a quiet office, for instance, will behave quite differently from a person hypnotized on a stage before an audience.

It is also known that a subject can experience different degrees of hypnosis. One investigator had listed over twenty such degrees. A person who is only slightly hypnotized may be more willing to do or to think whatever the hypnotist suggests. A person in a deep state of hypnosis will see and hear things that do not exist and will ignore things that do exist. That person may see pink elephants, or put on a coat that doesn't exist.[4]

In spite of our increased knowledge of hypnosis, we are still unable to understand it entirely. And hypnosis continues to be a fascinating subject.

1

dis   ly   less   re
able   un   ness

2

commercials   research
exclaimed   mileage   process

3

departments   features   information
unfortunately   vehicle   insulted
business   adequate   agreement
insisted   creative   patents

4

1. contract
2. mechanic
3. disassembled
4. clients
5. media
6. inexpensive
7. convince
8. grumble

5 # Preparing for the Campaign

Joe signed a contract with the advertising agency. According to the contract, he would receive twenty-five dollars for each car sold over three thousand that was sold during the year. Joe spent the next week studying all about the Niota model of car. He took the car to a garage and had a mechanic take it apart and put it back together. The process took over two days. When the car was disassembled, the garage was covered with parts—pistons from the engine, door handles, bumpers, nuts, bolts—thousands of parts. And Joe studied most of them. He asked * the mechanic at least a thousand questions.₁

Eight days after Joe had signed the contract, he was again sitting at the advertising agency conference table. Also sitting at the table were people from different departments of the agency. There was the man who headed the creative department. (That department makes up ads and commercials.) There was the woman who headed the marketing department. (That department does research for clients and studies marketing problems.) And there were the heads of the art department, the media department, and the new-business department.

"What have you come up with?" the president of the * agency asked Joe.

"Let's start with what we can't do," Joe said. "Then I'll tell you my plan."

"Sounds fair," the president said, and everybody else nodded in agreement.

"Here's what we can't do," Joe said. "We can't compete with the more popular Japanese imports because the Niota is not as good a product."

"It most certainly is!" the <u>president</u> insisted, standing up. "It's a fine product. I drive one myself."

"Look," Joe said, "you can either kid yourself or face the facts. You say it's a fine product. Sure, it's OK. It gets fair mileage, but look at the * big-selling Japanese imports. They get better mileage. The Niota handles well, but the other imports handle better. It has a pretty good engine, but that engine can't hold a candle to the Rondo. The Niota is fairly inexpensive, but it costs more than the Rondo.2 So what do we have to sell? Should we tell people that we have a good second-place car that's almost as good as some of the others?"

"It's got features that other cars don't have," the president responded.

"Sure it does," Joe replied. "And it's a nice little car, but it wouldn't do us any * good to try to convince people that it's better than other cars. So let's not try."3

The head of the creative department was on his feet. "Listen, I'm a busy man. I don't have time to sit in here and be insulted like this. You're telling us that we should throw up our hands and not even try to sell the product. You're crazy. What do you think we're here for?"

"I didn't say we're not going to sell the product. I said that we shouldn't try to convince people that it's a better car."

"What's the difference?" * the president bellowed.

"Why don't you settle down and listen to my plan? Then if you don't like it, I'll go my way and you can go yours."

"All right," the president said in a grumbling voice. "But try to make it quick. I have the distinct feeling that we're not going to like it."

"Here's the plan. We'll rename the car. We'll give it the kind of name that will force every other car manufacturer to advertise our car."

"What kind of name did you have in mind?" the head of the marketing department asked.

"Car," Joe replied. "We'll * call the Niota 'Car.' "4

The room became very silent. At last the president said, "I don't get it."

The head of the creative department said, "I think I do. If the product is called Car, all other manufacturers will say the name of our product when they talk about their products. Another manufacturer who says, 'This is the finest car on the road,' will be saying the name of our product."

"I get it," the head of the media department exclaimed. "Every time they say 'Car,' they're saying the name of our product."

"We can't get away with that," the * president said. "The word *car* refers to any car. We can't use that word just to refer to one brand of car."

"I think we can," Joe said.5

1 authentic specialize nation displeasure

2
purchased designers original exhausted
probably releases dealer displayed
billboard explaining imitations
campaign models middle-priced worth
advertising patent developed according

3
1. copyright
2. century
3. agency
4. commercial
5. import
6. frantic
7. budget
8. franchise

4

Car

Joe was explaining his idea to the executives of the advertising agency. He had proposed naming the Niota "Car."

He was saying, "I've been in touch with three lawyers who specialize in patents and copyrights. According to them, we can probably use the name 'Car.' And even if a lawsuit is brought against us, we'll probably be able to use the name for three or four years."[1]

"Car?" the president said. "You mean we'll just call the Niota 'Car'? That just doesn't sound right."

"Oh, no," Joe said smiling. "It sounds beautiful. It's different. It's something you'll remember. It's something * you'll think about.

The Car won't be just another import; it will be the talk of everybody. We'll get ten million dollars' worth of free advertising. Everybody will know about Car, and if enough people know about it, we'll sell a lot of cars and get a lot of new dealers." The marketing director was standing up. "It's great," she said. "If we can pull it off, it's the greatest idea of the century."[2]

The president was frowning and shaking his head. He said, "But it just doesn't sound right—Car."

At last the president agreed to the plan and * the work began. Joe spent the next three months working with the people at the agency. He developed names for the different models of Car. He named the cheapest line of Cars "Biggest Selling." He worked out commercials and billboards with the creative director. One billboard showed a very small picture of the Car. The message on the billboard said, "Now the Biggest Selling Car is in this country." (The word *is* was very small to make the message look as if it said, "Now the Biggest Selling Car in this country.") At the bottom of the billboard was another * message: "See it at your Car dealer."₃

Joe named the middle-priced line of Cars "The Number One in the Nation." One billboard showed a picture of The Number One in the Nation. The message said, "This Car is The Number One in the Nation. See it at your Car dealer."

Joe named the highest-priced line of Cars "The Original Imported." One billboard displayed the car and had the message, "See The Original Imported Car at your Car dealer."

Activity at the advertising agency was frantic for three months. Lawyers argued with each other. Designers and artists argued with * each other, as did the heads of different departments. And the president of the agency walked around shaking his head and saying, "It still doesn't sound right to me."₄

The agency planned to spend the entire advertising budget to put on a big show for one week. After that week, there would be no more money in the budget. Television time had been purchased. Ads had been placed in newspapers across the country. News releases were sent to newspapers and broadcasting stations. Billboards had been prepared.₅

At last the advertising campaign began. The first commercial came on the morning news * as the announcer said, "There's only one Car.

There are a lot of imitations. If you want to see the only car that is named 'Car,' where can you go? To your Car dealer. Don't be fooled, however. There are a lot of dealers who call themselves car dealers. Remember, there's only one Car, but a lot of imitations."

That commercial ran twenty times on national news broadcasts. On every television channel, there were also quick commercials throughout the day. All were the same— opening with pictures of more popular automobiles. As each automobile was shown, the voice said, "Is * this a Car? No." Then a picture of a Car flashed on the screen. "There's only one Car in this country. See it at your authorized Car dealer. Don't settle for imitations. The car you see in the picture happens to be the Biggest Selling Car. See it and the other authentic Cars—The Original Imported Car and the Car that is The Number One in the Nation. Call the toll-free number for the location of the real Car dealers."

Things went wild; a flood of calls came into the advertising agency before the campaign had been going three * hours.₆ Everybody from a senator to a group of local car dealers called and most were furious. "What are you trying to pull?" one dealer demanded. "I'm a car dealer, but I don't sell that thing you're calling Car. People are calling me and asking about Car."

Joe told the dealer, "The solution is simple. Keep your name and keep the cars you're selling. But add Car to your line. Then anybody who is interested in a Car will think of you first. We can give you an exclusive franchise in the city if you act immediately." The dealer acted * immediately and became a Car dealer.₇

1

commercial   reputation   glanced
undermining   dealership

2

1. hectic
2. exhaust
3. brochure
4. dealership
5. legal

6. vast
7. assess
8. talent
9. interview
10. violate
11. prior

3

resources   exhaust   campaign   industry
responded   national   specialize   official
product   manufacturers   protesting
committee   coughed   considering   directly

A Hectic Time

The advertising budget for Car was just over one million dollars. That budget was exhausted after a one-week advertising campaign. During that week, the advertising agency received nearly a thousand phone calls. The agency had to hire an answering service to handle the calls. Joe Kappas spent most of his time on the phone, talking to angry people.

Some of them were dealers of Car. "We're out of Cars," they complained. "We don't have enough brochures to hand out to customers. We need big signs so that people know where our dealerships are."[1]

During the week, fifty-three new * dealers were signed up to handle Car. About one hundred others were considering becoming Car dealers. Joe told each of the dealers interested in becoming a Car dealer, "Remember, as a Car dealer, you are entitled to display a sign in front of your showroom that says, 'The only real Car dealer in this area.' "[2]

Among the people who called the agency were reporters from the television and radio networks and all the leading national magazines. These calls went directly to the president of the advertising agency. He had meetings with reporters almost every day, starting on the second day * of the campaign. Joe was present during the first interview. Three reporters, two from local newspapers and one from a national magazine, shot questions at the president of the agency.

One reporter asked, "Is this campaign legal?"

"Certainly," the president responded. "Do you think we would do it if it weren't legal?"

"But," the same reporter continued, "isn't this campaign going to hurt other manufacturers and car dealers? They won't be able to refer to their cars as 'Car.' "

The president laughed. He then said, "Well, they can't call their * product cars because they're not Cars. There is only one Car that is sold in this country today."[3]

"Whose idea was this campaign?" the magazine reporter asked.

"It was a group effort," the president replied. "Our agency has vast resources and has a reputation for doing a creative job for our clients. We try to assess the needs of our clients and provide each client with the most creative and productive approach we can develop."

"What does that mean?" the reporter from the national magazine asked. "I mean, how did it really come about?"

The president coughed several times. Then * he said to her, "Well, it's difficult to describe how a total campaign is developed. As I said earlier, it is a group effort, with all

people putting their talent into the talent pool."

"But didn't somebody actually come up with the idea? Whose idea was it?"

The president glanced at Joe and cleared his throat. "I believe it came out of our creative department, but I can't actually remember. I don't believe that it was any one person's idea. As I recall, it was a group effort."

Joe understood that the president was trying to make it look as * if his agency had created the Car campaign, and Joe didn't really care. After all, Cars were selling, and Joe would receive twenty-five dollars for every car over three thousand sold during the year. Besides, Joe knew who created the advertising campaign.[4]

The interviews with reporters went on and so did the campaign. By the second week, Joe was beginning to tire of reading about Car in the newspaper and of watching TV reports on it. A government committee was investigating the situation. The labor union made a strong statement protesting the slogan, "The only Car in this country." * The union said that Car wasn't even made in this country and that it was undermining the nation's automobile industry.[5] A leading automobile manufacturer indicated that it was considering a lawsuit against Car. Another auto company indicated that it did not intend to drop the word *car* from any of its advertising and that it did not feel that it was violating any rights by referring to its automobiles as "cars." One company said that it had prior rights to the word *car* because it had used the word in advertising that dated back more than fifty years. A railroad car * manufacturer was considering a lawsuit against the makers of Car because the manufacturer had made railroad cars before automobile cars were invented.

In all, the weeks that followed the launching of the Car campaign were extremely hectic.[6]

1 un less sub
ness pre able ly

---

2 furthermore motionless
executives disguised

---

3 survival easily exact concerned
production instead convert
months situation convention
guarantee Kamigo estimate

4
1. launch
2. translate
3. facilities
4. associates
5. profit
6. colleagues
7. thorough
8. devote

5

Just Too Much

Two months after the Car campaign had been launched, six executives from the Niota factory in Japan came to the advertising agency. Only one of them could speak English very well. Joe and four people from the advertising agency met with the six Niota executives. During the meeting, the one who could speak English talked to Joe and the others. She then translated what was said to the other Niota executives, who would shake their heads either up and down or from side to side.

"We are concerned," the English-speaking executive said, "because we do not have facilities to * produce for export more than five hundred thousand Cars each year. Already, we are at full production. And already the orders from your country are greater than we can fill."[1]

"That's kind of a nice problem to have," the president of the agency said and laughed heartily. Several other members of the agency laughed, too.

Joe didn't laugh. He said, "I took one of the Niotas apart and I found out that it's almost an exact copy of a Miyada model that was built around 1995."

"You say we copied Miyada!" the Japanese executive said.

She quickly translated Joe's comment * to the other executives, after which they shook their heads from side to side and said, "No, no, no!"

The president said, "Joe, what are you trying to do? We're not here to insult Ms. Ogura and her associates."

"That's not the point. The point is that Niota could contract with Miyada to build more Cars.₂ I've looked into the situation and I've talked to the executives at Miyada. According to them, they can convert part of the Kamigo plant into making Cars within only three months. Furthermore, there are currently enough Niotas around to fill all orders between now * and then. There are nearly thirty thousand of them in France, where they are not selling well. We could easily pick up twenty thousand and have them shipped here within a month. With the other shipments that are scheduled, we should have enough Cars to last us until the Miyada plant starts producing."₃

Ms. Ogura was busy translating to the other Niota executives. Two were nodding their heads up and down. Ms. Ogura then smiled broadly and turned to Joe. "You are very thorough. However, we must know what it will cost for us to have Niota produced by Miyada." *

Joe said, "You will make a profit of about five percent, which is less than you make on the cars you produce, but you will have no expense in the production of these cars. Miyada will pay for setting up and producing Cars if you can give them a guarantee that you will take one hundred thousand Cars."

Ms. Ogura's eyes became very large. "Oh," she said. "Oh, that's many cars. Many cars."

She translated for her colleagues. Four shook their heads from side to side.

"Too many cars," Ms. Ogura said. "What happens if we can't sell all Cars * produced by Miyada?"

The head of the marketing department for the advertising agency said, "Maybe I can help. I have done some figuring. Based on the sales that we have made since the beginning of the campaign, I would estimate that nearly half a million Cars will be sold in this country during this year. That means that we will need more than one hundred thousand Cars from Miyada this year alone."₄

A quick translation from Ms. Ogura to the other executives and their heads began to nod up and down. Ms. Ogura smiled. "Very thorough, very thorough," she said. *

Joe had known from the beginning that he was a super salesperson, but now he felt that the Niota situation was getting a little out of hand. It was becoming too crazy. Imagine Miyada producing Niotas that were to be sent here and called Cars. Imagine all the other major manufacturers in the country battling a second-rate import for survival. Imagine hundreds of pages of print in newspapers and hours and hours of broadcast time devoted to news on the Car situation. And imagine the amount of money Joe would make if half a million Cars were sold. He * would make twelve and a half million dollars!

During the meeting, Joe found himself thinking, "This is just too much!"₅

1 Death straight Africa zero India
Montana dioxide atmospheric Portugal
survive Rainier climate
Meghalaya carbon Valley

2
1. extreme
2. endure
3. annual

3

Climate

No matter how hot it is where you are, you're only a few miles from a place where it is bitterly cold. That place is high over your head. Jet planes fly there because the air is thin high above Earth. Therefore, there is less pull, or drag, against the plane. The temperature outside a high-flying jet, however, is typically −40°F (−70°C).

Sometimes the temperature there is even lower. In 1963, the lowest atmospheric temperature ever measured was recorded high over Kronogard, Sweden: −225.4°F (−143°C). At this temperature some gases, such as carbon dioxide, will freeze solid.₁

Although temperatures on Earth's surface do not approach those high above Earth, some places on Earth do become amazingly cold. A record low of −128.6°F (−89°C) was recorded in 1960 at the South Pole. It seems astounding that any creature could endure such cold, but there are animals at the South Pole who do just that.

At the other extreme, some places on Earth become extremely hot. In July 1913, the temperature in the shade at Death Valley, California, soared to a scorching 134°F (56.7°C). A temperature of 136.4°F (57.8°C) was recorded in 1942 in northern Africa. However, the all-time high reading occurred in Portugal in September 1933. The temperature there suddenly jumped to 158°F (70°C). It remained there for two minutes and then dropped to less than 100°F (38°C).₂

Here are some other interesting facts about temperatures:

A great temperature drop occurred in Montana in January 1916. During the day, the temperature was 44°F (6.7°C). That night the temperature fell to −56°F (−13.3°C).

The world's hottest weather year after year occurs in Ethiopia, which has an average annual temperature of 94°F (34°C).[3]

The place with the greatest annual amount of snowfall is Mt. Rainier, Washington. From early 1971 to early 1972, 1224.5 inches (3138 centimeters) of snow fell there. That's more than 96 feet (30 meters) of snow—enough to cover a ten-story building.

The record for the greatest rainfall during any period occurred in July 1861. More than 366 inches (9 meters) of rain fell in Meghalaya, India, in that one month. That's as much rain as will fall in New York or Chicago in eight years. The one-year record for rainfall in Meghalaya is more than 1041 inches (26 meters).[4]

1

specialize   article   countless
convinced   pressure

2

reporter   raises   colleagues   campaign
monster   discussing   unpopular   serious
suddenly   strategy   overheard   estimate
brochure   filing   creative   broadcasting
accurate   concluded   patents   honest

3

1. genius
2. domestic
3. intent
4. fraud
5. deceit

4

Sinner or Genius?

Joe felt that the Car campaign had turned into a monster, and he was right. The head of the advertising agency's marketing department was pretty close in her estimate about the number of Cars that would be sold in this country during the year. Nearly a quarter of a million were sold within six months. About the time the 250,000th Car had been sold, a reporter from *Moment* magazine found out that Joe Kappas was really the brains of the Car campaign. The reporter interviewed Joe, and two weeks later, Joe's picture was on the cover of *Moment*. Beneath it, * it said, "Joe Kappas, Brains Behind Car." Inside the magazine was a four-page story about Joe. The title was "Joe Kappas, Sinner or Genius?" The article pointed out that the Car campaign had hurt sales of domestic cars, that Joe had used a trick to turn an unpopular imported car into the second-largest-selling import in the nation, and that he had done this in one year.₁ The article concluded, "The campaign created by Joe Kappas certainly points out the power of advertising; however, it raises serious questions about the rights of companies to use Joe Kappas's type * of advertising. There was no truth in Kappas's campaign, only tricks. Yes, Joe Kappas could claim, 'We sell the Car that is Number One in the Nation.' He can point out that his statement is true. In fact, the name of the Car is 'Number One in the Nation.' But clearly the car has that name so that Joe Kappas and the manufacturers of Car products can lie.₂ As a matter of record, the model that is named 'Number One in the Nation' is not number one. It is the fourth-best-selling imported model and the seventh-best-selling * model of all cars sold in the country. The three top-selling models are manufactured here. The Joe Kappas campaign points out that truth in advertising involves more than words. It involves intent. Joe Kappas's intent was clearly fraud."₃

Joe read the article four times. It made him feel quite bad. Joe was not a person with dishonest intent. He was a super salesperson, not a fraud. He understood people and what made them tick. He had seen the Niota as a challenge. It was an opportunity for him to take a product that was not doing well and turn * it into a success. To Joe, that was a good thing because it didn't involve destroying; it involved building something. At least that's how Joe had felt earlier. Now, however, he had some doubts. Perhaps the *Moment* article was accurate in suggesting that Joe had used tricks and deceit to sell Niota cars. Although he had succeeded in turning the Niota into a huge success, he had hurt other people along the way.₄

After reading the *Moment* article, Joe decided that he needed time to think. He didn't accept any phone calls during the next day. In fact, he didn't * spend much time at the agency. He spent a lot of time walking around the city. Every time he passed one of the Car billboards, he stopped and examined it. They didn't look too clever to him now. "See the

Biggest Selling Car at your Car dealer," he said to himself. "What does that mean? It means see a little Niota at your Niota dealer. But that's not what it says."₅

He listened to people talking to each other about Car. "My daughter is an automobile dealer," Joe overheard one woman saying to another. "And you would not believe the * trouble that she has had since that ugly Car came on the market. She gets phone calls from people wanting to buy Cars. She's had to go to countless meetings. Her company is filing a lawsuit against Car. It's a mess."

Joe overheard a couple of young men discussing Car. One of them said, "I think it's great. I think this is just what we need to wake us up. Maybe now we'll get some laws to make advertising honest."

The more Joe listened to people talk, the more he became convinced that he had to do something to fix * the situation. But what could he do now? Nearly four hundred dealers were selling Cars. The campaign was legal— even if it was based on falsehoods. There was no way Joe could turn the clock back one year and change the events that had taken place. So what could he do?₆

Joe now had a new challenge, and he loved challenges. Although he didn't know what his strategy would be, he knew that he would do something to correct the situation. However, he didn't want to hurt the people at the advertising agency or the dealers who were selling Car. * That was going to be hard to do.

Joe had been walking, listening to people, and thinking for nearly a week when an idea hit him. He was walking through a park, past a small pond that was dotted with ducks, when suddenly, he stopped, snapped his fingers, and said, "I think I've got a plan that will work."

1

re   ness   dis   tri   ly   un   able

2

beneficial   whether   especially
prevailing   particularly

3

seriously   image   practically   accounts
curiously   remained   securely   implement
waddled   interrupt   created   individual
canceled   concealed   demand

4

1. stroll

2. receptionist

3. schedule

4. conference

5. bellow

6. resignation

5

All in the Same Pond

Joe sat down on a park bench, took out his pocket notebook, and began to make notes. He talked to himself as he wrote, and some of the people strolling through the park paused to look curiously at him. Joe remained on the park bench nearly all afternoon. At three thirty he got up and ran the four blocks back to the agency. He ran up to the receptionist and said, "Set up a meeting." He paused to take a deep breath and continued, "I want to speak with the president and the department heads."

"When do you wish to * schedule this meeting, Mr. Kappas?" the receptionist asked.

"Right now," Joe replied quickly.

"Oh, I don't believe that's possible."

"I don't care how possible it is," Joe said in a firm voice. "Do it." Joe hadn't intended to be so rude, but he wanted to get his plan into operation as soon as possible.₁

The receptionist made some calls and then informed Joe, "The meeting is set up in the conference room in five minutes."

"Look," Joe said. "I'm sorry—I—" This was one of the few times that Joe was at a loss for words.

The receptionist smiled at * Joe and said, "It's OK."

Joe went up to the conference room and waited for the others to arrive.

When everybody was present and seated around the conference table, Joe said, "We must deal with some facts. Fact: The Car campaign has created a lot of ill will. Fact: The campaign has hurt a lot of people. Fact: Articles like the one in *Moment* magazine give this agency a bad image."

"What are you trying to get at with these facts?" the president demanded. "I can give you a fact, too. The people at Niota feel that our campaign was * so beneficial that they have given us another two million dollars for advertising. That's the fact that counts."₂

"Sure they do," Joe said. "But we have to consider other people, too. Wouldn't it be a good idea to get some good will for Niota?"

"Sales are good will," the president said. "And we've made lots and lots of sales."

"Look," Joe said. "I was sitting in the park looking at the ducks swimming in a pond when I got this idea. Each duck is an individual, but they're all in the same pond. Niota is a duck. It is in * a pond with all the other car manufacturers. But Niota has turned on the other ducks. What I'm suggesting is that Niota should try to get along with those other ducks."₃

"I don't know anything about ducks," the president said. "One of our accounts is Mason's TV chicken dinner, but that's as close to ducks as we get."

Everybody laughed except Joe. "Well, let me tell you my plan, and please don't interrupt. We've got the dealers now, so we're sure of selling Cars. That means we don't need our campaign anymore. And we can get another ten million dollars' * worth of news if we do something to fix this situation with the lawsuits and the other manufacturers."

"So what's the plan?" the president asked.

"Here it is," Joe said. "We keep on calling the Niotas 'Cars,' but we do it a little differently. We call them 'Cars by Niota.' Then we sell every other car manufacturer the right to call their automobiles "Cars." We can sell them the right for practically nothing, because we're not interested in the money; we're interested in the good will and the news that we can create with this move."₄

"I like it," the * head of the marketing department said.

"I don't," the president bellowed. "That's like admitting that we were wrong in the first place. From the beginning, I said that we should stand behind the Car idea."

The head of the marketing department said, "But it's a good idea. As Joe says, we've got the dealers now. Why not do something positive?"

The president stared at the marketing director and said, "It seems that there are some people in this agency who don't think for themselves. If Joe Kappas has an idea they want to buy it, no matter how sour it * is."₅

The head of the marketing department stood up. Very quietly she said, "Well, I'll tell you this. I don't feel good about the way the Car campaign is going. I didn't know it would get so big or that it would get so far out of hand. That's thinking for myself, and if you don't take Joe's suggestions seriously, you'll have my resignation."

A deep silence fell over the conference room.

1 especially   headlines   audience   furthermore

2 creative   wandering   dealership   figure
announcement   details   several   outfits
additional   financial   hurting   basically
general   remained   official   purchase
furthermore   environment   country
representative   create   waddling

3
1. withdraw
2. rowdies
3. term

Car by Niota

Joe stood up next to the marketing director and said to the president, "I'll do more than quit if you don't take my plan seriously. So far, you owe me more than six million dollars on our contract. If you don't implement my plan, I'll take every cent of that money and turn it over to one of the outfits that is suing Niota. Furthermore, I'll get in touch with the major news reporters in the country and tell them that I withdraw from the campaign, that I will take no money from the campaign, and that the only reason * the campaign is continuing is because *you* want it that way."[1]

"What is this?" the president said standing up. "There's no need for shouting and acting like rowdies. I gather you must be speaking out of great anger to talk about anything as crazy as giving away six million dollars."

"I may be crazy," Joe said softly. "But I'm me. And I have to live with me. And I don't think I would like myself with six million dollars that I made by hurting other people. I think I would like me much better if I knew that I was * doing what I think is right. I'm a good salesperson and I'm going to sell you on my plan. Believe me, you'll buy it before I'm done."[2]

The head of the creative department stood up. "I'm with Joe," he said.

The art director stood up. "Me, too."

The president sat down. "Now, I don't recall saying that I was <u>against</u> any plan to create good will. I don't know why everybody is jumping to conclusions."

"Good," Joe said, sitting down. The others sat down, too. "Let's go over the details of the plan. First, we have to talk Niota into * changing the name of Car to Car by Niota. That should be pretty easy to do because they'll be happy to have their name advertised again."

"I see no problem on that count," the president said.

Joe continued, "Then, we'll have to fix up the signs at the Car dealerships, so that they say, 'Car by Niota.' I figure that should cost no more than one hundred fifty thousand dollars. We must have those signs within three weeks, so we'll have to move quickly."

The head of the marketing department said, "I think we can do that without much trouble."₃

Joe went through the rest of the details that would have to be attended to. After the meeting, Joe remained at the agency and made more than a dozen phone calls. He called several lawyers, two union leaders, and several executives from other automobile companies.

During the next three days, Joe made more than a hundred phone calls. He called reporters and executives from all the automobile manufacturers that had distribution in the country, telling them of his plan. He asked them to keep it a secret until the official announcement, which was to take place on Friday. Joe asked * for a representative from each automobile company to be present at the announcement. All the companies agreed to send one.₄

Friday was extremely hectic at the agency, with people running around carrying stacks of paper that would be handed out at the meeting. Reporters were wandering around asking thousands of questions. At last, representatives from twenty auto manufacturers, thirty-five reporters, and a dozen lawyers went to the agency's meeting room. The president of the advertising agency stood up and said, "The Niota Motor Works has decided to sell rights to the word *car*. These rights will be sold to * all other car manufacturers so that they can use the word *car*. Niota is charging each company that wishes to purchase the rights one thousand dollars per year. This money will be donated to the labor union. Finally, the name Niota will appear on all cars manufactured by Niota. The name will be Car by Niota."₅

As the president talked, flashbulbs went off and cameras clicked. Following the announcement, every reporter in the audience seemed to ask a question at the same time. They asked which companies were taking up Niota's offer. Joe told them that all had agreed to * the terms. Reporters asked whether any of the suits would be dropped against Niota. They were told that most of the major suits had been dropped.

There were a lot of headlines in the newspaper during the days that followed the announcement and a lot of articles. *Moment* magazine ran an article that referred to Joe as "basically a good guy." Sales of Car didn't drop off. If anything, they went up. And Joe felt a lot better about the whole situation.

On the day after the meeting, Joe went for a walk through the park. He stopped and looked * at the ducks swimming in the pond, and he said to himself, "That's the way it should be."₆

1 less ly ness re able

2 ailment surgery knowledge
sewer cleanliness penicillin

3 especially medicine referred disease
sickness snout patient diphtheria
viewed fragment effective bubonic
leather plague sweating advanced
invisible professional contrast dwellings

4
1. treatment
2. organism
3. microscope
4. infected

5

Medicine Years Ago

The doctors of today are professionals with a great deal of knowledge about the human body and what may go wrong with it. Doctors understand what treatments are effective. They treat some problems with surgery, which involves cutting into the patient's body. To fight a disease they may use some form of drug, such as penicillin. They know that germs spread diseases, and that germs are tiny organisms, so small they are invisible unless viewed under a microscope. It is fair to say that today's doctors have a great understanding of medicine—the science of curing ailments.[1]

The doctors of * 1850 did not know many of the things that today's doctors understand. They didn't understand that they should wash their hands before touching a patient. If you had been living then and had to go to a hospital, you probably would not have left that hospital alive. Over half of the people who entered a hospital died there, because hospital attendants and doctors didn't know as much as they do today.2

Let's go back much further than 1850. Let's go back to the year 1350 and let's visit a large city in Europe. The scene is quite similar in all * large cities. The first thing you probably notice is the smell of the city. Many cities did not have sewers, so the streets were used as sewers. Another thing you notice is that the people are very dirty and that they smell. They don't believe in taking baths. Even kings and very rich people bathe only once or twice a year. The city, you observe, is surrounded by a large wall and the dwellings are packed together. The great wall around the city was originally intended to protect it from attack by neighboring kings or princes. But packing people together * makes for terrible filth.3

You observe an interesting contrast between the filth of the city and the beautiful paintings, statues, and hand-crafted objects made by the talented artists and craftsmen of the city. Obviously, the people have a great appreciation of beauty. And some of the music you hear is still played today. What a contrast. On one hand, the people's understanding of medicine and cleanliness is far different from what we know today. Yet on the other hand, the people are similar to today's people in their understanding of the arts.4

As you walk through the crowds of people * in the streets of the city, you notice a man dressed in a very strange outfit. He wears a large leather coat and gloves. Over his face is a strange mask with a large circle of glass in the middle and a long snout. He carries a long metal wand, and as he walks down the street, the people run to get out of his way. The man is a doctor. He treats people who are infected with the most dreaded disease in the city—the bubonic plague. His costume is a special one, worn only in times of plague. *5

The bubonic plague, called the Black Death at the time of our visit, is the greatest single killer in the city. This dreaded disease spread throughout Europe in the middle of the fourteenth century (the 1300s) and killed probably at least one-third of the population.

Bubonic plague is not the only killer in the city. Smallpox and measles and diphtheria are common. You probably notice that many people's faces are covered with pitlike scars. These scars were caused by smallpox. Almost everyone in the city suffered from smallpox when they were children. Those who wear the scars lived.6 The * graveyards are filled with the thousands of children who didn't live. On the average, a baby born in 1300 could have been expected to live less than twenty years. (The baby's *life expectancy* was twenty years.) This was so because many would not survive the diseases of childhood. Even those who did might die from something as simple as an infected tooth. In contrast, the life expectancy of people in Europe and North America in the twentieth century is about seventy years— because most children survive childhood diseases.

As you stand in the street, watching people make way for the * doctor in the leather outfit, you decide to follow him and observe how he cares for those who suffer from the bubonic plague. Perhaps you will regret this decision.7

communication   Egyptians   official
long-distance   combinations   English
Mandarin   billion   intelligent
hieroglyphic   language   represented
carried   determine   inhabited   scenes

1. inscribed
2. tomb

Spoken Language and Written Language

Experts have not been able to determine exactly when people first began to use language. Experts agree that prehistoric people used language thousands of years ago. They expressed many ideas through pictures, one of the earliest forms of written language. Drawings in caves show scenes of animals and hunters. In the earliest type of pictures, each picture represented an object, an idea, or an action. Later the pictures stood for sounds, not things, but they were not symbols for words or syllables.

Burial tombs show that the Egyptians who lived four thousand years ago had a highly developed form of picture writing called hieroglyphics. Examples of elaborate hieroglyphic stories have been found inscribed on vases, boxes, and the walls of the tombs.₁

Spoken language, however, came long before writing. While all groups of human beings have speech, the patterns and sounds of speech can differ greatly from one group to another. There are about three thousand languages spoken in the world today.

In the United States, English is the official language, but many other languages—for example, Spanish, Portuguese, and Japanese—are used. In some countries, there is no single official language. People from one part of the country cannot understand people from another part because each group speaks a different language. In India, about 140 languages and more than 700 regional variations are spoken.₂

The language spoken by the greatest number of people is Mandarin Chinese. More than one billion people speak this language. The second most widely used language is English, which is spoken by about 400,000,000 people.

Of all languages, English has the greatest number of words: about 800,000. The average English-speaking adult doesn't use all these words, or even half of them. The average person probably uses only about 10,000 of all English words.[3]

There are some very long words in the English language. One has twenty-eight letters: antidisestablishmentarianism. The longest word in the English language is the name of a lung disease that people who work in mines sometimes get. That word contains forty-five letters. Here it is: pneumonoultramicroscopicsilicovolcanoconiosis.

1 un re ly able ness

2 breathing foul heavens official

3 perfumed squirming responded
poison sternly curtains wand course
patients plague servant victim
females gloved filthy bubonic
conscious hollow bedding indicates

4
1. unconscious
2. sprinkling
3. impure

5

The Black Death

You are observing a doctor who is treating victims of the bubonic plague in 1350. You follow the doctor down the narrow street where houses are crowded side by side. The doctor pauses in front of a house. A large black cloth hangs from the front door. This black cloth indicates that there is a plague victim in the building and that nobody can leave the building. Only a doctor can enter.

The doctor goes inside and enters the room of the victim, who is unconscious in bed. The room is very dark and foul smelling. The windows are closed. * The bedding is filthy.

The doctor walks over to the bed and pokes at the victim with his wand. He uses the wand so that he doesn't have to touch the victim with his hands or even his gloves. The victim does not move.₁

"What can we do, doctor?" the victim's brother asks.

"I will purify the air," the doctor responds, his voice sounding hollow through the mask.

The doctor takes a bottle of perfumed water from under his coat. He walks around the room, sprinkling the curtains, the floor, and the patient's bed with the perfumed water. He then * asks the patient's brother for a cooking pot. After the doctor places some spices in the pot and lights them, a powerful-smelling smoke fills the room.

"Should I bathe my brother?" the young man asks.

"Heavens no," the doctor replies through his mask. "The Black Death is caused by impure vapors that enter the body through the openings in the skin called pores. If you bathe the patient, the water will open his pores further and more of the disease will enter his body. The smoke of the spices will prevent any more impure vapors from entering his pores."*₂

"Doctor," the brother asks, "will my brother live?"

It is difficult to see the doctor's expression through his mask. "I don't know," he replies.

The doctor charges the healthy brother a fee for the services he performed, and then, without washing his wand, he leaves the building and continues down the street.

As you follow him, you notice a horse-drawn cart that is piled high with the bodies of plague victims.

The doctor's next stop is a large house near the city wall. This is the house of a wealthy family. The doctor is not allowed inside. A servant * meets him at the gate to the house.

"My master is feeling ill," the servant says. "It does not seem that he has the plague, but he wishes your advice."

The doctor takes off his mask and shakes his head. He looks very tired. "I will give you some pills that will clean out his system, but my best advice is quick-far-late."

"What does that mean?" the servant inquires.

"It means be *quick* to leave the city. Go *far*. And come back *late*—after the plague has run its course."₃

The doctor hands the pills to the servant. * The servant says, "I shall tell my master what you said." The master who owns the house has ten servants and a great deal of money. He is lucky because he can afford to leave the city during a time of great plague. Only the kings, the princes, and the wealthy are able to follow the advice of quick-far-late. Of those who can't leave, two-thirds become plague victims, and as many as eight out of ten victims will die.

The doctor wipes his brow with the back of his gloved hand and then puts his mask on * again. He doesn't know that the stroke of the glove across his forehead spread the germs of the bubonic plague to him. He will be dead within a week.₄

1

surgeon   <u>uneducated</u>   <u>lecture</u>   challenge

2

Ambroise Paré   Leonardo da Vinci
intelligent   barber   conducted   spirits
popular   advice   ailment   penicillin
medicine   butchers   anesthetic   haircut
Latin   wealthy   respect
schooling   dissected   anatomy
infected   recognized   unfortunately

3

1. wounds
2. sluggish
3. amputate
4. scalding
5. purify
6. ignorant

4

The Barber-Surgeon

Around the year 1500, there were three types of doctors. The three types were called *surgeons of the long robe, physicians,* and *barber-surgeons.*

The surgeons of the long robe, unlike the surgeons of today, never operated. They dressed wounds, gave out pills or drugs, and "bled" people. During the 1500s, people believed that some diseases were caused by blood that was sluggish. The surgeons of the long robe suggested that patients would recover from these diseases if some blood were removed from their systems.

Sometimes the surgeons of the long robe worked with physicians. Physicians did not do any * work on patients. They lectured at universities and gave advice to people who could afford to hire them. If a patient needed some kind of care, the physician would bring in a surgeon of the long robe. The physician would give the advice and the surgeon of the long robe would take care of the patient's ailment. The physician never touched the patient.

Both physicians and surgeons of the long robe went through a great deal of schooling. They spoke Latin and the books they read were written in Latin. The great majority of the people of that time could * not speak or read Latin. In fact, most of them couldn't read at all. Physicians and surgeons of the long robe were well-to-do and highly respected, even though they knew very little about medicine, by modern standards.2

The third type of doctor was the barber-surgeon. Most of the barber-surgeons were uneducated, even unable to read. Many had other jobs, such as tending pigs or cutting meat in a market. Most people had little respect for the barber-surgeons, who had learned their trade by working in a "barber shop." You could get a lot more than * a haircut in those barber shops. You could also get a wounded leg amputated or have a boil lanced. You could have your teeth pulled or a bullet removed. (Guns were just coming into use in warfare around this time.)3

Barber-surgeons usually had a number of charms hanging in different parts of their shops. One of the most popular charms was a stuffed animal that was hung from the ceiling. The animal was supposed to keep the evil spirits away while the barber amputated a leg or an arm. Amputations were frequent because the doctors didn't know how to * stop infections. They had no penicillin or other drugs of that type, and they didn't realize that wounds should be kept clean. When a wound became seriously infected, the patient would either wait to die from the infection or have the infected part amputated. The operation was conducted without any anesthetics because at that time anesthetics were unknown. The barber-surgeon would tie the patient to a chair and saw off the infected part. Then he would place scalding hot oil on the wound to stop the

bleeding and to "purify" the wound. If the bleeding did not kill the * patient, the scalding hot oil sometimes did.4

Although the barber-surgeons were not trained in the science of medicine, their knowledge was not much less than that of the physicians and the surgeons of the long robe. The surgeons of the long robe never operated because they knew that the patient would probably die from the operation. So they devoted their efforts to impressing people by speaking in Latin, blaming diseases on evil spirits, and attempting cures that did not work.5

The religious ideas of the times made it very difficult for doctors to find cures that did work. People * believed that a person would not reach heaven if the body were cut into pieces. It was, therefore, considered a crime for doctors to study dead bodies. The doctors knew very little about the parts of the body—the muscles, the bones, the nerves. And they were prevented from finding out any facts by studying dead bodies. In studying anatomy (the structure of the body), they were allowed to operate only on animals such as dogs or goats. Unfortunately, the human body is not the same as the body of a dog or a goat. So the physicians and surgeons * remained ignorant about the human body, and they were suspicious of anyone who tried to challenge their ignorance.6

There were a few challenges around 1500. One came from a famous artist, Leonardo da Vinci. Another came from a man named Ambroise Paré, who became a surgeon of the long robe, even though he did not go to a university. He began as a barber-surgeon and never learned to speak or read Latin. Both da Vinci and Paré learned a great deal because they sought the facts—not the beliefs that had been passed along for hundreds of years.

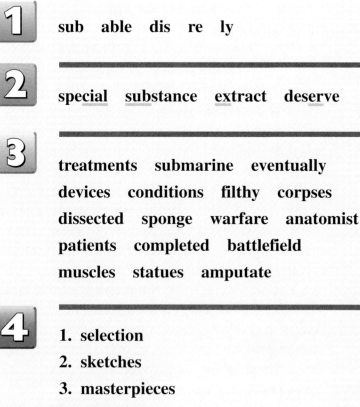

1

sub   able   dis   re   ly

2

spe<u>cial</u>   sub<u>stance</u>   <u>extract</u>   des<u>erve</u>

3

treatments   submarine   eventually
devices   conditions   filthy   corpses
dissected   sponge   warfare   anatomist
patients   completed   battlefield
muscles   statues   amputate

4

1. selection
2. sketches
3. masterpieces
4. anatomy
5. dressings
6. limbs

The Early Study of Anatomy and Surgery

After you read this selection, look up some of the paintings of Leonardo da Vinci. When you examine these paintings, look at the way Leonardo drew the human body. Leonardo understood the structure of the human body probably as well as anybody who had ever lived. And he reached this understanding of the body by studying its inner structure. He worked with corpses (dead bodies), and he dissected them (cut parts away so that he could study other parts). He recorded his findings by making sketches of the body parts. He made detailed drawings of muscles, bones, even nerves. He * hoped to publish a great work on the anatomy of the human body. Unfortunately, he died before he completed the book. All that he left behind were hundreds of notes and sketches. Many of these were lost after his death, but some were saved. These notes and sketches found their way to different parts of Europe.1

Leonardo also left sketches for another kind. Among them were details for building a submarine, an airplane, and other devices that would not be "invented" for hundreds of years. Besides the devices that remained on paper, he did invent machines that were actually used * to construct buildings, make statues, and create special effects for plays. He created paintings that are considered masterpieces. He helped open the door to the study of human anatomy. But he never saw some of his greatest achievements accepted by the world.[2]

A very different kind of contribution to medicine in the 1500s was made by a man called Ambroise Paré. Paré was not an anatomist or an artist. He began as a helper to a barber-surgeon in a hospital of more than one thousand beds. Conditions in that hospital were terrible even by the standards of that time. * Rats could be seen in every part of the building. The bedding and the dressings of the wounds were filthy. The odor was so bad that the attendants could not enter the sickroom unless they held a sponge dipped in vinegar over their nose and mouth. The patients were not fed regularly.[3]

After three years of working in the hospital, Paré became an army surgeon. Conditions for treating soldiers on the battlefield were as bad as those in the hospital. The surgeons would amputate limbs or try to extract bullets from gunshot wounds. Bullets were new in warfare, and the * surgeons did not know how to treat the wounds bullets caused. Some cut out the bullet and then poured hot oil into the wound.

These surgeons used the slogan: "If the wound is not curable by using the knife, use fire." (*Fire* meant hot oil.)[4]

Paré changed two things. First, he discovered how to tie off arteries in amputations so that the patient did not bleed to death. Second, he discovered that wounds healed better without boiling oil. Instead, he used clean cloth and mild substances like egg whites to cover the wounds. Paré's methods worked. Many of the soldiers * that Paré treated lived. Many didn't suffer as much as if they had received the usual treatments. They usually didn't develop fevers, and the wounds healed more quickly.[5]

People began to become aware of the work of Paré. He became court surgeon to three kings. In his day, many other doctors thought surgery was below their dignity. Paré helped raise the standing of surgery. But many physicians and surgeons resented Paré. They didn't believe in his methods. They thought he was an ignorant man because he didn't even know Latin.

Paré did a lot of things to advance medicine. He * developed new methods for delivering babies and cut down the number of deaths among mothers and newborn babies. The methods that Paré developed were eventually adopted by others. In fact, when he died, his methods were being used in the hospital where he had begun as a barber's assistant.[6]

1

able   ly   re

2

observations   posture   remarkable   breast
mentioned   courage   concerned   frequently

3

Vesalius   Galen   accepted   explanation
internal   scattered   challenge   miserable
managed   educated   conclusions   theories
indicated   ingredients   dissect   anatomy
humorous   community   conflict   prominent

4

1. suspicious
2. elaborate
3. proclaimed
4. trait

5

Galen's Theories

Around 1500, some doctors began to question the medical theories that had been accepted for hundreds of years. These doctors exhibited a great deal of courage because most people were suspicious of anybody who challenged established theories.

But a few doctors had the courage to record what they observed, even though their observations were in conflict with long-standing theories and with the accepted medical practice of the time. The basic theory of medicine around 1500 had been accepted for over a thousand years. It had been developed by a man named Galen, a Greek who tried to explain how * the body worked and how to cure its ailments.[1]

During Galen's time, doctors were not permitted to dissect (cut up) dead bodies. Galen realized, however, that doctors could not work with the human body unless they understood the anatomy of the body. (The study of anatomy deals with the structure of the body—the bones, muscles, nerves, and organs.) Galen wrote an elaborate work on anatomy. He drew conclusions about human anatomy by studying the anatomy of different animals. Since he couldn't work on human bodies, he dissected animals, such as pigs and apes.₂

Galen proclaimed that human hipbones looked * like those of an ox—a conclusion based upon his dissection of oxen. Galen thought that different human organs were identical to those found in the hog, the dog, the ox, or the ape. He made these mistakes because his conclusions about human anatomy were based upon animal anatomy instead of human anatomy.

Galen's views of anatomy were accepted as law for well over a thousand years. Few people questioned his findings; few surgeons made observations of humans and said, "Galen is wrong." Instead, physicians continued to teach Galen's theory and stood ready to fight anybody who challenged it.₃

We * have already mentioned one man who questioned Galen's theory—Leonardo da Vinci. His works, however, remained scattered around Europe for many years after his death. Another man who challenged Galen's views was Vesalius. He was a doctor and a professor at a leading university. Vesalius met Paré at one time. The two men had a great deal in common. Both relied more on what they saw than on what they were told. They were willing to question long-standing theories and were willing to see what was there, not what they wanted to see.₄

Another common trait of Vesalius and * Paré was courage. Remember, people were not encouraged to challenge accepted theories. If they did, they could expect trouble. Both Paré and Vesalius attacked practices of the day. Yet Vesalius was respected by many people. Toward the end of his life he became physician to two kings. His work helped lead the medical profession to a greater understanding of the human body.₅

1 corpus callosum greatest basically telephone estimates messages electric forehead halves dividing current hemispheres tracing lesion tremor melody damaged accurate fibers

2
1. composed
2. eliminate
3. function
4. logical

3

The Brain

The human brain is one of the greatest wonders in the universe. Basically, the brain is composed of nerve cells that are packed together. A nerve cell is like a wire. It has a long shaft that works like the wires that carry telephone messages or electric current. The best estimates hold that there are hundreds of millions of cells in the brain. Some of these are only a few centimeters long, but many are more than a meter long.[1]

If you were to draw a line from the tip of your nose, between your eyes, and up the middle of your forehead, you would be tracing the dividing line between the two halves of your brain. The fibers that join the two halves are called the corpus callosum, and the two halves are called hemispheres.[2]

Most theories state that each hemisphere has a different major function. A simple rule for describing what the two hemispheres do is this: The left hemisphere thinks and the right hemisphere feels. According to the scientists' theories, this rule is not exactly accurate, but it does tell the major function of the hemispheres. Language is usually controlled by centers in the left hemisphere. If these are damaged, you could lose your ability to speak and even to understand what others are saying. When you try to reason logically, you are primarily using the left side of your brain. But when you experience feelings, you are using the right hemisphere of your brain. When you listen to the melody of a song, your right hemisphere is involved. When you see a face in the clouds, you're using the right hemisphere. When you feel strong emotion, your right hemisphere is involved.₃

Although scientists understand a great deal about the brain, there is much they don't know. For example, there is the puzzle of the second lesion. A lesion is a cut. Let's say that you have a lesion on the left side of your brain, near the back. Your hands may shake so much that you can't hold a cup without spilling the contents. In some cases, this tremor can be eliminated by making another lesion on the opposite hemisphere. In this case, the lesion would be made on the right side, near the back. Why doesn't the second lesion make your condition twice as bad? Why doesn't the second lesion always work? These are very good questions; they haven't been answered yet.₄

1 able   dis   re   ly   less   ness   sub

2 challenging   disease   cautious   beneficial
emperor   unbelievable   starvation   certain

3 Servetus   dangerous   shortly   convinced
structure   superstition   accept   publish
observation   Vesalius   dissected
professor   sketches   opposed   obvious
described   designed   shipwrecked

4
1. gallows
2. criminal
3. liver
4. internal
5. cautious
6. predictable
7. position

5
Vesalius, Professor of Anatomy

Vesalius is called the father of anatomy. When he was a student at the university, he dissected a few animals and observed work on dead human bodies. Once he stole a human skeleton from the gallows. It was the remains of a criminal who had been hanged. If Vesalius had been caught, he would have been hanged himself. Vesalius studied the skeleton and made observations.

One of the first things he noticed was that the hipbones of the skeleton were not like the hipbones that Galen described.₁ Vesalius wrote down all his observations, but he was not yet ready to * publish them.

When Vesalius was only twenty-three years old, he accepted a position as professor of anatomy at a leading university. While continuing his study of anatomy at the university, he discovered many things that Galen had not noticed or described. Vesalius discovered that the liver and other internal organs were different from those in Galen's description. Vesalius carefully wrote down his findings and made sketches of their details. For five years, he wrote and studied and worked with artists who made detailed pictures based on human anatomy. Then, at the age of twenty-eight, he published his work. *₂

The response of many of the doctors of the day was predictable. Vesalius's former professor of anatomy accused Vesalius of being mad. The doctors agreed that Vesalius was both crazy and very evil for attacking the teachings of Galen. We can understand how these men felt when we remember that they had spent a great deal of effort learning to become doctors. They were convinced that they had special knowledge about how to cure diseases. The work of Vesalius said in effect, "You don't know much about the human body." Many doctors who read or heard about the work of * Vesalius continued to believe in Galen's work. After all, it had been accepted for centuries.[3]

However, Vesalius was very cautious about challenging long-standing beliefs. When he observed that human hips were different from the hips that Galen had described, Vesalius didn't say that Galen had been wrong. Instead, Vesalius suggested that people had changed since the time Galen wrote his work. He suggested that the shape of the hips had changed perhaps because people had been wearing tight clothing for so long.[4]

Vesalius probably did not believe this explanation, but he knew that it was very dangerous to challenge * long-standing beliefs. Shortly after Vesalius's work on anatomy was published, another man, Servetus, showed that the heart pumps blood to the lungs. Unfortunately, he wrote a book that was not in line with some of the religious beliefs of the day. All copies of that book were burned, and Servetus was tied to a stake and burned to death.[5]

Although Vesalius was not burned at the stake, he suffered many insults. The insults were so intense and frequent that Vesalius became depressed, quit his position at the university, and became the official doctor at a royal court. In the * course of his travels, he was shipwrecked on a small island, where he died of starvation. At the time of his death, he was still a fairly young man with a great deal to offer the world. He had tried to help the people of his day by adding to their knowledge about the human body. Doctors can't do much to cure a disease of the liver unless they understand some facts about the liver. Doctors can't do a good job of setting broken bones unless they know something about the structure of bones. Vesalius was not correct about everything * he observed, but the doctors of his day could not hide from the more obvious truths that Vesalius had pointed out. After his death, anatomy became a scientific discipline. And medicine became a profession. Vesalius helped to start a scientific revolution.[6]

Vesalius had opened the door to modern medicine, but the practice of medicine still had a long, long way to go. Vesalius got rid of some medical superstitions, but there were many more superstitions left to be fought. The pattern of these fights was often the same— long-standing beliefs had to give way to new knowledge.[7]

1 introduction specializes fright centuries

2 Semmelweis Pasteur Jenner fever
division infection garbage childhood
convinced pasteurization smallpox
improvements typhoid affects
diphtheria organisms poisoning purify

3
1. bacteria
2. vaccination
3. substance
4. explanation
5. life expectancy

4 Contributions of Jenner, Pasteur, and Semmelweis

Let's skip ahead in time to about 1850. During the 350 years since 1500, a number of improvements had come about in medicine; however, conditions were still very different from what we know today. The average life expectancy of people born in the cities was now about thirty-seven years. If people survived childhood, they could expect to live far beyond their thirty-seventh birthday; however, chances of living through childhood were not too good.

Diseases like smallpox, typhoid fever, and diphtheria still took the lives of thousands of children every year. Another killer was blood poisoning. Blood poisoning is * a serious infection that affects a person's whole system. A fever starts, and if the infection continues to develop, the person dies. The doctors of 1850 did not understand that blood poisoning is caused by tiny organisms called bacteria.₁

An Englishman named Edward Jenner had introduced a method for preventing smallpox about fifty years earlier. The method was called vaccination. Even by 1850 some people were not convinced that vaccination worked. They feared being stuck with a needle and having some strange substance injected into their body. Even some doctors were slow to accept vaccination.[2]

During the twenty-five-year * period following Jenner's introduction of vaccination, about six million people in Europe died of smallpox. The toll was especially great in the United States, particularly among the American Indians, who had no resistance to the disease. Entire villages of Native Americans died from smallpox. In fact, one hundred years after Jenner introduced vaccination, there was a severe outbreak of smallpox in the town where Jenner had lived and worked.[3]

One of the greatest of all medical scientists was Louis Pasteur. He discovered that diseases were spread by bacteria. He demonstrated that bacteria were living things and were born, like all * other life-forms. Until his theories were accepted, many doctors believed that flies and other small life-forms simply grew out of garbage or dirt. They didn't believe that these animals were born from a parent, like larger life-forms. Most of these doctors did not even believe that bacteria existed because they were invisible to the naked eye.[4]

Pasteur showed how to control the spread of disease. He demonstrated that harmful bacteria in milk could be killed by applying heat. This method, called pasteurization, assured a safe milk supply. His other great life-saving contribution resulted from his work * in the area of vaccination. He discovered that harmful bacteria (germs) cause some diseases by multiplying in the human body. He discovered how to stop this process by vaccinating a person with a weakened form of the germs. It is impossible to estimate the number of lives saved by Pasteur's work.[5]

A doctor named Semmelweis lived in Europe around 1850. He wasn't familiar with the work of Pasteur. But he showed that some problems of controlling bacteria could be solved by using common sense.

Semmelweis was in charge of a large hospital that specialized in caring for women who were * having babies. The women went into the hospital to have their babies, and a few days after the baby was born the mother and the baby went home—if the mother was still alive.

There were two divisions in the hospital. Semmelweis noticed a striking difference between them. In one division, one of every ten women died after giving birth. In the other, fewer than one of every thirty died.[6]

Semmelweis studied the figures and asked himself, "Why do more women die in Division One than in Division Two?" Division One was staffed by doctors and medical students. Division Two * was staffed by nurses. What was the difference between the doctors and the nurses?

An explanation had been offered by some medical officials. It might be that some women in Division One died of fright because Division One had a bad reputation. Some women might have died of heart attacks caused by fear.[7]

1 ly dis re able less un ness

2 occurred procedure solution arrange
resistance rejected laundry
examine weather consider

3 bacteria harmful explanation series
Semmelweis solve clue insisted
concluded dissecting childbirth contact
ridiculous patients indicated serious

4
1. diet
2. stale
3. punctured
4. frequently
5. resist
6. hostility

Semmelweis Solves the Problem

Semmelweis tried to figure out what caused the higher death rate in Division One of his hospital. He rejected the explanation that fear caused the higher death rate. He considered other explanations. One was that changes in the weather caused the higher death rate. Semmelweis pointed out that the weather was the same for Division One and Division Two.

Another explanation was that patients were crowded together in Division One. Semmelweis pointed out that deaths occurred in Division One even in areas where patients were not crowded. He also showed that high death rates did not occur in the parts * of Division Two where patients were crowded together.₁

Semmelweis considered a number of other possible explanations and rejected each of them. The bed sheets were equally dirty in Division One and Division Two. Semmelweis concluded that the condition of the bed sheets could not cause the difference in the death rates. Poor diet and stale air were also rejected as causes because both were present in both divisions.

Then something happened that gave Semmelweis a clue to the cause of the high death rate in Division One. A doctor who worked in Division One was dissecting a dead body when * his knife slipped and punctured his finger. Within a few days, he came down with a fever. It was the same kind that killed so many women in the hospital. It was called childbed fever. People had thought that the fever occurred only after childbirth, but the doctor's illness and death proved them wrong.

Semmelweis did not know that the doctor had been infected by bacteria that cause childbed fever (blood poisoning). But he assumed that something must have entered the doctor's body when he dissected the infected body.₂

Since childbed fever was more serious in Division One, where doctors * and students attended patients, Semmelweis concluded that the disease must be carried by the doctors and students, but not by the nurses in Division Two. So he began to examine what the doctors and students did. He found that they frequently dissected the bodies of women who had died of the fever. The nurses did not do this. The doctors and students frequently went directly from an operating room to deliver a baby without bothering to wash their hands. When they did wash, they used only soap and water.₃

Semmelweis took steps to cure this problem, but they were met * with a great deal of resistance. First, he insisted that all doctors must wash their hands in a solution that would kill the infectious material on their hands. Next, Semmelweis removed all dirty materials from the patients' rooms. Each room was cleaned frequently, and bed sheets were replaced when they got dirty.₄

The changes that Semmelweis introduced caused a great drop in the death rate in Division One. During the first year the new procedures were put into operation, the death rate dropped from one out of every ten women to one out of every hundred women—a drop of * ninety percent. During two months of that year, not one woman died in Division One.

Semmelweis should have been treated as a hero. Instead, he was greeted with hostility. Many respected doctors said that his procedures were ridiculous. They felt that he had no right to tell doctors how to wash their hands.₅ Semmelweis couldn't stand the constant battles, so he left the hospital. Shortly afterward he became ill and went to a hospital for an examination. He found out that he had infected his finger during one of his last operations. The infection was blood poisoning (childbed fever). Semmelweis * died of the very disease he had learned to control.

Semmelweis was a great man because he used common sense, facts, and figures. He didn't work out a cure for blood poisoning. He didn't work out ways to kill bacteria that had entered a wound. But he did a great deal for the field of medicine because he showed how cleanliness can prevent the spread of harmful bacteria. The techniques he introduced have been improved over the years, but they follow the same basic principle: whatever comes in contact with a wound must be clean.₆

1 identifiable   occurred   incredibly
meant   specialize

2 excellent   increased   rejected   surgeon
frequently   replace   function   infection
available   infantile   crippled   anesthetics
transplant   paralysis   assist   vaccine
doubled   thorough   punished   antiseptic

3
1. penicillin
2. attitude
3. symptoms

Medicine Now

A doctor's office of today is very different from the office of the barber-surgeon of 1500. It is also quite different from a doctor's office of 1900 because a great deal has happened since the beginning of the present century. Knowledge about medicine has grown like a snowball rolling downhill.

At first, the knowledge of medicine developed very slowly. Before the 1500s, few advances were made. Then the pace of change began to increase. By the beginning of the present century, doctors had far more knowledge than those of the 1500s. Doctors practicing in 1900 knew about germs, about * antiseptic procedures, and even something about anesthetics, which are drugs that kill

pain.₁ But there was no cure for the terrible disease that crippled young children—infantile paralysis (polio). There was little knowledge about heart disease, its symptoms, and how to prevent or treat it. Many diseases of the kidneys, heart, and liver meant certain death. Doctors didn't know how to transplant kidneys or how to replace valves that didn't function properly.₂

In the years since 1900, knowledge of medicine has snowballed faster and faster. New instruments, new operations, and new drugs have come to the medical scene almost yearly. * A vaccine was developed to prevent polio. The discovery of wonder drugs such as penicillin made it possible for doctors to control infections that had formerly killed patients.3

Another change that has occurred in medicine has to do with women. A little over one hundred years ago, all doctors were men. Women were allowed to assist doctors as nurses, and many women were midwives. (A midwife specializes in caring for a woman in childbirth.) Women, however, were barred from attending medical schools.

In 1849, Elizabeth Blackwell received her medical degree from a school in Geneva, Switzerland. She was the first * woman to graduate from a medical school. She was resented by the male doctors, taunted by other women, and rejected by her teachers, even though she was an excellent student. Although her problems did not end when she graduated from medical school, she set the stage for other women to become doctors. At first there were only a few, but the number of women doctors slowly increased. The attitude has changed—today, at some medical schools, there are nearly as many women students as men.4

The snowballing of knowledge in medicine has made it difficult for the average doctor to * keep pace. When there were only a few diseases known and a few types of treatments, it was not difficult for doctors to keep pace with the available knowledge of medicine. As the amount of information about treatments and the number of identifiable ailments increased, doctors were required to learn much more in order to keep pace with the available knowledge. Some experts have estimated that the amount of medical knowledge doubled between the years 1900 and 1940, doubled again between 1940 and 1960, and yet again between 1960 and 1970. These experts estimate that it will continue to double * at a faster rate, making it very difficult for a doctor to have a thorough understanding of medicine. Doctors are humans, and humans can learn only so much during the time that is available to them.5

To solve the problem of snowballing information, many doctors no longer attempt to deal with all medical problems. They specialize. Some specialize in ailments of the nose and throat; others specialize in a particular type of surgery, such as brain surgery. There are eye specialists and bone specialists, foot specialists, and of course dentists. These specialists are able to keep pace with the medical * knowledge of their particular field. There are still doctors who deal with all ailments; however, after reviewing symptoms, these doctors often refer patients to specialists.6

The medical profession has grown through the work of many brave people who said what they thought to be true, even though they knew their ideas would not be popular. We've looked at a few of these people—Paré, Vesalius, da Vinci, Pasteur, Jenner, Semmelweis, and Blackwell. There were many others. You can read about them in books on the history of medicine.7

1

Rochetain   funambulist   frightened
gorge   endurance   daring   Blondin
swayed   Niagara   bowed   impressed
Canadian   feat   balance   fad   crews
stroll   incredible   agent

2

1. casually
2. secured

3

Famous Funambulists

Nearly everybody who lived in the year 1885 knew what a funambulist was. Although the word is not used much today, it stood for feats of great daring to the people of the late 1800s. A funambulist is a tightrope walker. Tightrope walking became quite a fad after Charles Blondin performed his incredible walk 160 feet (49 meters) above Niagara Falls. The rope was three inches (a little less than eight centimeters) in diameter and was 1100 feet (335 meters) in length.₁ The crews experienced great difficulty in securing the rope, and Blondin's agent wasn't satisfied that the rope was adequately secured for his scheduled walk on July 30, 1885. Blondin, a famous French funambulist, was apparently not worried. He tested the rope, which swayed more than 29 feet (9 meters) from side to side in the middle of the span, and indicated that the crowd of people that gathered for the event would not be disappointed.

With the wind blowing and the silent crowds on both sides of the river, Blondin walked across as casually as one would stroll on a sidewalk. He stopped in the middle, put down the long pole that he carried for balance, and bowed to the crowd. Then he continued. What impressed people more than anything else was how easy Blondin made the walk look. Others attempted the same feat. According to one story, a man who had never walked a tightrope before in his life made a bet that he could walk across Blondin's rope, and he did. According to the report, he walked from the United States side to the Canadian side of the river at night.

Blondin, however, was not to be outdone. Five years later, he crossed above Niagara Falls with his agent on his back. His agent had never been on a tightrope in his life and was so frightened that he became quite sick after the walk had been completed.[2]

The longest tightrope walk was recorded in France in 1969. To cross from one side of a gorge to the other, the funambulist Rochetain walked 3790 yards (more than 3 kilometers). The walk took almost four hours.

The endurance record for being on a tightrope is 205 days, set by Jorge Ojeda-Guzman of Orlando, Florida. The previous endurance record for being on a tightrope was 185 days, and was set by Rochetain. Doctors were puzzled by his ability to sleep while balanced on the wire. During the 185 days, he walked to stay in condition. In all, he walked about 310 miles (500 kilometers). Food was brought to him regularly, but he never left the wire.[3]

One of the strangest tightrope exhibitions occurred in New York City in 1974. A French funambulist walked a wire between the twin towers of the World Trade Center. When he crossed between the towers, he set the record for the highest crossing—1350 feet (405 meters) above the street (110 stories). He was charged with trespassing.

Glossary

abnormal not normal

abruptly suddenly

accurate correct

achieve attain

acoustics the quality of sound in a place

adapt get along

adjustment slight change

advantage upper hand

agency a business that represents clients

aggressive quick to fight

alert paying close attention

amusing funny

anatomy the study of the body

ancient very old

announce tell something new

antics clowning behavior

anxiety worry

apparatus equipment

apparent obvious

approval an OK

area a region; a place

aroused awakened; stirred up

arranged made plans

assess evaluate

associated related

associates people who work together

assuming supposing

assured guaranteed

attained reached

attentive paying attention

bacteria germs that produce disease

bargain try to buy something at a reduced price

barge a long, flat-bottomed boat used for carrying things

beaker a container used in chemistry labs

bellow shout loudly

beneficial good

bill of lading a list of everything in a truckload or carload of things

bombardment shower

bonds forces that hold things together

bounding jumping and leaping

breadfruit a large, tropical fruit

breaker a big wave

brilliance sparkle and shine

brittle breaks; doesn't bend

brochure folder

buckles folds; collapses

budget a breakdown of how money is to be spent

buoy a float that marks something in the water

calculate figure out

campaign organized effort

canopy roof

cascading falling or tumbling

champion a person who is the best at something

charred burned and blackened

chores daily jobs

chowder a thick soup

churned stirred up very hard

claim pick up something you own

clients people who pay a company for work

climate weather conditions

coastal along the edge or coast of an ocean

coincidence something that happens by chance

collapse fall apart

colleagues associates

collide crash into each other

comment say something

commission money paid for selling something

composed made up of

computer program set of directions that tells the computer what it is supposed to do

concealed hidden

concerned interested

conference meeting

confidential secret

confirm   show that something is right

considering   thinking about

continue   keep doing

contract   pledge

convert   change

convey   get across

convince   make someone believe

coordinated   working together smoothly

copyright   the right to make copies of something that is printed

craft   boat

crease   a mark that's left after something has been folded

crest   top

data   facts

deadlocked   when neither side can win

deafening   very loud

deceit   lying

deceive   trick; fool

deceptive   misleading

delicately   gently and carefully

demand   need

demand   insist

descended   came from

deserve   earn

detect   find

determined   firm in your decision

develop   invent

device   an object made to do something special

devote   give a lot of attention

diet   all the things you eat

disassembled   taken apart

dismantled   taken apart

distinguish   tell how things are different

disturbed   worried or upset

doctor's degree   the highest degree you can get

domestic   not foreign

dressings   bandages that cover a wound

ducts   tubes

duplicated   made a copy

dwellings   places in which people live

efficiently   without wasted movements

elaborate   complicated

electromagnetic   very small waves that travel through space very fast

eliminate   get rid of

emerge   come out of

encounter   come up against

endure   put up with something unpleasant

enlarged   made bigger

erupted   suddenly burst

estimate   a smart guess

evolution   slow change

exaggerated   stretched the truth

examine   carefully look over

exceed   go beyond

exceptionally   unusually

exclaim   cry out

executive   a person who runs a company

exhaust   use up

expectations   thoughts that something will happen

expert   someone who knows a great deal about something

extension   something that is added

extinct   no longer living

extracted   pulled out

extreme   far from normal

facilities   things built to be used for a special purpose

faint   very weak

faked   pretended

fascinated   really interested

fault   something wrong

feat   a great achievement

fidget   twist and turn

fierce   very violent

figurehead   a carved figure on the front of a ship

filtering   straining

flail   swing around like crazy

flexible   bends easily

flounder flop around

flutter move back and forth rapidly

focused concentrated

foliage leaves on a bush or tree

formal stiff and polite

formulas sets of rules

fossil remains of a living thing from a past geological age

foul-tasting bad-tasting

franchise the right to sell something

frantic very excited and upset

fraud a trick to cheat somebody

frequently often

fret worry

function purpose

futile cannot succeed

gale a strong wind

gallows a device for hanging people

gamble risk

gash a deep cut

gasping breathing with short, fast breaths

gear equipment

genetic a living thing's inherited pattern of growth

gimmick trick used to do something

glance bounce off

glands parts of the body that produce important chemicals

glimpse a quick look

glistening sparkling

grade slope

graduate student someone who has an undergraduate degree and is working on a higher degree

grant money that researchers receive for doing a particular job

grazing eating grass

hailed called to

hazy not clear

heave throw

hectic frantic

hesitate pause for a moment

Himalayas the largest mountain chain in the world

hoist lift

holster a pouch for carrying a gun

hostility unfriendliness

hulk a person who is clumsy and overweight

hull body of a ship

humiliating very embarrassing

hurl throw

hurtle fling; hurl violently

husks the dry outer coverings of some fruits

ignore not pay attention

illegal against the law

image picture; reflection

impatient tired of waiting

impish full of mischief

import bring into the country

impressive exceptionally good

impure not pure

incident something that happens

incredible very hard to believe

incurable can't be cured

incurred caused

indeed for sure

indicate point out

infected diseased

inhabitants people who live in a place

initial first

innocent not guilty

inscribed written

insist demand

inspect look over carefully

instant very fast

intent aim; purpose

internal inside the body

interpretation explanation

interruption break

intriguing interesting

intruder someone who goes where they aren't wanted

invent develop

invoice   a list of prices for things that are being sold

irritated   a little angry

jostled   tossed around

keen   sharp

laboratory   a place where experiments are done

lava   hot melted rock that comes out of a volcano

ledge   a narrow shelf

leisurely   at a slow and easy pace

life expectancy   the number of years the average person is expected to live

limbs   arms and legs

lingered   hung around for a long time

location   a place

logical   makes sense

mammal   a warm-blooded creature that has hair

manner   way

marine   sea

masterpieces   fine works of art

matted   pushed and flattened

mature   full-grown

microscope   an instrument used to look at things that are very small

mission   serious duty

modeled   demonstrated

moderator   a person who runs a meeting, discussion, or debate

modified   changed

mole   a small animal that spends most of its life underground

momentary   lasts for only a moment

motive   reason

mounting   base

nervous   edgy or jumpy

nitrogen   a gas that has no smell or color

nonsense   something that makes no sense

nudge   a gentle push

nutrition   the food needs of the body

occasional   once in a while

official   backed by an authority

offspring   descendents; children

organism   something that is living

original   first

outfit   a set of clothes

outskirts   the areas on the edge of a town

paleontologist   a scientist who studies fossils and ancient forms of life

panic   sudden fear

particularly   especially

patent   a license that protects the person who invents an object

peak   the highest point of a mountain

peeved   irritated

penetrate   go through

perch   a small fish

personality   character

physicist   a person who works in the field of physics

physics   the science of how nonliving things behave

plead   beg

plumes   fancy feathers

plunge   dive

podium   a high desk used by speakers on a stage

potent   very strong

pounced   jumped on

prance   step high and move in a frisky way

precious   very special and rare

predator   an animal that kills other animals

presentation   speech

prevented   kept something from happening

prickly   sharp and will sting

prior   before

procedure   a series of steps for doing something

proceed   go ahead

process   a series of steps

proclaimed   announced

productive   achieves a great deal

profit   money left after all expenses have been paid

programmed   always follows the same steps

264

prominent   well known and important

property   trait; feature

proposition   plan

protection   something that guards

protest   speak strongly against

provides   gives

punctured   poked a hole in

puny   small and weak

purify   kill germs

range   the spread of differences

reaction   response

receipt   a paper that proves that something was paid for

recommend   suggest

referred   directed attention to

refused   turned down

reinforced   strengthened

rejected   turned down

related to   has to do with

reliable   can be counted on

remarkable   surprising or amazing

remarked   said; commented

remodel   change the way something looks

represent   stand for

reputation   what people think of you

request   ask for

researcher   a person who tries to discover new facts

resignation   statement that one quits a job

resist   not give in

respected   treated as a special person

respond   answer

resume   begin again

retrieve   recover

rig   device

rigged   fixed up

roamed   wandered

routine   something that is presented in the same way over and over

salvage   valuable objects saved from someplace

scan   look over very quickly

scarcely   only just

scavengers   animals that eat what other animals leave behind

scent   odor

schedule   set up a time

scramble   to move quickly

screens   keeps out

scurried   moved fast

sea level   the height of the ocean at the edge of land

secluded   well hidden

secured   put firmly in place

selection   a portion of something

sensed   felt

serious   important and not funny

severe   very fierce

sheer   very steep

shimmering   seems to be covered with shiny, moving lights

shorings   things that are used to hold something up

shortage   not enough

shrill   high-pitched

silt   very fine mud

site   place

situation   what goes one

slanting   not flat or level

slime   slippery coating

slither   to slide along

sluggish   slow

smoldering   burning and smoking without flame

snaked   twisted

solution   answer

sound   in good condition

sprawl   stretch out

sprouts   new shoots or buds

staggering   very hard to believe

stale   not fresh

stern   back end of a boat

stout   strong and heavy

strain   put forth too much effort

stranded   cannot move

strategy   procedure

strewn   scattered

strides   long steps

stunt   a hard trick done to get attention

subsided   died down

substance   material

suggests   hints

suitable   just right

summary   a short version of a speech or writing

superb   very, very good

surface   the top

surge   sudden movement

surpass   outdo

survive   live through

suspended   hanging

sways   moves slowly back and forth

swirl   twist around

symptoms   signs

tantrums   fits of anger

taut   stretched tight

term   a part of a contract

termites   bugs that eat wood

theory   explanation

thrash   to move about violently

tick   an insect that sucks blood

tiller   handle that steers a boat

tingly   a slightly stinging feeling

tomb   a building for the dead

topples   falls over

trace   track down

trample   stamp into the ground

trance   daze

transform   change

transmit   send; convey

trough   a container with its bottom shaped like a long V

typical   predictable

unconscious   asleep; knocked out

unconvincing   weak

undergraduate   a student who is studying for a regular college degree

unfortunate   unlucky

unison   at the same time

urge   a desire to do something

valves   movable parts that let air or liquid in and out

vast   very big

vegetation   plant life

vein   a thin line in rocks

venom   the poison that poisonous snakes spit

venture   a risky situation

verses   the parts of a song that are not sung over and over

viciously   fiercely

violate   break

visible   can be seen

volume   book

wail   cry out in pain

whir   a soft humming noise

wispy   very light and dainty

withdraw   take back